Screening Fears

Screening Fears

On Protective Media

Francesco Casetti

ZONE BOOKS · NEW YORK

2023

ZONE BOOKS
633 Vanderbilt Street
Brooklyn, NY 11218

Printed in the United States of America.
Distributed by Princeton University Press,
Princeton, New Jersey, and Woodstock, United Kingdom

Library of Congress Cataloging-in-Publication Data
Names: Casetti, Francesco, 1947– author.
Title: Screening fears : on protective media / Francesco Casetti.
Other titles: On protective media
Description: Brooklyn: Zone Books, 2023. | Includes bibliographical
    references and index. | Summary: "A historical and theoretical
    investigation of the unexpected ways screen-based media protect and
    excite viewers' fears and anxieties of the world." Provided by publisher.
Identifiers: LCCN 2022049958 (print) | LCCN 2022049959 (ebook) |
    ISBN 9781942130871 (hardcover) | ISBN 9781942130888 (ebook)
Subjects: LCSH: Digital media — Philosophy. | Mass media — Philosophy. |
    Surfaces (Philosophy) | BISAC: SOCIAL SCIENCE / Media Studies
Classification: LCC B54 .C37 2023 (print) | LCC B54 (ebook) |
    DDC 302.2301 — dc23/eng/20230110
LC record available at https://lccn.loc.gov/2022049958
LC ebook record available at https://lccn.loc.gov/2022049959

Contents

The Projection/Protection

Complex

Delights and Fears

One of the most beautiful testimonies to the values attached to the classical cinematic experience is Antonello Gerbi's "Initiation to the Delights of Cinema."[1] Gerbi's essay, published in 1926 in the authoritative Italian journal *Il Convegno* and only recently returned to the attention of film scholars, highlights the fascination exerted both by projected images and by the setting in which they are projected — a dual focus that fifty years later, Roland Barthes would reiterate in his famous contribution "Leaving the Movie Theater,"[2] with which Gerbi's essay can be associated for its orientation and sensitivity.[3]

Gerbi starts by describing not the spectators' exit, as Barthes would do, but their entrance into the theater. There is an economic transaction: "The delights of the cinema begin immediately after buying your ticket."[4] And there is a physical transition: "They begin as soon as the usher, seeing you arrive across the lobby, opens the velvet curtain so that you can enter [the theater] without having to slow down, without a moment of pause or the smallest obstacle." Those who go to the cinema must cross a threshold, both real and symbolic. The boundary is less pronounced when the spectator enters before the beginning of the film. In this case, the "tangible and three-dimensional reality"[5] is left behind through successive steps, which begin with the waiting for the film and end with the gradual fading of the theater's architectural elements: "Absorbed by the darkness, first every shape, every outline, every structure disappears: farewell, plastic forms!"[6] The boundary, on the other hand, appears much more marked when the spectator enters during the show. Here we have a "sudden leap"[7] between two profoundly different universes, marked respectively by light and darkness and in open struggle with each other. Not by chance, the usher who stands at the door of the theater

> opens the jaws of the shadows . . . just a little bit—I don't know if it's out of fear that the outside light would disturb or wound the sacred darkness or that the darkness collected in the room, having found some small opening, would spread out into the lobby, would hinder a careful checking of tickets, would pour out into the street and would shortly flood the entire city.[8]

If the light of the world threatens the room, the darkness of the room threatens the world. This is why we need a closed space, separated from the world. We need an antiworld, capable of "swallowing up the real, mundane world."[9]

Once in the theater, the spectator's gaze "springs to the security lights, grazes the luminous reflections that touch the rows of patrons' heads, and settles trustingly on the screen."[10] The already settled spectators, "subdued by the darkness," appear "dull, wan, and weighty without light inside, lacking any space around them or a bright background behind them." They almost seem to escape the new audience member's gaze. In return, the latter is especially attracted by the cone of light that comes out of the projection booth. It is "a very sharp electric ray, which with a shock awakens the little images in their squared cells of celluloid, and one after another, in rapid succession, throws them out of the little window only to flatten themselves out—enlarged by terror—against the canvas."[11] This divine, essential light is "a sort of domestic Milky Way that contains in embryonic form billions of worlds."[12] These worlds blossom when they are projected onto the screen—"a large cut of canvas" that is "ready to take in all of the impressions, and ready to forget them"[13] and that in this game of conquest and abandonment reveals its masculine nature: "Impassable and untiring, the screen is the last incarnation of the spirit of Don Giovanni."[14]

Devoid of images, the screen "is so stupid and useless that it is irritating. It doesn't justify itself. It doesn't explain itself."[15] But when the light from the projector hits it, the screen transforms: "What was a large bandage strewn with talcum powder is reborn as an altarpiece for the liturgies of the new times."[16] And like an altarpiece, the screen returns in all its richness the reality that spectators have left behind them, or even a reality they have never experienced. Indeed, the canvas, miraculously, "changes color, trembles, grows pale, flees into the background, approaches in close-ups right under the nose of the worshipper, passes through a number of hurried and temporary reincarnations, changes its face and soul a hundred times a minute."[17] What takes shape on the screen is the flowering of life.

Such a transformation of the screen is fully apparent at the beginning of the screening. While the title of the film and the names of the actors could still evoke literature and theater, with the first images, it starts a completely different experience: "The last, very thin veils are evaporating. . . . And, in a twilight of emblems, there appears the living divinity of Movement."[18] The theater is welcoming and relaxing: "Spectators make themselves comfortable in the deep of their chairs; their eye governs the focus of their gaze; their feet finally find the support they were looking for; their elbows marry the line of the armchairs."[19] It is in this restful and secure space that spectators witness, without "the light murmur of a prayer," in "perfect adoration," the appearance of a "new Epiphany."[20] Gerbi wonders, "Are we buried in the deep or hovering among the stars? I don't know anymore: certainly, we are very close to the heart of the cinema."

Despite the delights, however, there is no shortage of reasons for concern. Waiting for the film to start, for example, creates anxiety; it is then when we experience "the unexpected sensation of finding ourselves suspended between two worlds — the fantastic one of cinema and the real one."[21] A similar anxiety emerges when the projection is not well centered on the screen: "Everyone yells 'Frame! Frame!' with the same anguish of a person who sees a crazed horse coming from the end of a deserted street and yells 'Stop! Stop!'"[22] An even stronger anxiety takes shape when, for whatever reason, the pace of the projection slows down: "No patience could resist the slow, corroding, continuous dripping of images."[23] The projection can even stop: "A yawn. Just one. But in that boundless yawn the entire Universe will be swallowed up. That is how I imagine the end of the world."[24]

This fear that the world on the screen may dissolve, giving way to nothing, has its counterpart in the terror that the world on the screen may instead become real and merge with the everyday world. Here, Gerbi's imagination becomes apocalyptic: "The nighttime-reveling phantasms would come down from the screen and would attach themselves, deformed, contorted, grimacing, to the bodies of the spectators, to the bare walls, to the skin of the ladies, to the backs of the chairs, to people's heads, to their collars, to the newspapers."[25] A direct projection toward open space instead of a screen would produce similar anxiety.

> A disturbing thought: If a projection took place without the screen—onto open space—where would it end up? Seemingly it would vanish into the air, it would dissolve into a vague, luminous nebulosity. But if it is true that nothing is lost in the Universe, how can characters who are so alive and so animated disappear like that? Their fate worries me. If you were to find them close to you, so thin and silent, one night when you're returning home, there would quite a bit to be afraid of.[26]

The materialization of images is frightening.

Confronting the World

Gerbi's description, full of literary and religious echoes, hits the mark. Cinema is not just a movie; it is an optical-spatial dispositif that couples two fundamental elements—an enclosed space, separated from the everyday world, and a screen whose moving images reestablish contact with the reality from which spectators have been severed or to which they never had access. Conveyed by a powerful beam of light and in sharp contrast with the darkness of the theater, images acquire unusual intensity and strength. Hence the idea of a miraculous epiphany: the world on the screen ends up being more detailed and more encompassing than what direct sight can capture.[27] The consequence is that what was lost is given back with interest.

This interpretation of cinema as an optical-spatial dispositif is at once revealing and challenging. Why this retreat from the world? And why this reconnection with reality through images? The fears that Gerbi discusses—more than the delights—offer a clear answer. Direct exposure to the world triggers discomfort, to which spectators attest when they flee from their everyday milieu, when the movie is slow to start, when troubles in projection break the enchantment of the spectacle, and when screened images are mistaken for actual people. Reality can be threatening; hence the need for a physical enclosure that works as a sort of shelter and for screened images that work as a sort of filter.[28] The world must be kept at a distance. At the same time, the situation in which spectators are put—the relaxation of bodies and the heightened attention to the screen—allows reality to reappear through images that look like epiphanies and that can even be taken as direct perceptions.[29] Contact with the world is reestablished, a contact that appears safe and that remedies or remediates the distance and deferrals previously created.

Once we look at cinema from this point of view, an entirely new perspective surfaces. Cinema is not primarily a medium that expands our senses, an "extension of man," as Marshall McLuhan famously stated.[30] On the contrary, it is a *dispositif of protection* that spares individuals direct exposure to the world—or at least the world in which they usually live—without interrupting their interaction with reality. As such, cinema belongs to a lineage of modern media that perform this task thanks to the association of screened images and sounds and physical or psychological enclosures, a lineage that emerges in the late eighteenth century with the projections in a dark theater of the Phantasmagoria[31] and that finds its most recent example in the imaginary bubbles in which we find refuge from the immediate surroundings when we immerse ourselves in an online conversation or in a web navigation on our laptop or smartphone.[32]

At first glance, it seems odd to include the bubble in the same lineage with the Phantasmagoria and the cinema; unlike the other two examples, the bubble has no physical walls, no communal audience, and no projector. Yet despite these significant differences, all three dispositifs share the same basic operations: they rely on an intentional severance from reality and on screened images and sounds that at once accentuate and compensate for such a severance. Individuals are disconnected from their physical milieu and safely reconnected with the world through other means; they switch from immediate encounters with things and events to a mediated immediacy.[33]

This basic set of operations, which equally affects other modern media, including mid-twentieth century television[34] and the recently emerging virtual reality, unearths the presence of what I want to call the *projection/protection complex* — where, echoing both its psychoanalytical and economic meanings, "complex" stands for a set of interrelated processes and components here aimed at creating a "protected" confrontation with the world and at the same time at "projecting" individuals beyond the safe space in which they are located. The projection/protection complex plays hide-and-seek with reality. While creating a retreat from the surroundings, ostensibly because of their potential disturbances, it provides a safe reconnection with the world thanks to new channels that allow it to reemerge. The distancing from the closest context acts as a premise and condition for a reappearance of reality in forms that are no less dense, but more manageable. Such a state of security makes it possible to reintroduce the fears from which the spectators and users are safeguarded: images can be frightening, yet they are not threatening, unless they change their status and become physical entities, as Gerbi ironically remarks. While recalling traditional or even mythical places that merge enclosures and images, such as Plato's cave, religious rituals based on spatial deprivations and transcendental contacts, and forms of play that imply detachment and reconnections, including the Freudian *Fort-Da*,[35] the projection/protection complex is first and foremost a modern mechanism, a mechanism that responds to the challenges of a world that is perceived as increasingly difficult and taxing[36] with technologies that make available new forms of confrontation.

By tracking screens, the dedicated spaces where they are located, and the fears that accompany their presence, this book examines the projection/protection complex both in its general mode of working and in its most representative instantiations. It will bring to the fore the Phantasmagoria's ability to offer an escape from the pressures of a politically and socially turbulent age to make room for the exploration of a threefold universe, the natural, the spiritual, and the inner; the cinema's talent to compensate for the difficulties of spectators' existences with a comfortable setting and pleasurable images and sounds; and the electronic bubble's capacity to isolate individuals from their milieu and engage them in a face-to-face encounters at a distance. The complex does not cover the entire life of these three dispositifs (think of the origin of cinema as mere reproductive tool), and it often overturns situations in which separation from the world is considered dangerous (think of the suspicion of the film theater in the first years of its history). Yet the analysis of these three dispositifs in a specific stage of their existence will be able to detail the complex's mode of working and, more generally, the rationale underlying *protective media*. Their action not only combines spatial deprivation and sensorial excitation, persistent anxieties and forms of defense, and intentional retreats and bold explorations, but also prompts two possible outcomes, the emergence of disciplinary systems that create a well-ordered world instead of the chaotic one where we live and the rise of immune procedures that provide a sort of "vaccine" against potential threats.[37] The book will discuss the influence of both the disciplinary and the immune paradigms on the complex. Remarks about the dangers of overprotection (does the idea of safeguarding imply as much violence as the threats that we want to avoid?) and about the need to balance safety and exposure (how can a severance become productive?) will complete the complex's portrait. In this framework, the basic oppositions on which the complex relies—exterior and interior, reality and representation, individual and world, and even danger and safety—will progressively appear for what they are: not ontological constants, but rather parameters that depend on the complex's mode of working and respond to contingent and conjunctural situations.[38] In this light, they are an effect of the complex as much as they are its premises.

Straddling the mechanical and the electronic, industrial and postindustrial societies and the rise and decline of mass culture, the projection/protection complex emerges as one of the key mechanisms in the history of modern media. While underscoring the spatial nature of our mediation with the world, it also reveals the intimate processes that characterize this mediation, from the need to create thresholds to the empowerment of our forms of communication at a distance and from the dynamics between fears and threats to the dialectics between protection and control. In a world that is rapidly changing and that prefigures its and our extinction, the projection/protection complex enables us to grasp what ultimately is at stake and to imagine alternate ways of confronting reality.

I spent a great part of my scholarly life investigating the cinematic experience, first in its connections with the spectatorial address, then in its cultural relevance, finally in its persistence in face of technological change. With this book, I expand my scope to modern screen-based media, and I investigate the experience they elicit against the backdrop of the processes of mediation. Only a genealogy of the screen as dispositif and an engagement of modern forms of mediation can cast light on questions first raised by cinema and now reshaped by the current media landscape.

CHAPTER ONE

Screens, Space, Fears

The Visual and the Spatial

An end-of-eighteenth-century Parisian *citoyen* crosses the garden of the disreputable Couvent des Capucines and enters a dark room where a physician-magician summons ghosts that materialize out of nowhere and that seem to fly through the air. One hundred years later, still in Paris — but with some variations, the scene might be placed in Berlin or New York — a crowd lines up to enter the Salon Indien of the popular Grand Café on the Boulevard des Capucines, where ten short animated pictures are projected onto a piece of canvas. A little more than a hundred years after that, somewhere in the world, in a coffeehouse that offers a Wi-Fi hotspot, a customer isolates himself from his immediate surroundings to direct all of his attention to what appears on his laptop. To these examples we can add others: during World War II, an American soldier, surrounded by maps, sits in front of a console with a wide array of technical devices and looks at a circular monitor on which a pulsing light signals the presence of a potential target. In the 1950s, a suburban family gathers in front of a TV set to spend some time together. At the beginning of the 1990s, in a room filled with surveillance monitors, a police officer scans the images to find areas of the city that require her intervention.

These scenes, which respectively make reference to a Phantasmagoria show,[1] an early film séance,[2] an internet café, a radar station,[3] a television broadcast,[4] and a control room,[5] are quite puzzling. They have almost nothing in common: some involve a spectacle, other surveillance processes; some mobilize analogical representations, others, digital images; some address collective audiences, others, separate users; some occur in a unique site, others can or even must coexist in many different places. Yet two elements return in each of these scenes. All of their protagonists deal with surfaces on which mobile and impermanent visual data appears, and in doing so, they not only adjust their expectations and their reactions to what the surfaces continuously display, but they also alter their physical postures and their actions in response to the dynamic environment in which these surfaces are located. In a word, they confront a *screen* that visually addresses them and at the same time affects the space in which they are contained.

This emphasis on both optical and spatial connotations might sound strange. When we think of a screen, the immediate characteristic that stands out is a perceptual activity, whatever form that might take: to gaze, to stare, to glance, to check, to trace, or to monitor.[6] Yet today's prevailing optical disposition of the screen emerged only at the beginning of the nineteenth century, in connection with devices such as the Phantasmagoria and the magic lantern.[7] Since the fifteenth century, the English word "screen," as well as the French écran, the Italian *schermo*, and the German *Schirm*, have denoted objects that perform functions other than attracting visual attention. A screen was a contrivance for warding off the heat of a fire or a draft of air; it was a partition of wood or stone dividing a room or building into two parts, a wall thrown out in front of a building to mask the façade, a tactical deployment of soldiers to conceal the movement of an army, or an apparatus used in the sifting of grain or coal. It was a filter, a divide, a shelter, and a form of camouflage.[8] Outside the Western tradition, the Chinese term *ping* denoted a containing wall before being associated with a displaying surface.[9] These meanings underscored not so much the optical qualities of a screen, but rather its nature as a prop to be used within and upon a space and, consequently, its environmental character.

Quite paradoxically, the progressive explosion of the number and kinds of screens throughout the twentieth century—an explosion that became fully apparent with the advent of the new millennium—lends a new currency to the old and seemingly antiquated meanings of the word "screen." Think of our initial examples. Radar systems scan skies and seas thanks to outposts located near a territory's borders, and when they detect an intruder, they activate barriers. Surveillance monitors, especially those supposed to protect public or private buildings, reinforce the division between an exterior and an interior and control movement from the former to the latter. The laptop in the internet café creates a space of intimacy in which its user can find a private refuge within a public space. Screens have once again become filters, shelters, divides, and means of camouflage.

This reemergence of environmental connotations[10] calls us to pay closer attention to what is at stake in screen-centered situations. To what extent does an address to the eyes imply an action in space, and vice versa? Does the convergence between the visual and the environmental elicit forms of synchronization, or does it create disjuncture? And why does the visual dimension sometimes take the lead, especially when supported by accompanying sounds, and other times a step back? To answer these questions is crucial, especially if we want to capture not only a common ground for different screen-centered situations, such as the ones I listed at the beginning, but also the different forms of alliance between the optical and the spatial.

In the next pages, I explore the convergence of screen and space, at first in general terms and then in the particular combination that mobilizes screened images and physical enclosures. This combination characterizes all our initial examples. While creating a spatial break with the immediate surroundings, it reactivates the relationship with the outside thanks to visual or audiovisual cues. Such

21

a double movement seems to respond to the recurring anxieties related to direct exposure to the world and at the same time to the desire to reconnect with it in a safe way. It emerges with particular strength in modernity, in coincidence with an increasingly aggressive and elusive reality, against which it offers relief and protection. Yet in order to understand why and how screen and space converge and what kinds of effects this convergence elicits when the space is an enclosure, we need to take a step back and reconsider, in a fresh and hopefully unconventional perspective, what a screen is.

Becoming Screen

We often assume we can identify the screen with a particular group of objects. Yet no device possesses the status of the screen independently from its functioning within a specific context. In a certain sense, and quite scandalously, a screen "as such" does not exist. A screen becomes a screen when it interacts with a group of elements and is connected with a set of practices that produce it as a screen. Habitual exposure to screens may well have an effect of naturalization, causing the process underpinning its production to withdraw from perception. Screens then look like something available for an already established use, something ready-to-hand, in Heidegger's terms. Yet following suggestions from Gilbert Simondon,[11] if we focus not on the screen's use but on the screen's mode of working, what comes to the fore is the presence of a heterogeneous set of elements that develop mutual interconnections and functionalities and that configure what has been called a *dispositif* or an *assemblage*.[12] It is in the framework of this set of elements and their reciprocal feedbacks that a screen finds its status, like every other individual component of the ensemble.[13] This status depends on the assemblage's organization and inclination — its *disposition* — as well as on the concrete action it performs — its *operations*. In our case, it depends on the assemblage's propensity and capacity either to display a representation or to sieve external elements, to offer a refuge, to divide a space, or to conceal a component. Each of these options defines one mode of working of the assemblage; Simondon would say it defines a dispositif's *technical essence*. The screen reflects this technical essence and performs consequently. It responds and contributes to the assemblage's mode of working, and in exchange, it discovers its own function and position, either as a support, or a filter, a shelter, a partition, or a camouflage. That means that it is only when integrated into an assemblage that a screen comes fully into existence. Only then does it become "*a*" screen and "*that*" screen. In principle, everything can become a screen: what matters is not its materiality, but the dispositif's capacity to make a component act as a screen in the framework of an oriented and operating assemblage.

An example may be useful. If in the Phantasmagoria the screen gained a role and an identity, it arose from the physical and functional arrangement of the whole aggregate. The Phantasmagoria's mode of working implied the source of the projected images be fully concealed while making the images themselves fully available to spectators. The translucent surface fulfilled both conditions. Occupying an intermediate position between lantern and audience, it was able to hide the former thanks to its partial opacity and to materialize the apparitions for the latter thanks to its partial transparency. The name "screen," which the translucent cloth rapidly gained at least in English, reflected this double function: it referred directly to the capacity of the intermediate element to act as a filter, as if the surface were another instantiation of the barrier type of screen that sits in front of a fireplace, and at the same time, it carried a new visual connotation due to the dispositif's propensity to display images. It was this contribution to the assemblage's overall design that made the screen a recognizable and recognized presence, in contrast to previous optical devices that used reflective surfaces without assigning them a structural role.[14] As the act of showing became more and more important, the screen's optical aspects became prevalent and independent from the need to hide the source of the images; hence the consolidation of the screen as a tool and as a term in dispositifs such as the magic lantern or the stereopticon.[15] With the advent of cinema, the screen's role and name came to be familiar and even taken for granted. The white canvas *was* a screen. This naturalization obscured the fact that the screen always had to *become* a screen in the framework of a network of well-connected components. The fact that in cinema's first decades many surfaces were equally eligible to perform as screens, once adapted to the projector's performance, the theater's layout, and the spectators' sight — among them, there were transparent sheets, mirrors, opaque fabrics, and white walls — bore witness to the screen's persistent dependence on the assemblage's configuration and way of working.[16]

The process of becoming screen does not necessarily reflect a deterministic design. What matters is the congregation of the components and the orientation of the ensemble, rather than an abstract project. It was the way in which the Phantasmagoria's parts came together that defined the function assigned to each part and to the whole, and not the contrary. Even if the convergence of components is conceived in advance, the assemblage's composition and propensity become clear only when its components actually meet — and they meet not only when the time is ripe for their coalescence, but also in ways that are often unexpected.[17] This means that the emergence of a dispositif responds to *contingency* and *conjuncture*, more than to necessity. What is needed is just the presence of a collection of favorable, though often coincidental conditions that make the congregation of components possible and at the same time recognizable as such. In this sense, assemblages fully belong to their epoch.

The Screen and Its Milieu

In this process of becoming screen, do the connections of the screen with its surrounding space play a special role? To answer these questions, I rely again on Gilbert Simondon: whose idea of a "technical object" provides a theoretical background that can lead our investigation.

According to Simondon, "the technical object is situated at the meeting point between two milieus" — the technical and the geographical milieus — "and it must be integrated to both milieus at once."[18] This means that a device at the same time belongs to the universe of machines and occupies a physical place in the world. This double orientation leads to the creation of a complex terrain in which artificial and natural elements find a point of contact: Simondon calls it a *techno-geographical* or *associated milieu* ("milieu associé") and characterizes it as the actual context within which the technical object performs its action.[19] The associated milieu is not the simple sum of two already given realities. On the contrary, when a technical object puts in contact the world of machines and the natural world, it forces both worlds to redefine their affordances. In particular, the technical components improve the territory with their presence, and the natural components provide the resources the device needs to complete its action (the wind or the water for the mill).[20] In this sense, the associated milieu is more than the place of a technical object: it is the component that finalizes the technical object's mode of working.[21] Triggered by the technical object, the associated milieu allows the technical object to become what it is — to find its own *individuation*.[22]

The screen perfectly fits this design. In order to work properly, it needs to be connected to a physical space, one that can accommodate both the screen and one or more observers. This involvement with a physical milieu gives rise to two forms of association. The first path sees screens spread across a territory and somehow "occupy" it. Such an "occupation" is far from being neutral. While accommodating themselves within a physical space, screens exploit the resources of the territory and in exchange endow it with characteristics and functions that it did not have before. This is the case of early cinema. As the then-famous critic Louis Delluc noted at the beginning of the 1920s, film's rapid and widespread success in an age of flourishing transportation allowed distant audiences to enjoy the same movie almost at the same time, connecting otherwise isolated points and transforming our world into a site of exhibition.[23] Our current networked society is just one step forward. The spread of surveillance cameras and monitoring facilities transforms our world into a series of sentinel posts. In these cases, while the territory uncovers its breadth, screens become an *infrastructure* that engages and reshapes the territory.[24]

The second path sees screens "appropriate" part of the surrounding space and transform it into the setting where they perform their action. This is the case, again, of the Phantasmagoria. Its basic scheme recalled ancient rituals, hence the need for secrecy, surprise, and control. The answer was a theater that was kept sealed and in darkness—a piece of world that did not simply host the show, as in the magic lantern shows, but that was intimately part of the spectacle and its "machine." The apotheosis was reached in 1799, when the famous impresario Robertson (Étienne-Gaspard Robert) moved his performances to the grounds of an old nunnery. The new location's history and atmosphere accentuated the dispositif's propensities, to the point that it became the Phantasmagoria's emblem.[25] What is apparent for the Phantasmagoria is also true for many present-day screens. There are urban spaces such as Times Square in New York City or Federation Square in Melbourne that change their traditional functions and become ancillary to the presence of gigantic screens. They allow the screens to address the crowd that they gather and accommodate—a crowd made no longer by passers-by, but by bystanders. The physical context is not only adapted, but is literally included in the screen-based dispositif, which in this way becomes an *optical-environmental compound*.

Either as elements of an infrastructure or as parts of an optical-environmental compound, screens find a strong connection with their physical context. They work within and upon a space. Conversely, this space finds its specificity in screens; be it an environment that hosts screens and consequently responds to them or a now-specialized site that envelops screens, this space becomes an accomplice of screens' action and a component of their assemblage. Screen and space merge, and the landscape becomes a *screenscape*.

Innervation

In addition to Simondon's idea of a mutual exchange of their respective resources, there are different theoretical models that can be summoned to explain the merging of screen and space. In the first decades of the twentieth century, the biologist Jakob von Uexküll was interested in animals' and humans' perceptual worlds, where each organism perceives the same environment differently and transforms it in a specific field of action.[26] We can consider technical objects active entities that, not unlike living organisms, "read" their surroundings in their own way and transform them into their own *Umwelt*. The screen's ability to detect a territory in order to "occupy" it is a perfect illustration of this process. A second model is offered by historian and philosopher Michel de Certeau. In the 1970s, de Certeau explored the ways in which we convert a generic place into a specific space thanks to social practices such as walking, telling stories, and mapping.[27] According to de Certeau, these practices recall the process of enunciation by which a speaker takes possession of the possibilities of a language and creates her own discourse, thereby inscribing herself into the utterance as its ideal source.[28] Again, we can apply this interpretation to screens. In particular, the cases in which a screen "appropriates" a place and transforms it into its own setting is in some ways an act of enunciation. Without dismissing these two models, I want now to engage another framework, suggested by Walter Benjamin's idea of *innervation*.[29]

Benjamin speaks of innervation as a multistep process. To innervate means to open a pathway into an individual or a collective body and by becoming part of it to reconfigure its organization, to enhance its performance, and to assign to it new tasks and goals. A technical component provides a social or biological entity with new organs;[30] the entity's orientation and sensibilities change;[31] and its action takes a new course, with new practices replacing old ones and new predispositions coming to the fore. Finally, a new kind of interplay between elements emerges.[32] The consequence is a leap forward of the entity; whether this entity is a human being or a collective body, it now moves toward an unprecedented identity.

In a screenscape, we detect a similar process. When screens occupy or annex a space, they penetrate its fabric, develop its potentialities, and change its nature. In particular, screens transform a territory into a space where visual data can circulate and be accessed. They create points in and upon which we convey, approach, rework, check, retrieve, and share this data and connect the data with social discourses and collective behavior. The territory finds new configurations based on its own ability to support this kind of action and ultimately adheres to the screens' presence. If screens become the backbone of a new environment, the territory becomes the counterpart of the screens' presence.

Television's infiltration into domestic and into public spaces illustrates how screens can be a means of innervation. In postwar America, the penetration of television into the household elicited a theatricalization and a specularization of the family space, as Lynn Spigel demonstrates.[33] The TV console constituted a new and alternative point of attraction; it brought public space into the private space of the home; and it facilitated the purchase of other appliances, providing a more general "technicalization" of the household. At the same time, sitcoms and other kinds of shows literally staged family life, transforming it into a spectacle and providing a sort of mirror for their audiences. As a consequence, the living room underwent a deep transformation: from a space of aggregation, it became a space of vision and a space of performance, able to "domesticate" a technology that had crept into it.

In the 1990s, the penetration of television into public spaces, be they coffeehouses, bars, restaurants, shopping malls, stores, medical waiting rooms, stations, and airports, followed a different path, which Anna McCarthy explores.[34] While still offering points of attractions, TV screens engaged people who were doing something else. Buyers, customers, and travelers had the opportunity to become spectators while remaining buyers, customers, and travelers. To achieve this goal, television screens did not need to appropriate a space and to convert it into a site of vision, as they did in the household. They just needed to spread into the territory, to mark its nodes, and to build an ideal network. Innervation here prompted a modulation of spaces, rather than a conversion of previous sites. Yet in both cases, what emerged was a new screenscape: in one case, it was centered at sites where the screen played the role of a centerpiece; in the other, it was dominated by places where the screen worked as potential connector. It's worth noticing that this process was brought forward by what we are used to consider the same technical dispositif, television; however, the two different forms of encounter with an associated milieu and the two different screenscapes that surfaced might suggest that television acted as it were as two different dispositifs.

Despite their potential differences, all screenscapes represent a crucial point of junction between the optical and the environmental. In a screenscape, screens intercept the gaze and at the same time shape the space in which visual data are available.[35] They address eyes and mobilize feet. Conversely, the space hosts screens and at the same time adapts itself to them. Geography and visibility thus overlap. The consequence of these convergences is twofold. On one hand, the screen gains new opportunities. It no longer works alone and for itself; it annexes its own context and reaches a high level of performativity thanks to this "ecological" appropriation. Its ability to interact with spectators and users increases, as does its ability to spread and to rework visual data. The screen becomes an "extended medium." On the other hand, the presence of screens changes the territory's inflection, and the space is no longer a simple container, but rather becomes part of the screen's action. It determines and produces positions, postures, ranges, points of view, and so on, and consequently, it sustains and models the screen's interactions and

29

visibility. In this sense, it becomes an essential component of the process of mediation.

An Ecology of Operations

The ways in which screen and space overlap, thanks to the inner-vation of the latter by the former, bring to the fore the *operations* that undergird a screenscape. They are *hybrid operations*, since they synchronize and merge different elements, including mechanical tools, human bodies, environmental elements, and mental attitudes. They are *interconnected operations*, since they respond to each other, either for a specific purpose or in a more stochastic way. They are often *invisible operations*, when they are directly performed by machines and consequently bypass human eyes, such as facial recognition systems (think of Facebook's DeepFace) or the images taken by military drones.[36] Finally, they are *located operations*, since they ultimately define the screenscape's range and extension. Indeed, they constitute what Bernard Geoghegan has termed an *ecology of operations*, that is, the assembly of processes that define a dispositif's playing field.[37]

Apparently each technospatial dispositif performs a distinct group of actions. Let's think of our initial examples. The Phantasmagoria, while summoning the kingdom of dead, worked equally on the physical space of the theater, the emotional space of spectators, and the social space of the audience. The postwar television gathered the family, reinforcing its sense of privateness. Cinema offered, and still offers, imaginary worlds that challenge the real world in which spectators reside. Radar scans a wide territory in order to prevent both internal risks and external intrusions. The laptop allows connections at a distance. Each dispositif works in its own way, according to its purposes, its range, and ultimately its terrain of action. Yet there are recurring operations that these dispositifs share.

A first group regards the ways and the degree to which technology penetrates the territory. Our initial examples imply a progressive technologization of space: the Phantasmagoria relied on a single screen located in an enclosed space in front of a unique audience; control rooms bear witness to the widespread presence of cameras, sensors, detectors, observers, experts, and so on within our environment. This increase highlights a process to which Luciano Floridi calls attention, in which technological innervation favors the creations of "envelopes," that is, spaces already structured in order to accommodate a technology, at the expenses of "environments," that is, territories to which the technology must adapt itself.[38]

A second set of operations regards the shape of the territory. This shape is seldom stable. The settings in which a screen takes place tend to change their format. This is the case of film theaters, which underwent dramatic transformations from nickelodeons to cinema palaces to multiplexes. Indeed, screenscapes are characterized by and endless genesis—like Simondon's technical objects, whose lives display a persistent "coming-into-being."[39] Screenscapes' multistage self-realization often consists of an expansion: optical devices tend to multiply (think of the progressive occupation of the domestic space by monitors, displays, terminals, and so on) or at least to create new spatial connections (think of television and its capacity to put spectators in contact with the entire universe outside the domestic walls). Yet the self-realization can also take the reverse path: national firewalls are an example of screenscapes' intentional delimitations.

A third group of operations defines the forms of access to both the visual and aural data. Our examples highlight the crucial role of the setting in which spectators and users are accommodated, as well as the different ways through which visual data can be approached. There are spaces that offer full visibility and others affected by blind spots, areas in which images are made public and others in which they are intended for only a few, points of contact and forms of seclusion. Jacques Rancière coined the expression *distribution of the sensible* to designate how different media share their content — with modern media tending to create egalitarian access.[40] Screens are a paramount element of the contemporary distribution of sensible. While widening the spread of visual and aural data, especially thanks to the networked images of the web, they also retain forms of restriction due to economic, social, or power inequalities.

The question of access highlights the connections between screen and space. Its different forms generally rely on a double manipulation. There are operations on the spectator/user, who can be pushed, halted, attracted, channeled, and so on, and there are operations on the screen itself, which can be located, relocated, put at a certain distance, kept closer, or removed from our sight. Whatever their shape, the resulting settings underscore how "looking-at-ness"[41] is not only *embodied* in a perceptual organism and *embedded* in a cultural configuration; it is also *grounded* in a territory.

Screens merge with territory to provide the public exhibition of images, domestic entertainment, strategic visual data, control of urban areas, military detection, and so on. From this point of view, they are multifunctional objects. Film theories have understood this characteristic very well. While focusing on the main metaphors of the screen as a window and as a mirror, they also have explored the idea of the screen as a slate, as a sensitive surface, as an installation, as a filter, as a divide, and as a concealment.[42] The current ubiquity of the screen further multiplies the functions that it takes on when it merges with space. Yet below these functions, there are always the operations we have talked about. They guarantee the merging of screens and territory and define the playing field of each dispositif.

Screens and Enclosures
Returning to our initial examples, one characteristic that deserves attention is the recurring presence of spatial enclosures that intentionally exclude the immediate surroundings and screens that, thanks to their images, reestablish a contact with the world — be

it a factual or a hypothetical world, one at hand or distant, the one that individuals have left behind or one that they are not able to reach, and so on. The Phantasmagoria did this by projecting ghosts in a space that was sealed at the beginning of the show. Cinema offered, and continues to offer, screened stories in a theater. Postwar television combined domestic interiors with news from around the world. Radar brings together a sentinel post and the width of the airspace. Surveillance control rooms align the space of a closet with an exterior that is potentially under threat. Finally, the screen-elicited bubbles that we create around us when immersed in our laptop or smartphone merge a space of intimacy with public content, including online conversations. What does this convergence of enclosed spaces and screens imply in terms of operations? And what is its ultimate meaning?

The crucial action that the optical-environmental arrangements above perform is to highlight the presence of a perimeter and to transform it into a defense against the outside world. The borders of the space in which the screen is located are either concrete walls, as in the Phantasmagoria, cinema, radar station, and surveillance rooms, or invisible, self-imposed confines established by the individual in front of the screen, as in digital bubbles. In the first case, the borders physically frame the viewers; in the second case, they wrap the viewers in a zone of intimacy; in both situations, they place in opposition an inside and an outside. The territory is split and becomes dualistic. In general, the separation of inside and outside creates a contrast between a space that is private, or sacred, or autonomous, or ruled and a space that is common, or profane, or heterogeneous, or unconstrained.[43] Here, instead, what emerges is the idea of a *space of retreat* that is opposed to a *space of exposure*. The inside is a sort of refuge, the outside a threatening zone. This is quite clear in the case of the radar station and the surveillance room, whose main function is to detect external threats, yet it also applies to the Phantasmagoria, to cinema, and even to personal space — an imaginary bubble — in which online individuals seek respite from their everyday engagement with an often demanding milieu.

Between the two spaces, there is no lack of circulation. In the physical walls of our dispositifs, there is always a door, which is replaced in the digital bubbles by the constant possibility of reverting one's attention to the immediate surroundings. This door allows the outside to reach inside, and vice versa. When it is closed — something that happens once the spectacle starts, or duty calls, or the immersion in the laptop is complete — it is replaced by another breach that puts the internal space in connection with the external one. This breach coincides with the surface that hosts images and sound from the world "out there" and that displays them "inside." Rather than a window or a door, a conduit — since it grants circulation rather than transparency and admission — this breach provides a replacement for the exterior world when the physical openings are closed. The outside returns in the form of screened images and sounds, whose sensorial qualities compensate for the spatial deprivation. Consequently, individuals can avoid direct exposure to the outside world. They can enjoy it as an effect of these images and sounds in a space of retreat.

The *projection/protection complex* is my term for this mechanism of disconnection and reconnection with reality that emerges thanks to enclosures and screens. It highlights the fear of dealing directly with the world — a fear that is not uncommon in modern Western culture. To limit myself to the twentieth century, I am thinking of the celebrated sections of *Being and Time* in which Martin Heidegger speaks of the anxiety of being-in-the-world, exposed to a reality that, in turn, exposes itself to us, as well as the fear elicited by the impending presence of external menaces.[44] Taking up a recurring topic of philosophical anthropology, Arnold Gehlen underscores the threats of the natural environment for that "underdeveloped animal" that is man and the need for the latter to build an artificial but safe milieu.[45] Focusing on modernity, Georg Simmel describes an extremely intense and taxing age characterized by an excess of sensorial stimuli that affect the "mental life" of city dwellers.[46] Expanding upon Simmel's comments, Walter Benjamin speaks of an epoch of shocks and traumas that leave the individual astounded and often speechless.[47] Finally, Paul Virilio suggests that modern technology shrinks space and accelerates time to an unprecedented scale and consequently makes the world unmanageable.[48] Despite their different theoretical contexts, these voices converge in describing the difficulties of directly coping with reality. The radical threats of the twenty-first century — especially global pandemics and climate change — make the sense of insecurity even more palpable: the world "out there" is a deadly menace. The projection/protection complex responds to the fears elicited by this world with a space that works as a *shelter* and a screen that works as a *filter*.

At the same time, the complex expresses an equal and contrary desire to preserve interaction with reality. Spectators and users reengage it by proxy, but it is a proxy that keeps or recreates the world's liveness and density and that consequently allows it to reappear. What was left behind is not lost. This reengagement of the world completes the picture. The filter provided by the screen is also an *interface*[49] that puts in contact two separate universes, the inside and the outside, letting each influence the other. And the shelter provided by the enclosure is also a *niche*[50] that, while maintaining a sort of autonomy, is nevertheless part of a wider environment. The outcome is a mechanism that balances distance and proximity, direct acceptance and possible withdrawal, intervention and caution. The fear of dealing directly with the world finds a positive answer in a protection that does not produce isolation.

Taken in itself, the projection/protection complex appears akin to what Simondon calls a "pure schema of functioning";[51] it is a sort of abstract design that displays the rationale underlying a series of dispositifs as different as the Phantasmagoria, cinema, radar, surveillance control rooms, and electronic bubbles. The dispositifs that embody the complex, instead, are "historical types" whose lives are characterized not only by a recurring configuration — an enclosure and a screen — but also by the presence of inevitable variations, accidents, and adjustments that connect them to their times and contexts. While the "pure schema" defines the basic profile of the "historical types" and consequently what they have in common, the "historical types" display the concrete ways in which the "schema" works and consequently the particular outcomes it can reach. Indeed, the dialectical relationship between "schema" and "types" illuminates both poles. On the one hand, the projection/protection complex gains its full meaning: like the "complexes" in psychoanalysis, it is a recurring mechanism that exerts a strong influence on different situations, and at the same time, like the "military" or "economic complex," it becomes visible as a set of components that respond to the same finality. On the other hand, the instantiations of the complex, starting from those that I listed at the beginning of this chapter, are defined at once by a repeated configuration and by their idiosyncratic composition.[52] The complex covers them insofar as they activate a disconnection and a reconnection with the world, no matter how they perform the two operations. When a dispositif ceases to do this, it slips out of the coverage of the complex.[53] Hence the emergence of a family of media — we can call them *protective media* — in which the bonds are both solid and precarious. We can always add a new member when its performance is pertinent,[54] but we can also expel an old member when its performance is directed to other ends. The outcome is an idea of media history in which convergences and alliances are meaningful, but not constrictive. The projection/protection complex with its instantiations offers a good example of such an idea of media history.

Screenscapes and Mediation

It is easy to read the projection/protection complex, with its replacement of reality with images of reality, in the light of the Heideggerian prophecy of the world being transformed into a picture.[55] There is no doubt that the complex reflects an age characterized by an increasingly alienated reality, an overwhelming presence of technology, and a progressive transformation of the natural space into a map or a set of data. Yet more than confirming the Heideggerian dystopia, the projection/protection complex helps us to understand better the extent to which screenscapes intervene in our mediation with the world.[56]

I have already underscored that the convergence of screen and space, far from being a simple addition, creates a new landscape in which what comes to the fore are the ways in which individuals access images, recognize situations, map territories, manipulate possibilities, and follow specific courses of action. In this scenario, the screen becomes an essential element in the confrontation of an individual with the world (real or possible) and with others (physically or virtually copresent). Correspondingly, the territory becomes a dedicated space where confrontation with the world and with others reaches the point of its full realization. This means that in a screenscape, screens reveal the very essence of media: they are tools for a situated mediation. Conversely, the space acquires a certain quality of mediation: space becomes a medium unto itself.

The screenscapes elicited by the projection/protection complex fully exploit their nature as *spaces of mediation*. Indeed, their constitutive elements are at the core of the ways in which we negotiate reality, instead of being "exposed" or even "prey" to it. First, the convergence of screen and enclosure that characterizes the complex bears witness to the composite nature of our mediation. To interact with the world is an activity that engages a plurality of resources and that depends on their mutual convergence. We do not cope with reality just through a single sense or a single channel. We do it in multimodal ways, depending upon what is available and what is functional. And we do not cope with reality exclusively with means that are external to it. We often use reality itself.[57] In this sense, the merging of screen and space is exemplary: it offers a playground in which we can deploy multiple strategies and in which we use a portion of world to mediate with the world. The effect is to bring to the fore the whole picture of our mediation, including its environmental components. Connotations such as those tied to an atmosphere or an ambiance become then crucial—I am thinking of the "visible darkness" in the Phantasmagoria,[58] the comforts in cinema, or Zoom fatigue in virtual bubbles.[59]

Second, the projection/protection complex relies on a separation that paves the way for a reconnection, since we drop the external reality in order to reach it. This situation reflects the presence at the core of the process of mediation of an exclusion that demands to be mended. Not by chance, when we approach things through media, we experience a sense of distance that paradoxically helps things to come closer[60] but that nevertheless persists. This means that we regain the world by accepting its absence. Our examples are inhabited by presences that bear the sign of the absence: from the Phantasmagoria's ghosts to the Zoom's talking heads, images of liminal entities bring to the surface the "included exclusion" that characterizes our mediated encounters.[61]

Third, the sense of fear that permeates the complex reveals a largely underestimated aspect of mediation. Indeed, our confrontation with the world does not necessarily imply an expansion and a conquest; on the contrary, it is often a form of defense against potential threats. Hence the relevance of media, and especially screen-based media, that represent a safeguard against external menaces rather than an "extension of man," as Marshall McLuhan famously claimed, with a formula that implicitly emphasized the process of appropriating reality.[62] Today, a hostile Anthropocene highlights the role of these *protective media*.[63]

Finally, by highlighting the role of situatedness, separation, and fear in the process of mediation, the projection/protection complex puts the very notion of the world under scrutiny. The world is no longer taken for granted, nor it is simply encapsulated in the opposition between being "as such" and being "for us." In a more complex game, the world emerges at the intersection of nonbinary couples such as being "out there" and "on screen," or being "at hand" and "at a distance," or being "given" and "given back."[64] Its nature — as indeed ours — and its configurations, including the couple "interior" and "exterior," are ultimately determined by and within the mediation itself.

The projection/protection complex embodies these issues in a technoenvironmental mechanism that stages a process of separation and rapprochement, of rejection and defense, of acceptance and replacement. This peculiar way of working puts the two key elements of the complex — the space and screen — exactly in the middle of the process of mediation. If individuals and the world confront each other, and if the former finds the means to manage the latter, it is because of the physical presence of enclosures and screened images. Their action is the only immediate element of the mediation, and the world and individuals ultimately emerge as a consequence of it.[65] Indeed, this is the paradox of the complex: it can give back what was left behind only as mediated reality. In exchange, it displays its own work of mediation in full view. We will once again enjoy the world from a safe harbor, but we will not be able to do this without also enjoying the process of its restitution.

In the early modern and modern age, there are other complexes that model the way in which screenscapes work. I am thinking of the *exhibitionary complex* that Tony Bennett sees at the roots of the museum[66] and that can cover different forms of display, from paintings in a gallery to commodities in a window, from bodies in a pageant to data on a slate. I am equally thinking of the *communicative complex* — the name is mine — that Raymond Williams describes while speaking of the flourishing of the press, the telegraph, and the telephone in the nineteenth century[67] and that ultimately covers most of the forms of circulation and exchange of material and immaterial objects in a territory. The projection/protection complex has tangential relations with these other complexes, which not only share some of its traits, but moreover are partly applicable to the dispositifs I have discussed — think of cinema and its exhibitionary components, or the digital bubbles and their communicative orientation. Yet the peculiar way in which the projection/protection complex brings together screens and enclosures, its attempt to respond to the modern need for a safe encounter with an increasingly aggressive and elusive reality, and finally its capacity to be in the middle of a process of mediation make of it a particularly relevant and enlightening case study.

In the next chapters, I focus on the three main examples from which I started and that perfectly exemplify the nature of the projection/protection complex. I will analyze in detail the Phantasmagoria, cinema, and the digital bubbles, with their settings, their ecologies of operations, and the fears they negotiate. At the same time, I will keep constantly in the background the ways in which these three examples imply and affect processes of mediation. Projected on this wide horizon, these three examples reveal the extent to which the merging of screen and space is part of the modern attempt to capture the world without suffering the consequences of a direct exposure to it.

Bunkers

Matinee, directed by Joe Dante (USA, 1993), develops a series of striking parallels. Set in Key West during the Cuban missile crisis, the movie tells the story of a teenager, Gene Loomis, whose father is an active serviceman and who has an overwhelming passion for horror movies. The terrifying images of the films that Gene loves mingle with his nightmares, which center on fears that his father will be killed. Still uncertain about his father's destiny, Gene becomes excited by the news that the producer Lawrence Woolsey will screen a preview of his latest B-movie, *Mant!*, in Key West. The implausible plot of Woolsey's movie revolves around the idea that in a world that has been contaminated by atomic pollution, X-rays turn a dental patient into an ant man, or "mant"; the fear of an impending atomic conflict between America and the Soviet Union is echoed in the unlikely story told by the film. The way in which Woolsey arranges the preview creates further equivalences. The movie is offered in a new format called "Atomo-vision"—a sort of 3-D that will "put spectators in motion," as Woolsey puts it—and with new special effects called "Rumble-Rama," consisting of buzzers inserted into the spectators' chairs, flares that burn in front of the screen during explosion scenes, sound pitches that create vibrations, and an actor dressed as the Ant-Man inside the theater. Badly performed, the special effects make the spectacle go awry. The buzzers are too forceful and threaten the audience; the actor dressed as Ant-Man becomes angry when he sees his girlfriend flirting with another boy; and the vibrations of the sound, combined with an excessive crowd, cause the balcony to collapse. When on the screen an atomic blast apparently stops the projection, the audience is led to believe that the Third World War has begun. While fleeing the collapsing theater, Gene and his friend Sandra end up in an atomic shelter that the theater's owner built in the basement in anticipation of the war, and, likely, out of fear generated by the horror movies that he regularly screens.... At last, Woolsey frees Gene and Sandra from the bunker, and the Breaking News on TV announces that the Cuban missile crisis has come to an end.

This plot, with its dense set of coincidences, makes *Matinee* an apologue. There are innumerable threats "out there": a father in danger, families in trouble, jealous boys, arrogant classmates, obsessive teachers, and moreover an impending war. Against these threats there is also a line of defense. It includes not only the ships that encircle Cuba, the restricted areas where servicemen and their families live, the antiaircraft batteries deployed on the shore, the bunkers and casemates that are everywhere, but also the basements transformed into shelters, the duck-and-cover drills that students undergo repeatedly at school, and finally, the movie theater. The theater provides a safe refuge from external dangers. It is like the caves in which our ancestors sought protection from the ferocious animals they then drew on the walls, as Woolsey explains to Gene. Similarly, the theater is where a crowd of anxious boys and girls find a relief from their fears by watching movies that depict impending menaces through harmless images. The bunker in the basement is then a reasonable extension of theater's protective nature.

While recalling that against a dangerous exterior it is possible to build a safe interior, the defense system that spans from barracks to theaters is strongly embedded into the geography of Key West: it crosses restricted military zones, the school where students practice air raid drills, and the spaces for civilians. In a word, it is deeply territorialized. In exchange, the territory is weaponized: the city is under alarm, the school mimics the military training camp, malls are besieged by citizens who want to stock up on food, and every basement can hide a shelter.

This double shift — a territorialized defense and a weaponized territory — perfectly echoes the modern evolution of the battlefield. As Virilio underscores in his book on bunkers, the wars of the twentieth century no longer imply preexisting grounds where armies physically collide; on the contrary, they cover much wider areas. Conflicts create a new multidimensional space that includes zones of friction and ordinary premises, pieces of land as well as skies and oceanic depths, and even a new climate in which air mingles with deadly gasses and the waves of explosion.[1] Technologies of war innervate every milieu, and the whole landscape becomes a *warscape*.[2] In this battlefield that englobes the globe, the line of defense is not necessarily located at the border of the nation, nor does it necessarily consist of thick walls that combat the physical attacks of the enemy. As bunkers exemplify, on the one hand, there are still buildings that perform a protective function, but their presence extends to the heart of the cities, and their function can be accomplished by the most diverse architectures — and ultimately by the most diverse media.[3] On the other hand, there are still layers and filters that preserve an interior from the external threats, but these filters and layers can be replaced by more immaterial tools, such as a firewall, when the conflict is based on intelligence and data.[4] In modern war, the defense system includes everything, and it is everywhere.

Through the tender story of a teenager, *Matinee* shows what Virilio writes in his book, which mingles personal memories, the history of architecture, and technologies of warfare. In Key West, a movie theater is equivalent to an atomic shelter as they both protect from a widespread danger, and they both are immersed in a territory that is inevitably exposed. In this sense, the movie is even more than an apologue. It is a precise diagnosis of contemporary conflicts and ultimately of contemporary life conditions, with their fears, the need for protection, and the implication of space. The climax of this diagnosis is paradoxically reached in the apparently crazy teaser of *Mant!* that *Matinee* englobes into its story. This wonderful example of what Christian Metz called "mirror construction"[5] states simply the truth: atomic blasts have already polluted the world; they have affected and changed our atmosphere. A gigantic Woolsey addresses the audience from the screen and states": "Today there is no safe place to be"—except the movie theater, where explosions are transformed into spectacle.

Matinee's utopic component comes only at the end. Freed from the bunker in which they were driven—and where they experienced a first kiss that their friends experienced in the movie theater—Gene and Sandra run on the beach while the helicopters that were deployed to Cuba are coming back. Maybe, one day, the atmosphere will clear again. . . .

CHAPTER TWO

The Phantasmagoria:

An Enclosure and Three Worlds

The Vaults of Memphis

In chapter 7 of his *Mémoires*, Étienne Gaspard Robertson, who became famous for popularizing the Phantasmagoria in 1798, recalls an episode that despite being generally overlooked by scholars, sheds new light on his main achievement. While researching the occult sciences, the young Robertson discovers "an engraving with the illustration of the rituals that initiates have to be submitted to, following the four elements, in the subterranean vaults called Memphis"[1] and reproduces and explains the engraving (fig. 2.1). The first initiation test required the initiate "to sink into the earth, at an unknown depth, by a narrow path."[2] Then the initiate entered a large hall consumed entirely by fire, except for a passage over an incandescent grid. The following test consisted of swimming in a channel in absolute darkness, and finally the initiate, suspended on a drawbridge in a noisy hall, had to jump from one big wheel to another until he reached the exit. Robertson describes in painstaking detail the initiation rituals, the characteristics of the environment, the machines that the initiate encounters, and the fear and the excitement that permeate the situation. What he portrays is a grandiose scene that mixes natural elements, technological devices, suffering bodies, labyrinthine passages, darkness, and sound in

Figure 2.1. "The subterranean vaults called Memphis." In Étienne Gaspard Robertson, *Mémoires récréatifs, scientifiques et anecdotiques du physicien-aéronaute E. G. Robertson,* inserted between pp. 162 and 163.

which the initiate gains new knowledge and new life after leaving behind his usual milieu. This engraving and the complex world it depicted would exert a permanent influence on Robertson's career as an inventor, lanternist, and impresario. In his words, "it is in these subterranean vaults that the old Phantasmagoria was born."[3]

Overflowing with anecdotes, documents, gossip, and overstatements, Robertson's *Mémoires* are more a boastful self-celebration than an accurate report of facts,[4] yet a critical reading of this text is still useful. Chapter 7, in keeping with the whole book, is relevant not only for its silences (Robertson fails to acknowledge the merits of a certain Filidor, who produced an early instantiation of the Phantasmagoria in 1792 and who, under the name of de Philipsthal, brought the show to London in 1801) and for its contradictions (while he praises science for dispelling superstition, Robertson is still captured by the deceptive power of magic), but also for its unexpected revelations. Indeed, Robertson's statement that the engraving would be a source of lasting inspiration changes our perception of the Phantasmagoria. Instead of a show with ghosts — the characteristic for which the Phantasmagoria was and is best known — the etching directs the reader's attention toward a separation from the everyday world, an immersion into a space filled by strange machines, a confrontation with the four natural elements — earth, water, fire, and air — and the acquisition of new abilities and skills. What comes to the fore is not a mere parade of spirits, but a composite and sophisticated dispositif that, while depriving initiates of their usual points of reference, underpins an exploration of new universes and a testing of initiates' emotional endurance.

In reading the Phantasmagoria this way, I will move away from its traditional interpretations. Laurent Mannoni has seen in the Phantasmagoria a smart application of the magic lantern.[5] Terry Castle has underscored its place in the history of imagination and ultimately its capacity to transform thoughts into spectral realities.[6] Stefan Andriopoulos has argued that the Phantasmagoria was an attractive reference and finally became an epistemic figure in the German philosophy of the first half of nineteenth century.[7] Tom Gunning has retraced the state of astonishment that the Phantasmagoria consolidated and that film would later inherit.[8] Noam Elcott has emphasized the sense of copresence of images and spectators that the Phantasmagoria's hallucinatory perceptions elicited.[9] In all these approaches, apparitions are the centerpiece. My goal is different: following the engraving, I will contend that the Phantasmagoria was an *optical-environmental dispositif* that, in addition to screened images, included a peculiar site, a space split from the external world and yet arranged as a sort of eccentric and exciting microcosm.

This convergence of the optical and the spatial—due to the merging of the display on the screen and the venue around it—triggered a counterintuitive effect. While restraining the audience within a self-contained space, the Phantasmagoria gave viewers the opportunity to explore and appropriate at least three realms: the kingdom of the dead, experienced in its projections; the physical fabric of our world, displayed through atmospheric effects and physics experiments that were associated with the show; and the interiority of spectators, bolstered by the situation in which they were immersed. Each of these three worlds represented liminal realities—spirits, nature, emotions—that late-eighteenth-century culture investigated with fascination and suspicion. The Phantasmagoria helped to manage these emerging worlds. An early modern medium, it provided what media tend to offer: an interface between observers and observed reality, an environment in which to experience it, and a repository of data and content that represents it. Hence the conclusion that the Phantasmagoria was more than a ghostly entertainment with multiple paraphernalia. It was a new form of mediation with the world, with others, and with the self, based on spatial deprivation and visual reward. Such a task made the Phantasmagoria a perfect instantiation of what I have called the projection/protection complex, that is, the mechanism

that in certain modern media exempts spectators from an immediate exposure to the world and that returns reality to them in a
more manageable form. At a time when the world became at once
more challenging and more volatile, the Phantasmagoria was the
first modern medium to refer to this complex, becoming part of a
peculiar lineage.

In the following pages, I will outline the Phantasmagoria's mode
of working before turning to a close examination of the roles of
both the screen and the setting in creating a seclusion from external reality and three worlds that surprised, delighted, and finally
rewarded spectators for their loss of contact with everyday life.
I will conclude my analysis with some brief remarks on the way
these worlds were represented—as the Phantasmagoria worked as
an unconventional cartography of unexplored territories—and a
consideration of the Phantasmagoria's association with other media.

The Phantasmagoria's Assemblage

As I have mentioned, the Phantasmagoria was born three times.[10] It
first appeared in Paris in December 1792 as a short-lived attraction
offered by Paul Filidor—also spelled Filidort or Philidor—with
the promise of evoking the shadows of celebrities and with the
assurance that the show had "no dangerous influence on the organs,
no unpleasant odor, and persons of all ages and sexes may view
it without inconvenience."[11] It reappeared in Paris in January 1798,
performed by "the citizen E. G. Robertson,"[12] accompanied by
experiments with electricity and in a format that found its can-
onization the following year when the show moved to the former
Couvent des Capucines. Finally, it arrived in London in December 1801 as a patented spectacle by Paul de Philipsthal, without the
alleged didactic purposes that had characterized its two previous
versions—an omission that raised some complaints.[13] Especially
in England, the show was almost immediately imitated by similar
presentations with similar names.[14] Despite its sudden initial success, by late 1810s, the Phantasmagoria began to decline; although it

survived until midcentury, it was mostly as a single attraction — the "Phantasmagoric scenes" — inserted in more composite spectacles.[15]

From the technical point of view, the Phantasmagoria was a development of the entertainments based on the magic lantern. In the second half of the eighteenth century, projections had improved and expanded with new devices such as Edmé-Gilles Guyot's "nebulous lantern" and new kinds of shows such as the ceremony described by Friedrich Schiller in his novel *The Ghost-Seer*.[16] The Phantasmagoria exploited this improvement and expansion, adding two crucial innovations that changed the dispositif. Both innovations were perfectly captured by the English journalist Francis William Blagdon, who in a letter from Paris dated December 20, 1801, claimed to be able to reveal the Phantasmagoria's secrets.[17] The first innovation was the mobility of the projector: the lantern was mounted on wheels, and once it moved closer to the screen, or on the contrary away from it, images would respectively shrink or grow. Adjustable lenses allowed the figures to remain consistently in focus, transforming them into actual presences.[18] The second innovation was that the lanternist's "operations and optical instruments" were hidden "from the eyes of the public."[19] Images were projected from the rear, giving the sense that the apparitions came out of nowhere. We must add that the slides had a black background and, consequently, the screened figures were frameless. Audiences had the impression that they were seeing real ghosts, materialized by miracle, moving freely in the theater.

The mobility of the lantern and the effects of the retroprojection required consummate skills. Robertson was especially proud of his ability. He claimed that his show offered "the veritable proceeding of ghosts, instead of a discontinuous and awkward movement, the lifelike and the vividness of the bodies, a wise distribution of light and shadow, a proper size of the specters, their gradual decline, and finally their almost immediate rapprochement under the eyes of spectators, on whom they seem to rush."[20]

A detailed description of the first Phantasmagoria's instantiation, published in the revolutionary journal *La feuille villageoise* on February 28, 1793, two months after Filidor's opening in Paris, perfectly conveys the sense of astonishment elicited by the dispositif.[21] The chronicle begins in an ironic tone: an "English Physicist" is resuming the old necromantic practices in a spectacle open to everybody and payable in the new revolutionary currency.[22] Yet the description soon becomes more dramatic. After a pedagogical introductory address, the physicist ushered the audience "into a room covered by black drapes, with images of death on the wall and enlightened by a sepulchral lamp."[23] A magical draft blew out the candle, leaving the room in complete darkness, then a clap of thunder exploded and the spectacle began. Mirabeau's ghost first surfaced as a luminous spot, circumfused by a sort of cloud that made his figure indistinct; his countenance gradually became more and more distinguishable. The ghost walked in the shadow; he came so close that spectators could almost touch him; then he disappeared. "Twenty other ghosts follow one another. . . . Sometimes the earth seems to produce them; sometimes they seem to pierce the vault and descend from the ceiling; other times it's the wall itself that seems to open to let them pass."[24] The climax coincided with a hallucinatory scene: "Finally, I saw my own image; I saw myself, go, come, and get excited in front of me."[25]

In his memoir, Pierre-Jean-Baptiste Chaussard, a prominent figure in the French Revolution, adds a more reassuring note. Speaking of Robertson's show, he says: "There is something for everybody. We see the Bleeding Nun and Robespierre, Henry IV and Mirabeau, Franklin and Voltaire, Samuel's and Macbeth's shadows, smart and stupid people, magicians without malice and characters who are surprised to be in the show."[26] Consequently, the audience's reactions varied: "These representations, despite their grim look, go cheerfully. Laughs follow silence and boos alternate with applause, according to the grace that ghosts put in their roles or according to the ideas that they raise."[27] The show, which was complemented by the eerie sound of a spinning glass harmonica, concluded with experiments in physics and a performance by a ventriloquist. Finally, the audience could take liberties. "The fear, the mischievousness, and a bit of licentiousness make spectators move their feet and hands closer to other spectators' feet and hands. The living are no less busy than the dead."[28] Hallucination gave way to mere amusement.

Other, almost forgotten documents provide further information. For example, the almanac *Les ombres, ou, les vivans qui sont morts: Fantasmagorie litteraire* underscores an additional reason for the Phantasmagoria's success: with "a happy and truly lucrative idea, the citizen Robertson ... partly achieved what we read in ... the black novels that have been published for several years."[29] An audience already familiar with a new narrative form flocked to enjoy what the page simply alluded to.[30] The notice ends with an ironic poem that recalls Chaussard's chronicle:

> One cannot count the number
> of specters of all kinds;
> to laugh, we show the shadow
> of the most hideous scoundrels,
> and, without fear of blame,
> after their death, we bring back
> the spirit and the soul
> of people who had neither.[31]

Blagdon, the *La feuille villageoise*, Chaussard, and *Les ombres* bear witness to the Phantasmagoria's complexity. To an already innovative form of projection, the Phantasmagoria added a peculiar ambiance, a composite program, a prolific series of cultural references, a shrewd ticket-pricing policy, and a special ability to keep spectators at bay — after having bombarded them with images to the limits of hallucination. Within this sundry assemblage of elements, three components came forward: the screen, the setting, and the audience. While each played multiple, even contradictory, roles, together, they helped define the Phantasmagoria's mode of working — in particular, its ability to create different forms of enclosure that severed spectators from their everyday reality and to summon the three worlds that filled the emptiness created by this severance: the kingdom of the dead, the domain of the nature, and the interiority of spectators.

The Screen

There is no doubt that the Phantasmagoria found in the screen its pivotal element. Both in his *Mémoires*[32] and in his own patent,[33] Robertson notes the importance of creating a perfectly transparent screen, a goal that he proudly achieved thanks to an original mix of Arabic gum and white starch. Yet what matters is not the screen's materiality, but its structural role — the position it occupied in the assemblage of elements and the functions it performed.[34]

As I have already mentioned, in the Phantasmagoria, the screen's most immediate function was to hide the presence of a projector and at the same time to host the images cast by it. The screen was at once a *blind* that concealed part of the technical apparatus and a *support* that materialized the rear-projected pictures. One single object thus allowed for these two functions — to conceal, to reveal — that underpinned the Phantasmagoria's mode of working.

As a blind, the screen created a *divide* between two spaces. There was a backstage area, where the technical apparatus did its work, and an area in front in which the specters gained substance. The former was the operator's domain, the latter the space where spectators sat. The splitting was physical, delimiting two different portions of the theater. It was also sensorial, opposing the visible and the invisible. Finally, it was metaphorical, since it provided a separation between the site of production and the site of consumption and, in a general sense, between the space of technology and the space of imagination.

As a support that hosted projected images, the screen appeared as a *luminous spot* — the only one in a darkened room. The anonymous chronicler of *La feuille villageoise* describes the surprise and attraction exerted by this spot, which first "pierces the deep night from afar," then "moves, approaches, grows at the same time, and takes on a configuration that becomes more distinct with each step it takes," and finally, "once it got four or five feet away," reveals the identity of the convened ghost.[35] While the darkness of the room marked a discontinuity with the external world — reinforcing the symbolic closing of the doors that occurred at the end of the conjurer's preliminary speech — the screen's luminosity granted access to a new kind of reality. The realm of the dead reached into our world thanks to a point of passage — an *interface* — between the two territories.[36] We have already heard in the *La feuille villageoise* and from Chaussard a description of the ghosts' parade: for some spirits, it was an opportunity to live again, for others, especially for the heroes of the Revolution, a way to recall their procession to the guillotine.

However, the screen was also a paradoxical object. While allowing ghosts to become visible, the screen eluded spectators' perception. Before the show, it was masked by a curtain; during the show, it disappeared under the images that it hosted. This condition assimilated the screen into the technical apparatus, which also withdrew from spectators' eyes. In exchange, specters gained a sort of independence. They moved freely, back and forth, often as if they were suspended in the air, invading spectators' space. A late English report published in *The Portfolio* vividly describes the audience's reactions: "Some thought that they could have touched the figures, others had a different notion of their distance, and few apprehended that they have not advanced beyond the first row of the audience."[37] Chaussard is even more vivid. Recalling the show's climax, he says: "Surprised by the harmonica's sound and by unexpected apparitions, [spectators] try to hit the shadows with their cane. Shadows flee away screaming."[38]

The sense that the ghosts possessed agency not only gave substance to the world of the dead. It also elicited a sense of close contact with spectators. Noam Elcott speaks of an "assembly of bodies and images in real time and space,"[39] yet rather than a form of coming together in which bodies and images were equalized, this assembly was permeated by forms of communication, and even of transaction, that enabled the real world and the other world to be in touch without losing their different natures. Chaussard recalls the back-and-forth of the ghosts, to which the audience responded with an equal movement of expectation and surprise: "You named [a ghost], she appeared ... then you uttered a cry of dread and dismay."[40] At the same time, the exchange was also an appropriation. For a supplementary fee, patrons were able to have an extra ghost of their choice among those in display.[41] Such a commodification reveals the Phantasmagoria's ideological propensity: the other world ultimately was a territory to be explored and exploited. Spirits were partners in commerce.

A blind that masks the apparatus, a divide that defines the theater's physical organization, a support on which apparitions gain life, an interface that puts two worlds in contact, and a point of confluence of spectators' gazes that remained invisible in itself. While playing a multifaceted role, the Phantasmagoria's screen systematically coupled two tasks, hosting images and shaping the space where it was located. We must now look at this interplay between the optical and the spatial from the perspective of the Phantasmagoria's setting.

The Setting

With the Phantasmagoria, it is impossible to speak of the screen without speaking of the theater where the audience gathered. The latter was at once the premise and the complement of the former's action.

On the one hand, the auditorium and its immediate extensions were closed spaces, severed from external surroundings. In becoming an audience, spectators lost contact with their usual world. Such a separation, which complemented the separation between the theater and the backstage area, was foundational with respect to the screen's performance: if apparitions were able to become

actual presences, it was also because the loss of contact with everyday reality left a void that ghosts filled. On the other hand, the
auditorium and its extensions were not only a *recess*, but also an
environment — a space where the nature that spectators were asked
to leave behind reappeared in its more expressive aspects, such as
in thunder and in the sound of rain, or in its basic laws reproduced
by technical devices or exposed by physics experiments. The emergence of an ecological universe hosted by the setting complemented
the emergence of the kingdom of the dead triggered by the screen
in a sort of mutual relay.

The double nature of the setting as recess and as environment, as
well as its relations with the screen's action, were already apparent
in Filidor's Phantasmagoria. Not by chance the anonymous chronicle
in *La feuille villageoise* starts from a description of the ritual closure
of the theater and the imitation of natural events that immediately
took place afterward. While the shutting of the doors and the
sudden darkness created a separation from spectators' usual milieu,
this separation was immediately redeemed by overwhelming special
effects. "Suddenly thunder rumbles; the flashes dazzling your eyes
at intervals, seeming to shine only to make the darkness blacker. At
the same time all the signs of thunderstorms are heard; rain, hail
and winds form both the opening and the symphony of the act that
is about to begin."[42] A new world — at once aural and visual — came
to the fore.

The setting's double nature as recess and as environment became
even clearer with Robertson's Phantasmagoria. On January 3, 1799,
Robertson moved his show from its previous location, at the Pavill-
lon de l'Échiquier, to the Couvent des Capucines. The new site, a
nunnery that had been expropriated by the Revolution in 1789 and
transformed into a populated and sometime tumultuous Maison
Nationale, added further fascination to the spectacle, if only for
the presence of numerous old graves and for the memories tied to
the former residents of the site — an order of nuns known for their
strict discipline. Yet it was the general arrangement of the space

Figure 2.2. "Expériénces physique de Robertson." In Robertson, *Mémoires récréatifs, scientifiques et anecdotiques du physicien-aéronaute E. G. Robertson*, vol. 2, frontispiece.

that was the real key to the new location's success. Robertson's *Mémoires*[43] and the "Instructive Program" distributed to the public[44] allow us to cast a glance at this arrangement through the layout of the new site and the attractions that were offered.

To reach the Phantasmagoria, spectators had to leave Rue Neuve des Petits Champs and cross part of the convent's garden.[45] Once they reached the site, they lingered in a vestibule called the premier Salon de Physique or moved to the passage called Galerie de la Femme Invisible. While the latter entertained waiting spectators with an acousmatic Invisible Woman who answered every possible question and with a ventriloquist, Fitz-James, who exhibited his celebrated abilities, the Salon de Physique was more austere (fig. 2.2). It housed a prism "reflecting the seven primitive colors," several anamorphic and illusionistic paintings, a microscope, beetles and fleas, distorting mirrors, and a set of electrostatic devices that produced discharges between two poles. Despite its appearance as a traditional cabinet of curiosities, the items on display and the presence of scientific experiments—experiments that Robertson widely heralded in his frequent advertisements—gave a slightly different color to the Salon de Physique: it was a sort of microcosm, exhibiting natural specimens and natural effects.

At some point, the public accessed the Salle de la Fantasmagorie, where the apparitions took place. There were seats, but spectators could also stand. After a brief speech by the conjurer, the doors were closed, and a complete darkness enveloped the spectators—a "darkness visible," as David Brewster called it.[46] The theater became a sealed space within an already enclosed site in a not easy to reach building—producing a Russian doll effect. It was in this sealed space that ghosts made their appearance in a ceaseless procession. Despite the triumphant arrival of the kingdom of the dead, the natural world did not disappear. It emerged no longer due to visual experiments, as in the Salon de Physique, but due to sound and tactile effects. Robertson speaks of three devices that were employed during the show, a tool for the imitation of the noise of rain, a tool for producing thunder, and a tool for the simulation of wind and a hurricane.[47] While detailing the technical specifications for each machine, Robertson gives a functional explication for their use. He notes, for example, that the rain noise "puts thought to sleep, so to speak; all ideas seem to be recalled to a single object, to a single impression."[48] Such a state of mind allowed spectators to direct all their attention toward the show, but at the same time, it recalled the situation that they encounter when confronted with nature. What is more natural than essential atmospheric elements such as rain, thunder, a hurricane, and the darkness of the night? Framed in a sealed space, detached from reality, the Phantasmagoria's audience was able to enjoy a natural environment by means of technical devices.

So we find an esoteric screen and an atmospheric setting. While confining spectators within a restricted space, both the screen and the setting gave them the opportunity to face more complex worlds, respectively, the other world of the ghosts and the natural world of weather and, in the Salon de Physique, of optics and electricity. The two universes may seem to be at odds with one another. Yet in the Phantasmagoria, they coexisted: they were both "marvels" and, at the same time, they were perfectly factual in a blend that the plate with the vaults of Memphis had already foreseen.

Fears

But why a severance from immediate surroundings, followed by the emergence of new realities? Why an enclosure that brought forth what spectators left behind or never accessed? As I already mentioned, the Phantasmagoria may be considered an early instantiation of the projection/protection complex as it embodied a mechanism that exempts spectators from direct exposure to the instability, unpredictability, and irrationality of modern life while providing alternative access to the world based on different and safe means of experiencing those qualities. The sealed space of the Phantasmagoria, combined with the materialization of liminal entities that spectators were asked to negotiate, bears perfect witness to how the projection/protection complex works.

The key element of the complex is the fear of immediate reality. We tend to think that the fears that permeated the Phantasmagoria were elicited by the screened ghosts. This is undoubtedly true, yet the Phantasmagoria also dealt with other kinds of anxieties related to direct exposure to the world. Robertson's *Mémoires* offers recurring claims, and sometimes purported testimony, about the terror elicited by the encounter with ghosts in real life or with natural forces set free. Parallel documents, such as booklets on alleged apparitions and the calamities they bring with them bear the same witness.[49] To these fears, we can add the concerns raised by the political and social revolutions of the time — after all, Filidor's Phantasmagoria was contemporary with the Reign of Terror — as well as the tensions triggered by the rise of new lifestyles. These anxieties required an answer. Jonathan Crary, in his analysis of visuality from the eighteenth to the nineteenth centuries, identifies this answer in heightened forms of self-control and social restraint.[50] To counterbalance an overstimulating atmosphere — to which they nevertheless contributed — optical dispositifs summoned forms of discipline that at once generated limitations and offered protection. This was clearly the case not only of the Panorama, analyzed by Crary, but also of the Phantasmagoria. Spectators were alerted in advance that the show was not dangerous.[51] They were channeled in their path toward the show.[52] Once in the theater, a conjurer reassured them that the spectacle was exclusively based on optical tricks.[53] And finally, special attention was paid to the female spectator because she was supposedly more sensitive to the illusion than her male counterpart.[54] The Phantasmagoria was meant to be reassuring; and precisely because it was such, it could harbor frightening effects. I must add that the whole building in which show was located was an emblem of this contrast between danger and reassurance. After its expropriation, the former Couvent des Capucines gave rise to a tumultuous environment; reports penned in the early years of nineteenth century by Antoine-Charles Aubert, Architecte de la Regie des Domaines Nationaux and supervisor of the entire complex, provide vivid evidence of a constant control.[55]

The creation of a safe site was highly beneficial for the show. The new worlds that were offered, despite their dramatic tone, did not appear as dangerous as if they were experienced directly. And the crowd, gathered in this safe site, found a collective energy for facing their fears, as a reporter noticed.[56] This was true for facing the ghosts on the screen and nature in the theater. It was even more true for facing the third world that emerged at the crossroads of the two: the spectators' *interiority*.

Interior, Interiority
The second half of the eighteenth century saw the reemergence of the idea of interiority through a partially new set of references.[57]

On the one hand, the concept found fertile ground in literary essays that explored and promoted the "inner world" of human beings. Jean-Jacques Rousseau's *Confessions*, published posthumously in 1789, was the book that contributed most to this perspective, with its mélange of memories, revelatory experiences, and fears. It proved that the French Enlightenment was deeply interested in the ways in which individuals come to terms with their deeper emotions and thought and thus to know themselves. On the other hand, German philosophy brought attention to the process of mental apprehension and appropriation of empirical reality. Rather than a space of intimate thoughts, the almost brand-new German term *Innerlichkeit* (usually translated as "inwardness") designated a site where external data are reelaborated into a subjective experience and where subjects are able to return reflexively to this process.[58] Finally, interiority took on a spatial connotation. It was associated with a location separated from the outside, in particular, the interior of a building, especially the house, and consequently promoted as the emblem of intimacy and privateness.[59]

Against this backdrop, the Phantasmagoria dealt with spectators' interiority in a twofold way. First, it offered a place where patrons faced their inner world. The chronicles of the show converge in describing a highly emotional experience. In front of the screen, astonishment, surprise, longing for the deceased, political animosity, and especially fear were common and heightened feelings. Without attempting to make claims about spectators' psychology, we can nevertheless say that viewers had to cope not only with ghosts, but also with their own way of coping with ghosts. In other words, they had to deal with their own emotional reactions and with the necessity to accept them. The sentence above by the anonymous chronicler of *La feuille villageuse*—"Finally, I saw my own image; I saw myself, go, come, and get excited in front of me"—testifies not only to a hallucination, but also to the strength with which the show pushed its spectators to confront themselves and their interiority. The Phantasmagoria apparently was a site of self-discovery.

Figure 2.3. Robertson's gravestone in Paris's Père Lachaise Cemetery.

Second, the Phantasmagoria made this inner world *publicly visible*. Although experienced individually, interiority can be put on display, if only in the effects that emotions elicit. There is no lack of testimony of how spectators' emotional expressions and outbursts were part of the show. Robertson recalls that in Bordeaux, a professor of physics, Cazalès, fell prey to his anxiety and tried to strike the projected ghosts: the audience immediately ridiculed him, creating a sort of spectacle within the spectacle.[60] Such a display of emotions finds its perfect illustration—again, in a gendered way—on Robertson's gravestone (fig. 2.3). On the left side, we see ghosts in the form of frightening creatures and medieval monsters; on the top, there is a flying skeleton with the trumpet of death in his mouth; on the right side, the patrons are gathered. Some of them stare at the amazing creatures on the stage, as if they were accepting the challenge; others seek comfort in someone else, as a toddler and a woman do, hugging respectively his mother and her partner; a woman in the foreground covers her eyes, overwhelmed by the apparitions but still experiencing the spectacle; a boy on the right simply turns his back to the show, as if he has renounced his place in the audience. In this modulation of gazes, spectators' inner worlds come to the fore.

Located in a safe space and displayed on behalf of others, interiority became a realm like the other world and the natural world. It became the third world — after the natural and the spiritual — to which the Phantasmagoria gave rise in its spatial enclosure.

The emergence of this third world gave a further boost to the dispositif. The Phantasmagoria is often associated with immersive media because of the intensity of the visual cues and the hallucinatory effects of the screened images.[61] Yet, if the Phantasmagoria was immersive, it was not only because of the role of the optical components, but also because of the construction of an enclosed and enveloping space and the mobilization of spectators' reactions. This last component granted the sense of a shared experience; in a certain sense, it was the glue that held together the different worlds — almost a multiverse — that the Phantasmagoria revealed. From this point of view, the display of interiority was a key element in the process.

Mapping the Multiverse

While being performed in a sealed space, and as a consequence of being performed there, the Phantasmagoria gave access to the other world (where ghosts originate), the world outside (the natural milieu), and the world inside (where spectators' emotions reside). But what kind of reality was made available in such a multiverse? And what kind of access to that reality was eventually granted?

Let's go back to the kingdom of the dead. Under the general heading "Petit Répertoire Fantasmagorique," Robertson's *Mémoires* recalls a list of the most successful acts he exhibited over the years.

The extent and variety of the topics are impressive. The catalogue includes premonitions such as "Lord Littleton's death"; legends related to saints such as "Saint Nicholas's pilgrimage" and "Saint Antoine's temptations"; historical sets such as "Druids' procession and sacrifice"; biblical episodes such as "Samuel's spirit appearing to Saul" and "David and Goliath"; and classical myths such as "the rape of Proserpina," "Medusa's head," and "Orpheus and Eurydice." The main attractions obviously were witchcraft, as in "Macbeth's witches," "Departure to Sabbath," and "Witches' dance"; necromancy, as in "the gravedigger" and "Saint Bruno's convent"; and prurient episodes, as in "the bleeding nun" and "Venus cuddles a hermit."[62] Due to the political climate in which Robertson wrote his *Mémoires*, he does not mention other acts that, according to direct witnesses, he had certainly performed; in particular, the parade of great men that included Rousseau, Lavoisier, and Voltaire, and the recollection of the main personages of the French Revolution, starting with Robespierre.[63]

Because of their success, many of the original Phantasmagoria's acts would be adapted and reproduced by other performers. The surviving Phantasmagoria slides—generally produced later and characterized by a popular style—bear witness to the persistence of the topics listed in Robertson's "Répertoire." We find slides of the bleeding nun, the head of Medusa, witches and devils, skeletons, and skulls but also mythological scenes and portraits of political figures, including Bonaparte.[64] Their graphic quality is a little rough—after all, the slides were miniatures—but once projected and moving, the figures were effective.

What surfaces is a world where religion, the supernatural, mythology, current events, and voyeurism converge and often merge. It may look like an implausible world, due to its overloaded and chaotic composition. And it may look like an unreal and insubstantial world due to the content and style of its representations. Yet its fabric is not distant from the other worlds that the Phantasmagoria summons. Like the inner world, the kingdom of the dead brings to the fore spectators' recurring anxieties and wishes, intimate thoughts, and uncertain beliefs. And like the natural world—let's think of the experiments in galvanism—it ceaselessly moves back and forth from secrecy to full visibility and from death to life.[65] These similarities allow us to make a decisive step: in bringing to the fore its three worlds, the Phantasmagoria fully retains the *imaginary* that surrounds them; that is the imaginary made by expectations and interpretations that according Edgar Morin constantly filters the reality of the facts and that consequently nourishes our experience of things as much as a direct relationship with them.[66] Despite the pedagogical address at the beginning of the show or the praise of applied physics in the "Instructive Program," the Phantasmagoria never cast an objective look at its worlds; on the contrary, it included the imaginary in its *repository*, and in doing so, it offered its objects along with the full resonances—a halo?—that accompanied their social presence.

In exchange, the Phantasmagoria's three worlds surfaced not in all their details, but in their landmarks. This choice reduced the intricacy of the territory on behalf of its saliences. If we look again at Robertson's gravestone, we can see how it displays canonical states of mind: a fearless attitude, a hesitant gaze, a retreat from reality. Likewise, the nature summoned by the spectacle is reduced to its elemental components: weather, electricity, optical illusions. The episodes listed in the "Petit Répertoire Fantasmagorique" recall recurring themes: unexpectedness, heroism, pain, and fate. The slides, allegedly so naive, visualize emblematic moments: Medusa addressing the audience; a skeleton exiting his tomb; a nun with a dagger in her hand; a hero seducing a beauty, a father burying his son. The Phantasmagoria's audience did not encounter full narratives, as in the theater or literature, but the essential pieces of a world disclosed in its cardinal points: loss and desire, death and life, threat and salvation, greed and sacrifice, bravery and fear. In this respect, more than reviving traditional legends, well-known biblical stories, worrisome visions, or magic tales, the Phantasmagoria primarily provided a system of signals that oriented spectators within the labyrinth of the imaginary worlds it was exploring. In doing so, it ended up drawing a basic map of the three domains of its multiverse — neither a miniature replica of the countries, nor a systematic record of the properties, but the sort of chart recalled by James Carey[67] that is simply sketched, or even danced or sung, and that nevertheless, with its essential directions, allows the members of a community to orient themselves within their own territory.

It is thanks to this map that the Phantasmagoria was able to negotiate between the unveiling of new domains and the necessity to provide a clear picture of them, between an unprecedented complexity and the urgency to offer points of reference, between the pleasure of exploration and the need to feel safe. Like its contemporaneous explorer La Pérouse, mentioned by Bruno Latour as a key example of a new idea of geography,[68] the Phantasmagoria charted unknown territories to provide reproducible representations able to grant full recognition and possession of new lands. Neither a narrative nor a description, neither an epic nor a comedy, the Phantasmagoria ultimately was a *cartography*.

The nature of the Phantasmagoria as map explains a final switch. After he ceased the show, Robertson bought a hot air balloon and dedicated himself to aerial explorations. The choice was apparently due to economic reasons. As Robertson confesses, "an ascent is visible to a wider crowd and can quickly provide a huge take."[69] Yet, the passion was authentic. The second volume of *Mémoires* documents Robertson's numerous exploits and includes the reports that the author addressed to various scientific societies; in particular, the long account sent to the Imperial Academy of Saint Petersburg about nine experiments performed during a long ascension in Hamburg on the physical and physiological effects of the altitude.[70] Beyond a lack of precision and rigor of the experiments — later contested by Joseph Louis Gay-Lussac, as Robertson candidly confesses — the account displays the same spirit we found in the Phantasmagoria: it mingles scientific terms and the language of wonder, barometer readings and personal thoughts, the sense of a challenge and the desire to keep things under control. Now enclosed in his gondola, no longer on or below but above the surface of the earth, Robertson again reckons with nature, the other world, and interiority and tries to describe the worlds he confronts in cartographic terms. His old show still shines high in the skies.

The Phantasmagoria's Legacy

After a very successful decade,[71] at the end of the 1810s, the Phantasmagoria started to decline. As it waned, though, its name flourished. It came to define any sequence of images seen in a dream or in a state of excitation, as well as different kinds of premonitions and apparitions, murder or mystery stories,[72] particularly vivid poetical or musical compositions,[73] and generally any work permeated by imagination.[74] In Feuerbach, it would offer a metaphor for defining a form of knowledge;[75] in Marx, it would designate the illusory value of commodities;[76] and in Benjamin, it would summarize the complex and kaleidoscopic cultural world of Paris in the nineteenth century.[77] Lewis Carroll entitled an 1869 collection of his poems *Phantasmagoria and Other Poems*,[78] and one of the first animated cartoons — a movie by Émile Cohl dated 1908 and characterized by spectral figures — would be entitled *Fantasmagorie*.

This paramount connotation confined the Phantasmagoria to a specific and narrow area. Its essence would be an excited, overloaded, and deceptive vision. Its ancestors would be the dispositifs that produced illusion and hallucination. Its inheritance would be what Tom Gunning calls, after Eisenstein, "attraction."[79] Against this reductive definition, to maintain that the Phantasmagoria was an optical-environmental dispositif in which an artificial enclosure elicited the cartographic exploration of a threefold world — the spiritual, the natural, and the inner — not only preserves its historical authenticity, but also sheds new light on its connection with other media.

First, it clarifies the Phantasmagoria's relations with previous dispositifs, in particular, its capacity to remediate[80] traditional rituals into modern means for the examination and appropriation of a multiple universe. It suffices to compare it to the Forty Hours' Devotion, a Roman Catholic practice extremely popular during the Counter-Reformation. Characterized by a luminous ephemeral decoration of the altar,[81] a strong delimitation of spaces, and a compelling ritual based on imaginative homilies held every hour[82] designed to move the faithful to the extreme emotion in order to relive the passion of Christ, the Forty Hours' Devotion shared with the Phantasmagoria the visual-spatial arrangement, the attempt to regain possession of an otherwise lost reality, and the appeal to the inner world of the beholders. Yet the multiplicity of the Phantasmagoria's worlds, the complexity of its machinery, and the typology of its audiences entailed significant changes. While the Forty Hours revolved around religious practices, the Phantasmagoria aggregated social, economic, and communicative technologies aimed no longer at the redemption of believers, but at the enjoyment of customers; while the former was unidirectional, the latter was a multifaceted and flexible constituent of a then-emerging capitalistic economy. The Phantasmagoria was a modern machine that responded to modern needs and distress.

On the other hand, the Phantasmagoria anticipated the future optical-environmental dispositifs that characterize the contemporary forms of mediation. The most obvious reference is to cinema, with its enclosure that severs spectators from everyday reality and its flow of sensorial cues in order to summon a world that is "larger than life." What connects the two dispositifs is not so much their theatrical vocation as the interplay of losses and compensations, closures and openings, gazes and postures, that underpins forms of experience in line with an increasingly elusive world that becomes available only as image. The Phantasmagoria and cinema are both instantiations of the projection/protection complex.

Finally, a full portrait of the Phantasmagoria helps better grasp

68

its relations with other symptomatic dispositifs of its time. As James Chandler and Kevin Gilmartin have proven,[83] the turn from the eighteenth to the nineteenth century was characterized by spectacles such as the Eidophusikon[84] and the Panorama[85] and by wide-format paintings such as Thomas Girtin's *Eidometropolis*,[86] to which I want to add a less analyzed entertainment such as La Veillée, a Parisian building that hosted several reconstructions of picturesque scenes.[87] They were all devices that challenged the limits of visuality through the potentialities and constraints of space.[88] The Phantasmagoria was at once part of this landscape and an excessive presence: its radical imbrication of a screen and a setting, its ability to summon a multiple universe, and its working on spatial deprivations and optical compensations, made it a model for modern forms of mediation. Although its life was ephemeral, its role and legacy were profound.

The Ballistics of Perception

The big-game hunter and author Robert Rainsford is cast ashore on a small island when the yacht on which he was traveling is wrecked. He is the only survivor among the passengers and crew. On the island, he is welcomed into the castle of the Russian expatriate Count Zaroff, who is a passionate hunter and admirer of Robert's books. Robert befriends Eve Trowbridge, another guest of the count and the survivor of another wreckage, along with her brother, Martin. Zaroff hides a horrible secret: he causes the ships that pass near his island to sink so that he might procure the human prey of his hunting. After Robert and Eva discover the secret, Robert refuses Zaroff's proposal to join him in his next hunt. Consequently, he will be the next prey. If he survives, he and Eve will be allowed to leave the island; otherwise, Eve will be kept prisoner forever. Robert, under threat, is forced to accept, even though none of the previous victims survived such a "dangerous game." The hunt begins, and Eve flees with Robert. Chased by Zaroff, the two set a trap and then find refuge in a dark cave. Zaroff detects the trap and disables it. He approaches the cave, but stops on the threshold. He knows that Robert and Eve are hidden there, but he is unable to see them, while Robert and Eve see him in full light. Zaroff draws the Tatar bow that he has chosen for the hunt, and shoots an arrow into the dark....

The sequence in which Zaroff tries to hit Robert and Eve, hidden in the cave, although he cannot see them, is a key scene in the movie *The Most Dangerous Game*, directed by Irving Pichel and Ernest B. Shoedsack (USA, 1932). In an influential close analysis of the sequence, the French scholar and experimental video artist Thierry Kuntzel underscores the similarity of the situation depicted by the movie and the situation in which filmgoers find themselves:[1] in both cases there is an enclosed space in which observers, concealed in the dark, see someone in full light that is unable to see them. In this respect, Robert and Eve are perfect spectators, and Zaroff the epicenter of the show.[2] I will further develop the analogy—which Kuntzel interprets in psychoanalytical terms as the reemergence of the "primal scene" in which children secretly spy on the sexual act of their parents[3]—with a focus on the elemental components of the episode. Indeed, the disposition of the spaces, the confrontation between the hunter and his prey, and the logic underlying the hunt provide a powerful metaphor for the mode of spectatorship that the projection/protection complex elicits, especially when it works on physical enclosures that are shaped as a theater, as it is the case not only of cinema, but also, prior to it, of the Phantasmagoria. I will push the metaphor to the very end, and I will do it in four steps.

First, the cave is where Robert and Eve find shelter from the dangers that come from "out there." External reality is a source of anxiety, and the only protection comes from an enclosed space. Yet the cave is not a perfectly sealed place. After Zaroff disables Robert's trap, the way ahead of him is clear. Inside the cave, Robert and Eve perceive that the menace is approaching. Unexpectedly, Zaroff stops at the cave's threshold, and by doing this, he reveals the presence of two distinct "regimens of light," to use an expression by Gilles Deleuze.[4] The entrance of the cave is a bright zone compared with the darkness of the space in front of it. Lingering on it, Zaroff is almost glowing: when in close-up, his face is well lit; when in medium or long shot, his silhouette is located in a white spot against the more opaque background. Robert and Eve, on the contrary, are immersed in the dark; their faces reflect a faint light that comes from the cave entrance, but around them, everything is covered by a thick shadow.

The instantiations of the projection/protection complex, in particular those that include a physically enclosed space, rely on the presence of a dark recess (the theater) and a luminous threshold (the screen). By doing so, they not only create a contrast between spectators in the dark and a brilliant spectacle, but they also fully exploit it. Will the light prevail over the darkness — and the spectacle overwhelm spectators — or will the darkness resist the onslaught of the light? The projection/protection complex is a site of tension between these two poles. Its "economy of light," as Ruggero Eugeni calls every arrangement in terms of luminous energy,[5] is deeply conflictual.

Second, being in full light does not give any advantage to the hunter. In the cave, Robert and Eve look out and see Zaroff approaching, while Zaroff, on the threshold, cannot see them. And when he draws his Tatar bow, the arrow is launched into the dark. It is as if Zaroff were blind. Uncertain whether he hit Robert or not, Zaroff replaces the arrows with words, and he addresses Robert directly: "Come out of there, Rainsford!" No sound or noise comes from the cave. Zaroff is not only like a blind man, he is also like a deaf man. This double deficiency spoils Zaroff's ability as a hunter. In a sense, it makes him a prey. Robert, on the other hand, sees and hears Zaroff, who is in full display in front of him. This position could transform Robert, the prey, into the hunter, yet he does not possess any way to deal with Zaroff directly — he has only a knife with which he originally set the trap — nor does he want to reveal himself by moving out of the dark.

Again, this situation clarifies the kind of experience elicited by the projection/protection complex, especially in its theatrical instantiations. What we have is a confrontation between two components — spectacle and spectators — whose qualities are inverted:

the spectacle addresses spectators, but it cannot see or hear them, and the spectators are ready to deal with the spectacle, but they lack any direct way to do so.

Third, Zaroff and Robert have different means of contend with each other. Standing in the light, Zaroff relies on his gaze to penetrate to darkness (which it cannot do) and his words to make Robert betray himself (words that, like the arrow he shoots, merely disappear into the darkness that he cannot penetrate). Conversely concealed in the darkness and silent, held within himself, Robert is safe as long as he remains there, though he still experiences the threat of Zaroff as real. So, there are projectiles that pierce — arrows, gazes, and words — and there are protective tools that shield — caves, darkness, and silence. The former are not always effective; the latter apparently work better. This ambivalent duality creates a sort of stalemate. There is a hunt, in which neither the hunter nor the prey can prevail. Projectiles are not deadly enough, and shields freeze the action.

The projection/protection complex reflects this balance of powers. It relies on a combination of weaponry and defensive systems, in which apparently no one of the two poles can take the lead. Spectators are challenged by the spectacle; yet, until they stay hidden in the dark, they can postpone any conflict.

Fourth, in the dynamics that oppose hunter and prey, there are not only confrontations, but also transformations. This is the case with Zaroff's and Robert's gazes. As the *Most Dangerous Game* illustrates, the gaze is part of a set that includes the arrow and the words. To cast a look is equivalent to throwing a projectile or addressing someone verbally: both are components of the same ballistic, as John Durham Peters would say.[6] Like the jungle in which *The Most Dangerous Game* is set, the modern world in which film spectators live is filled by a multiplicity of elements that hit and hurt: objects so fast that they harm, events so unexpected that they traumatize, people so aggressive that they threaten others, and stimuli so intense that they sting. In this world, of which Walter

Benjamin offers a prodigious portrait, visual sensations, starting from those that are directed at the spectators from a screen, elicit not contemplation, but shocks.[7]

Yet the gaze is also part of the system of defense against these shocks. To protect themselves against them, a spectators's main strategy, as Benjamin suggests, consists of accepting exposure to the shocks and using them to test one's own capacity for endurance.[8] Once again, the confrontation of Robert and Zaroff in the cave is exemplary. Robert is still prey, and he is under Zaroff's threat, yet he looks at the one who aggressively looks at him and learns how to frame a possible target. His action is deferred — after all, he is still on the defensive — but in the cave, he starts or restarts making his gaze a potential asset. Not surprisingly, by the end of the film, he will regain the initiative. Once he gets hold of a weapon, a rifle, he will prevail over Zaroff. Like him, spectators see and endure, and in the theater, they regain power against the shocks that challenge them.

CHAPTER THREE

Cinema: A Space for Comfort

King Kong's Jungle and Mr. Rockefeller's Temple

In 1925, the Austrian author Joseph Roth, then a successful film critic, dedicated a humorous review to *The Great White Silence*, a British documentary about Robert Scott's tragic expedition to Antarctica.[1] Roth writes:

> Snow, ice and the sky. Walls, castles, cities, worlds of snow. Sledges, dogs and a couple of people. Penguins, a tent, a whale. And we are sitting in a modern theater. All the so-called blessings of civilization are there: proper and clean girls in white aprons with program booklets; electric light; central heating and a film screen. Protected from all sides against all evil of nature, we look into a most impossible world in which the most impossible fate of the most impossible challengers takes its turn.[2]

This passage, in a tone that mingles irony and sadness, bears witness to a contradiction that has affected cinema from the beginning. If on the one hand film shines for its ability to record and return crude reality to the point that spectators feel themselves cast into it, on the other hand, it grants a sort of safe harbor, from which spectators can enjoy the situations depicted on the screen without the risks that actual participation implies. Hence a split: undetermined and undefined nature—an "open" entity by definition—finds itself replicated in the "closed" space of a theater on behalf of patrons who can follow extraordinary events while taking pleasure from the delights of a technologically advanced age.

Framed by a comment about the passion for the gigantic and the childish in the American society, a similar contrast reappeared in a 1933 review signed by the literary and film critic William Troy. Commemorating *King Kong*'s screening at Radio City Music Hall, Troy noted the paradox of "an audience enjoying all the sensations of primitive terror and fascination within the scientifically air-cooled temple of baroque modernism that is Mr. Rockefeller's contribution to contemporary culture."[3] Once again, we find in the cinema a wild world and a highly artificial space. Both provide excitement, but the former implies the risks of an exposure, the latter a sense of relief. If audiences fully enjoy the wilderness, it is because they are located in an upscale, technologically advanced setting.

These two short critical passages are remarkable. While candidly highlighting the puzzling situation in which film spectators are caught, they focus on three often overlooked aspects of the theatrical film exhibition — the most common way of showing a movie, at least in the Western world during the 1920s and 1930s, though not the only way films were presented.[4]

First, Roth's and Troy's comments underscore the nature of the physical site in which movies were screened: a *space of comfort* where patrons were able to enjoy all the "blessings of civilization," as Roth calls the heating system, the many electric devices, the usherettes, and the perfectly projected movie. He could have added relaxing seats, clean restrooms, lavish lobbies, expandable screens, and state-of-the-art technology. At the time he wrote his review, these utilities were crucial components of filmgoing as they provided spectators with a sense of physical and psychological well-being — "comfort," singular, while the plural, "comforts," describes all of these conveniences[5] — that was at the core of the cinematic experience.[6]

Second, the two short critical passages disclose the *meaning of comfort.* To experience a movie in a "modern theater" (the Berlin cinema palace attended by Roth) or in a "temple of baroque modernism" (the Radio City Music Hall attended by Troy) offered something more than a sense of pleasure. The comforts of the theater created a relaxing environment in which spectators were able to face the crudest aspects of the world—including their own milieu, often as challenging as the jungle and Antarctica and often dramatically represented on the screen as the setting of contemporary stories—without feeling any obligation to engage with them directly. From this point of view, the conveniences that were made available to spectators can be understood as a form of *exoneration* and *compensation.* On the one hand, they exempted spectators from a direct commitment with reality, now replaced by an artificial environment; on the other hand, they provided a reparation for the limited and frustrating existence that spectators suffered in their everyday lives.

Third, Roth's and Troy's reviews help us to uncover the *ambiguity of comfort.* The sense of well-being, and the amenities that made it possible, were duplicitous in themselves, especially if connected to ideas of exoneration and compensation. Indeed, just as exoneration implies a departure from a troubling situation, compensation implies some kind of loss that must be rewarded. Both provide relief by reacting to worries and threats. In this sense, comforts are always the counterpart of pain, especially pain linked to everyday existence. Are comforts able to heal this pain, or do they ultimately recall its inevitable presence? Do they underpin a utopian space of self-confidence and satisfaction, or are they accomplices of the causes of this pain?

In the next pages, I will engage these three issues—the amenities offered to filmgoers, their functions, and their contradictory nature—in the light of the projection/protection complex and its ability to spare individuals direct exposure to the world in favor of an interaction with it in a safe environment and by safe means. With a physical enclosure that severed spectators from their usual milieu and images on the screen that reconnected spectators to realities that they had left behind or had never experienced, cinema was a perfect instantiation of this complex.[7] Between 1925 and 1933—the two years in which Roth and Troy wrote their reviews and a period in which the Western model of film exhibition found its apex, as Douglas Gomery has proven[8]—comforts were structural components of this instantiation. The lavish atmosphere of the theater, the assistance offered by ushers, and the increasing pleasurable way of displaying images made it easier for spectators to leave behind their everyday world. And the sense of safety conferred by these comforts made spectators' reengagement with reality more productive. Filmgoers were able not only to find on the screen what they left behind, but also to test their ability to cope with puzzling situations without risking any real consequences.[9] At the same time, the next pages will uncover the ambivalent nature of these comforts. Although the projection/protection complex's ideal was to replace direct exposure to the world with a safer environment in order to make the mediation with reality more manageable, the amenities of the theater cast some shadows on this ideal. The modern world is hard to manage as it extends its own logic to the counterforces that intend to correct it. In this context, the amenities granted some help but fell short in alleviating a more radical distress. Spectators were safeguarded from the polar ice and the Great Ape, but not removed from the struggles they faced in everyday life. A final return to Roth and his novel *Antichrist*—a masterpiece of the cinephobic literature—will help us further understand the circuit of threats, relief, substitutions, and fears that encircled the comforts of the theater and ultimately substantiated cinema itself.

Modern Comforts

In its issue of December 1927, the popular-science magazine *Scientific American* hosted a richly illustrated two-page report aimed at updating its readers about the evolution of movie theaters.[10] The chosen example was the recently opened Roxy Theater, located between Sixth and Seventh Avenues, just off Times Square in New York. Nicknamed "the Cathedral of the Motion Picture," the Roxy was an ambitious project conceived by the film producer Herbert Lubin and realized by the entrepreneur Samuel "Roxy" Rothafel.[11] Indeed, with its seating capacity of 5,886 spectators, its luxury décor, its abundance of spaces, its technical dispositifs, and its final cost of twelve million dollars, it became the epitome of the movie palaces of the time.[12]

Scientific American was especially attentive to the technological applications. A photo shows the projection booth with at least five projectors, including the ones "arranged for the projection of the newest talking movies," either with the Movietone or the Vitaphone systems. Another vignette displays the totally mechanized pit elevator that "can be raised or lowered at will." Two pictures illustrate sound devices: the noisemakers "for accompanying the pictures" and the console of a gigantic organ. Equal attention is paid to the dispositifs aimed at spectators' well-being. Cool water to drink is available almost everywhere thanks to a refrigerating plant also documented in a picture. Huge fans provide perfect ventilation, with "a complete change of air in the theater at predetermined intervals." In the summer, "an efficient refrigerating plant" chills the air in the theater, making the usual promise of "20 degrees cooler inside" become true. A seat indicator allows the ushers to know which place is actually vacant. A "very complicated lighting switchboard" grants perfect management of the illumination of the entire complex. The most surprising vignette is dedicated to a hospital, hosted inside the theater and intended to respond "to every possible emergency" (fig. 3.1). The accompanying text, while offering further information on all these devices, also mentions the lobbies so spacious and sumptuously decorated "that persons visiting the theater for the first time are entranced as they enter, and often spend some time in viewing them"; the restrooms, furnished in the best of taste"; and the courtesy with which "the ushers conduct one to his seat." All these elements converge toward a single

ORGAN CONSOLE

S. L. Rothafel is here shown standing beside
one of the huge organ consoles of the Roxy
theater, New York City. From this and
other consoles, skilled organists control the
flow of air through the organ pipes located
in another part of the theater. Notice the
complexity of the various organ controls

THE HOSPITA

The really modern theater
every possible emergency. He
the completely equipped hos;
Roxy theater, where even a ma
can be performed if necessary.
all of the ushers carry small
for the treatment of fainting

▲ **PIT ELEVATOR**

The entire orchestra pit, with all of the
musicians, can be raised or lowered at will

◄ **NOISE MAKERS**

Various sounds for accompanying the
pictures are produced with these instruments

PROJECTION BOOTH ►

Standard projectors and those for "talking
movies" are part of the regular equipment

The "Movie" Theater Up-To-Date

NOT so many years ago, the average motion picture
theater contained only a series of seats, a screen,
(more or less smooth), and a projection booth. The manager gave little thought to the comfort of the patrons— in
the summer they might swelter, and in the winter be subjected to the vagaries of an inefficient heating plant. They
came to see the "movies" regardless, because they were
new. Patrons were not discriminating, and furthermore
there was not much keen competition. But as the art of
motion-picture production grew by leaps and bounds,
and the pictures to be presented became more pretentious,
the number of exhibition houses increased. Then, the
effects of competition came to be noticeable, and the
managers cast about for methods of attracting patronage
to their particular houses. First, only special attractions
were advertised as "drawing cards," but that was not
always enough. Then managers began to improve their
theaters and patrons became attracted to the various
personal comforts that were offered. The old style of

uncomfortable hard seats were replaced with
spacious and upholstered chairs that made sitti
a long program a pleasure rather than a verita
Soon the sign "20 degrees cooler than the stre
a common-place method of attracting the sum
to the cool, comfortable, darkened depths of t
But the end was not yet. The theaters became
more ornate, and still further attractions we
It might be said that the ultimate in theatri
for the presentation of motion pictures has
reached. In New York City there are se
houses dedicated to the presentation of motio
that are, in every sense of the word, palaces.
theater, the result of years of planning on th
S. L. Rothafel, well known radio entertainer,
cellent example of these. We reproduce on th
several photographs, specially posed for the S
AMERICAN, of the more striking features of
designed theater. It seems that nothing has be

Figure 3.1. "The 'Movie' Theater Up-To-Date: Many Modern Comforts Provided,"
Scientific American 137.6 (December 1927), pp. 516 and 517.

WATER COOLER

*er that is piped to the various
fountains located in various parts
water is first cooled to the correct
ure by means of the complete
ing plant illustrated above. This
at improvement over individual
-water fountains cooled by ice*

VENTILATION

*In order that the patrons may be in absolute
comfort at all times, it is essential to have
complete ventilation. In the Roxy, huge
fans of the type illustrated above take care
of this, effecting a complete change of air in
the theater at predetermined intervals, thus
completely getting rid of the stale, impure air*

AIR COOLER

*In summer, the air in the theater is cooled
by this large efficient refrigerating plant*

SWITCHBOARD

*A section of the very complicated lighting
switchboard is shown directly at the left*

SEAT INDICATOR

*In the balcony, this board of indicating
lights shows exactly which seats are vacant*

Many Modern Comforts Provided

every comfort of the patron has been thought
longer is the theater a mere place in which to
motion picture. Instead it is more of a place of
ament and a club combined. There are rest
urnished in the best of taste and equipped with
omfort that patrons could possibly wish for.
ies are spacious and are so furnished and decorated
·sons visiting the theater for the first time are
·d as they enter, and often spend some time in
them. Within the theater itself, the ushers
one to his seat with the utmost courtesy, and
ing seated, one finds that he is as comfortable as
i be in his own home. In the hot days of summer,
always coolness to be found in the modern theater.
provided by means of up-to-date refrigerating
and ventilating systems. At convenient places
re inviting drinking fountains where water of
right temperature may be obtained. Here again,
ating plants are employed and the cooled water

is circulated to the various outlets. Should it so happen
that a person be taken sick while in the Roxy theater, an
attendant is always at hand to render first aid, and if necessary, rush the ailing one to the completely equipped hospital that is an integral part of the equipment of the
theater. In the projection apparatus, many changes over
older types of projection machines are noticeable. The
booth is cool and well ventilated, and the machines are
of the latest types. Most prominent among them are
those which are arranged for the projection of the newest
"talking movies." Complete installations for the presentation of two different types of the latter are available.
Both of these systems have been described in this magazine. One is the Movietone, in which the sound record
is made directly on the motion-picture film, in a narrow
space at the side of the pictures. This was described in
detail in the September, 1927, issue. The other method,
described in the June, 1927, issue, is the Vitaphone, using
a disk record for sound recording.

point: the Roxy is a perfect illustration of the "modern comforts" that film exhibitors are able to offer to their patrons. It provides a rich and exciting ambiance, an appropriate microclimate, a clean space, continuous assistance, and high-quality projection.

Scientific American's insistence on spectators' comforts echoed widespread attention to the topic. While chronicling the opening of new movie theaters, trade journals such as *Exhibitors Herald, The Architectural Forum*, and local and national newspapers, systematically underscored the concomitance of technologically advanced devices and pleasurable environments. Good examples are the accounts of the opening of the Mastbaum Theater in Philadelphia in 1929 in *The Billboard* and in *Exhibitors Herald World*.[13] At the time, the eighth-largest movie theater in the United States, with over four thousand seats, the Mastbaum is celebrated by the *Exhibitors Herald World* as "the union of modern scientific efficiency with classic beauty." The theater's distinctive features were its grand foyer with brilliant chandeliers and a marble fountain imported from Italy, its eight floors opulently decorated, its mobile orchestra pit, and "public rooms so big and so handsomely decorated that waiting in them will indeed be a pleasure." Equally characteristic were "a separate cosmetic room, equipped with French plate glass mirrors," two spacious elevators that facilitated the spectators' access, and an extremely efficient cooling and heating systems that made available the climate that audiences desired.[14] *The Billboard* adds: "A great deal of machinery is required to run all the multitude of apparatus at the Mastbaum, but the patron sitting in his chair will not be conscious of it." The spectators' pleasure relied not only on the perfect coordination of a large number of technical devices, but also on their discreet way of working. "Modern comforts" were the outcome of an advanced *dispositif* that did not necessary reveal its own action. An assemblage of mechanical tools, furnished spaces, and functional equipment, cinema proudly converted this complex set of elements into a relaxing environment.

This combination of technologies, relaxation, and environment found its climax in the then-successful "atmospheric theaters."[15]

Speaking of the imminent construction of the Universal Theater in Brooklyn, the architect John Eberson—the leading figure in the field—described in detail the imaginary landscape in which the auditorium would be immersed, with one side representing an Italian palace and the other a terraced garden, "all set under a moonlit sky with stars twinkling and with clouds rolling by."[16] At the same time, "particular attention [is] given to lines of sight and acoustics" in order to let spectators to enjoy the movie and to a modern ventilating and refrigeration system that allows the theater to "practically control its own weather." Both design, décor, and appliances are intended "for the maximum comfort of patrons."

Yet comforts were not exclusive to the huge lavish theaters. Barry H. Holquist, a frequent contributor to *Exhibitors Herald World*, offered an iconic description of the ideal movie theater in a small city in which the magnificence of the cinema palaces was commensurate with the needs of a different audience.[17] Holquist's description starts from the outside, from the "impressive marquise" over the main entrance. "Going into the theater, we find that it has an attractive arched foyer. The floors are luxuriously carpeted. The walls and ceiling of the foyer are highly ornamental." Moving forward, we enter "the main auditorium where there is an effective system of cove lighting controlled by switchboard and dimmers." Lights literally sculpt the space, "bringing out the architectural beauty of the interior." The theater is ready to accommodate its patrons: it is "equipped with comfortable upholstered seats. There are retiring rooms for men and women, attractively furnished. A modern cooling and ventilating system keeps the auditorium comfortable under all conditions." In this ideal theater, the ambiance is not only gorgeous, but also relaxing and secure as "everything is neat, clean and sanitary." Holquist's depiction can appear to be a mere fantasy, a celebration of "the power of the motion picture theater ... extending itself into all corners of the land." Yet dozens of portraits of small theaters hosted by trade journals confirm that this model was an actual reference.[18]

We can find the same mix of elements aimed at the spectators' comfort outside the United States, though often with a local touch. Suffice it to recall the celebrated description of the Berlin film palaces in Siegfried Kracauer's "Cult of Distraction: On Berlin's Picture Palaces" (1926): big theaters such as the Ufa Palast am Zoo, Capitol, Marmorhaus, and Gloria are "shrines to the cultivation of pleasure," spaces animated by the "attempt to create an atmosphere," and ultimately sites where to enjoy a true "total artwork of effects."[19] One year before Kracauer, the literary critic Kurt Pinthus offered a similar description of the Ufa Palast, claiming that "in spite of its gargantuan size, it is more comfortable than a good number of intimate theaters."[20] Janet Ward has reconsidered German *Filmpaläste* in the context of German architecture and found them instrumental to an enhanced the film experience.[21] An ironic chronicle penned by Roth of his "conversion" into a perfect spectator while attending a movie in the Ufa Palast bears further witness to the ways in which these temples of entertainment responded to the needs and desires of their patrons.[22]

Manufactured Weather

Roughly speaking, the comforts of the film theater belonged to three main fields: they promoted an elegant, pleasurable, and safe environment, a smooth and efficient social gathering, and a functional and sensuous viewing experience. In this section I will analyze the first aspect, and I will discuss the others in those that follow.

The idea of a comfortable environment was first and foremost tied to the presence of an enjoyable climate prompted by air-conditioning and heating systems. The practice of cooling air in movie theaters dated back in the 1910s, when in many states, exhibitors were required by law to install systems of ventilation for the benefit of patrons' health. However, it was during the 1920s that theater owners improved these systems, first by purifying and then by refrigerating the air, paving the way for the spread of this technology in other public venues, such as offices and department stores.[23] As Gail Cooper underscores in her history of air-conditioning in the United States, this addition allowed the theater owners to go "beyond mitigation of discomfort to the creation of an attractive alternative to outdoor amusement."[24] Thanks to air-conditioning, in the summer—a season traditionally difficult for indoor entertainment—movie theaters became healthy spaces more attractive than parks and other natural sites, and the lower temperatures granted comfort that no other place was able to offer. Not by chance, speaking of Balaban and Katz's Tivoli Theater, a Chicago health commissioner considered its internal atmosphere "better than that on Pike's Peak," and he recommended to all that they go there for a few hours each week to really benefit by getting some fresh air in their lungs."[25] Movie theaters were advertised as safer than open air.

By the end of the 1920s, exhibitors' promises of either twenty degrees cooler than outside during the summer months or of a consistent seventy degrees all year round were deemed essential, as countless interventions in trade magazines testify. By providing stable internal temperature regardless the external conditions, air-conditioning allowed the theater to be filled at any hour and in every month of the year.[26] The comfort of a cooled atmosphere was thus beneficial not only for health, but also for business (fig. 3.2a). At the same time, the massive adoption of air-conditioning reinforced the idea—or the dream—that artificial weather could replace the unpredictability of the natural elements. A twenty-eight-page booklet published by the Carrier Engineering Corporation in 1925 goes to the heart of the issue (fig. 3.2b).[27] Once equipped with the company's system, theater owners would no longer be beholden to the natural climate; instead, they would be able to replace it with "manufactured weather" created according to their own needs. The Carrier system promised superior combination of temperature, humidity, and ventilation, as well as air circulation scientifically designed to bring fresh air to patrons' lungs and to remove stale air

Figure 3.2a. Advertisement in *Exhibitors Herald World* 29.5 (April 16, 1927), section 2, p. 34.

Figure 3.2b. Carrier Engineering Corp, *"Theatre Cooling by Carrier Centrifugal Refrigeration and Air Distribution: A Restful Refuge Summer & Winter"* (New York: Carrier Engineering Corp., 1925).

from auditorium, at which point it would be collected, rewashed, and cooled again. As the booklet noted: "the occupants of the theater are not conscious of the source of this constant supply of cool, refreshing air. They have only that sense of *perfect comfort* and this applies to every section of the house."[28] A technical device was thus capable of rivaling nature, and patrons were apt to mistake the manufactured weather insider for a natural state.

Parallel to the artificial climate, there is a constant concern for a clean environment. Once again, trade journals regularly underscored the quality of the restrooms and lavatories and hosted dozens of advertisements praising articles aimed at improving this quality. Yet an interesting point of view is offered by the theater management. The training manual for the Balaban and Katz Theater Corporation published in 1926 had a specific section on the topic.[29] First of all, the manual depicts a robust cleaning department in which every worker has specific competences and all respond to a chief janitor. Second, the manual scrupulously lists the items that must regularly be cleaned. These items not only include toilets and restrooms, but extend from the glass and walls to spectators' seats, from furniture to the floors, from carpets and draperies to the plants and birds that adorn the theater. They are clustered in sixteen classes, each implying specific procedures and the use of specific cleaners or products. All the actions—cleaning, polishing, scrubbing, waxing, dusting, brushing—are described in detail and each is assigned to one specific type of worker. In this framework, "special attention must be paid to lavatories, toilet rooms, and the sink rooms for the purpose of eliminating all disagreeable odors."[30] The use of disinfectants instead of simply soap—which "is food for vermin"—is prescribed. Toilet seats must be washed frequently, flush valves and nickel plates only twice a week. "During the fly season it is necessary to spray all toilet rooms at least twice daily with some insect spray." What is at stake is ultimately the quality of the experience and the welfare that the theater offers to its patrons. In this vein, "members of the cleaning force should take a personal pride in the condition of the theater and should be careful at all times in the handling or cleaning of it."[31]

Despite their differences, cooling and cleaning share crucial characteristics. Not only do both aim at creating a pleasurable and safe environment, but both also imply a separation between the interior and the exterior in order to avoid the exposure to something that is uncomfortable, be it painful weather or aggressive germs. In a word, both cooling and cleaning transform the theater into a *shelter* against the dangers of the outside world. The image of shelter is made explicit in many chronicles, reviews, and advertisements.[32] In the same years, it is also summoned by Kracauer to designate the spaces of entertainment, including film theaters, in which blue-collar workers can find a semblance of a decent lifestyle that in fact they had lost.[33] Finally, the idea of shelter resonates with one of the main meanings of the word "screen": prior to denoting a surface that hosts impermanent images, the screen referred to "a contrivance for warding off the heath of a fire or a draught of air."[34] The idea of shelter unifies the cooled theaters, their cleaned toilets, the venues that help to forget a miserable social status, and the capacity of screen to keep reality at a distance. It connects the comforts of the theater with a set of elements that connote a sense of protection.

The Rules of Courtesy

Ushers were another distinctive feature of the movie palaces at the end of the 1920s. A report in *The New York Times* underscored their relevance: "Soft-voiced young men with military postures to direct the crowd of costumers in Broadway cinema houses are among the attractions the owners offer their patrons."[35] Movie palaces were a space of flows: flows of cool air and fresh water for patrons' comfort, flows of images on the screen for patrons' enjoyment, and flows of patrons themselves. The first task of ushers was to manage the flows of patrons in the theater so as to minimize disruptions and preserve the comfort of those who gathered there. They did with the help of devices that allowed them to identify empty seats

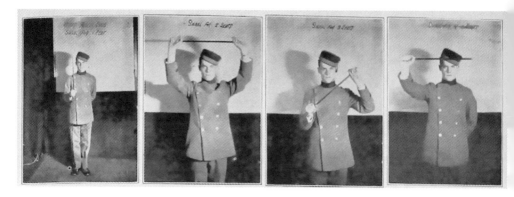

Figure 3.3. "How many, please?" From James D. Kennedy, "Problems of Theatre Management: Seating the People," *Exhibitors Herald World* 25.5 (April 17, 1926), section 2, p. 19.

USHER'S PLEDGE
I WILL TO THE VERY BEST OF MY ABILITY, TRY:

To be a gentleman.
To render 100% service.
To be courteous to PATRONS and to fellow employees.
To work willingly and cheerfully.
To be pleasant and wear a smile.
To be alert to anticipate PATRON'S desires and to surprise them with service and attention they do not expect.
To speak pleasantly, to say "yes sir" and "no sir," and "I thank you," and "please," in a pleasant way.
To obey our rules because I realize that rules are necessary in a business organization.
To interpret intelligently the policy of our organization.
To practice headwork and heartwork because I know that these virtues are indispensable to success.
To strengthen myself by study, observation and practice.
To keep my temper.
To avoid arguing with PATRONS.
To make every PATRON satisfied and happy.

Ushers Signature ....

Figure 3.4. "The Usher's Pledge," in "Try This on Your Ushers!—It's OK," *Motion Picture News* 41.23 (June 7, 1930), p. 160.

and of a system of signals that allowed them to be constantly in contact with one another during screenings (fig. 3.3).

Yet the ushers' job was more extensive: they had to offer patrons continuous support, answer their most disparate questions, avoid accidents, and prevent conflicts between spectators. A report on *Motion Picture News*, which included a satirical "Usher's Pledge" (fig. 3.4), recorded twenty-four obligations that they must keep in mind,[36] and the training manual for the Balaban and Katz Theater Corporation listed thirty-one specific duties to which ushers must be devoted.[37] Among these responsibilities, safety was a major concern.[38] The Balaban and Katz manual is adamant about the topic, with special regard for fire protection: "Each employee should feel deeply the very great responsibility that is ours in protecting the lives of our patrons. Rules and regulations are prescribed by law, and various supplementary preventive measures will be outlined from time to time by the management. It is the duty of every employee to see that every preventive measure is fully enforced at all times."[39] Safety also included preventing disturbances. The Balaban and Katz manual has a section on how ushers should deal with situations created by "annoying people." Among these situations there are "petting couples" who do not stop their flirting, "intoxicated persons" who are out of control, and "degenerates and morons" who literally threaten other spectators.[40] Ushers were requested either to stop the improper behavior or to bring the annoying people out of the theater under the guidance of their supervisor, and, if necessary, with the use of force. Yet there was no safety without courtesy. The core of ushers' obligations laid in always being polite and available, in looking generous and competent, and in understanding potential problems in advance.[41] First and foremost, they had to convey the sense of an organization that cared about its patrons.[42] Comfort was provided not only by the facilities of the theater, but also by a warm welcome and constant assistance.

In 1927, *The Baltimore Sun* hosted a delightful portrait of the perfect usher: "Suave and slender he stands, his polished hair gleaming, his erect shoulders molded into a well-tailored uniform, a jaunty swagger stick tucked under his arm. There is about him the military precision of an army lieutenant and a graceful tact of a diplomat."[43] However, behind the usher's appearance, marked by courtesy, efficiency, and dedication, there was a strict organization. Indeed, ushers were well trained, both morally and physically. Rothafel is particularly candid about this issue:

> The members should be drilled regularly, so that their movements and demeanor may be smart, snappy, and precise. They should be taught of the importance of personal cleanliness, so their uniform and general appearance at all time are immaculate. They should be given "institutional" talks which instill in them a sincere and wholesome interest in their work and pride in the institution which cannot help but be reflected in the attitude that "'the patron is always right.'"[44]

Special schools were often providing this education.[45] The strong and repeated training was paired by a functional specialization. While ushers knew how to perform many duties, each one was assigned to take care of a specific issue. *The New York Times* mocked such a specialization: "There is one usher, or one squad of ushers, to hand programs to incoming patrons; another group to hand announcements of future picture to outgoing patrons; a group of pages, smaller and younger boys, to run errands about the theaters."[46] Yet it made ushers' jobs even more effective. Finally, ushers followed a precise hierarchy. "With a staff of fifty or more, divided in two or more shifts, there are privates, corporals, sergeants, captains and so on up the line."[47] Hence a strict discipline: "Members of this department will be under the direct supervision of the chief usher and his staff, including assistant chief usher, floor captains and directors, and should at all times follow strictly instructions given by them."[48] There existed also a complex system for rising in the hierarchy: "There is a honor role and a demerit system by which those who have earned the right are automatically headed for promotion."[49]

As we have seen with *The Baltimore Sun*, in the press ushers were largely identified with the military, and the widespread presence of former sergeants as trainers helped this identification.[50] They also resembled workers and employees in factories and offices. The emphasis on the division of labor, efficiency, and identification with the firm were the same.[51] These comparisons allow us to uncover a relevant aspec. While organizing the attendance of the patrons and responding to their needs, ushers essentially acted as perfect agents of a disciplined society. The comfort that they provided was synonymous with order. Thanks to them, a crowd was transformed into an audience, that is, into a structured social body, and a gathering became a safe and ordered social encounter, that is, an appropriate social activity. Hence a further equivalence. This process of ordering applied also to the images on the screen. A film is the attempt to tame the flow of the images and convert it into a coherent story, just as a comfortable encounter is the result of a domestication of bodies. In this sense, however paradoxical it may seem, ushering and screening shared many aspects. How the comforts of the theater, with their ties with discipline, were equivocal and cinema itself could ultimately come to be seen as poisonous we will see shortly. For now, I will examine the third type of comfort, that related to watching the film.

A Perfect Vision

During the 1920s, the lavish picture palaces represented the ideal of film exhibition. It was there that most of the spectators' comforts were adopted. At the end of the decade, as a consequence of the Great Depression and of the move toward sound, a new model of film theater emerged: a more intimate, functional motion picture theater in which the accent was put on the best perceptual and psychological conditions in which to follow the movie. It was not the first time that theaters changed their arrangement and scope, and it would not to be the last.[52] The nickelodeon of the mid 1900s through 1910s was a bare room aimed at hosting an undifferentiated audience;

the multiplex and cineplex of the 1980s, with many screens under the same roof, would echo the configuration of malls; the Imax and black box theaters of the new millennium would address cinephiliac audiences, though by opposite means.[53] The picture palaces of the 1920s, with their multiple attractions and the huge number of spectators in attendance, apparently did not put emphasis enough on the enjoyment of the movie itself.[54] The more functional theaters of 1930s rebalanced the situation, giving the comfort of the actual viewing experience its rightful share.[55]

But what does the comfort of actual viewing experience entail? In its essence, it involves the creation of functional and sensuous conditions for viewing a film via the implementation of filmic representations and implementations in the architectural arrangement of the site. A few words on each of them.

One way to improve the viewing experience was to enhance visibility by improving the screen's size and performance. In the late 1920s there were attempts to increase the size of the screen, in particular with novel technologies such as the Magnascope and the Fox Grandeur. The former, inaugurated in 1926 at the Rivoli Theater in New York, employed variable screen masking and a third projector to modify the visible surface over the course of a film, maximizing the screen space during spectacular sequences. The latter, launched in 1929 at the Gaiety Theater in New York, used a wider screen (thirty-four feet or a forty-two feet wide, instead of the usual twenty-two to twenty-four feet) and a seventy-millimeter gauge. Though short-lived, the two devices were relevant episodes in the history of wide screens.[56]

The increase of the screen's size was potentially damaging to the image's resolution, hence there were simultaneous efforts to increase the screen's brightness. The most used surfaces were diffusive or matte and reflective or metallic. The canonical *Richardson's Handbook of Projection* in its fifth edition tested several materials and found kalsomine, a whitewash made with calcimine, to be the best for movie screens.[57] In her book *On the Screen*, Ariel

Rogers reconstructs with great accuracy the experiments aimed at improving the screen scale and brightness during what she calls "the long 1930s," as well as the use of rear projections and the emergence of new kinds of screens, including the television cathode tube, then in its first stage.[58] What she underscores is the constant attempt to search for the perfect balance between spectacular grandiosity and visual comfort—a task that was pursued through an increasing synchronization of sensorial stimuli and spectators' sensibility, as well as a progressive integration of screen and its environment.

The search for a more realistic and immersive experience is also worth of mentioning. An interesting thread is the early discussion of stereoscopic cinema. In 1929, the press announced that Dr. Herbert Ives of the Bell Telephone Laboratories—"who has brought television in the last five years from a dream to the commercial stage"[59]—was experimenting with 3-D. The *New York Herald Tribune* looked at this experimentation as a decisive step toward a truthful and lifelike picture of reality that would surpass the movies' current rendition. "This projected system for taking pictures in relief could be theoretically combined with color processes and with talking picture mechanism, making possible the ultimate illusion of figures in natural color moving freely in space and talking, thus superseding the shadowy ghosts which now speaks with supernatural effect from the black-and-white two-dimensional screen."[60] Such a quest of realism gave way to the dream of mobilizing other senses beyond sight. In the same years, we find announcements of systems able to activate smell—in a futuristic vision of a cinema not as Nietzsche's "total art," but as total environment.[61]

Yet comfort while viewing a movie also was ultimately tied to a radical redefinition of theaters' layout. While promoting a more comfortable visual experience, this redefinition echoed "concurrent practices in modern art and architecture, which themselves reflected the social and sensorial changes arising with urban-industrial modernity."[62] Among them, there was a progressive synchronization of spectators' body and mind with their main task: watching a movie. One champion of such a change was the architect Ben Schlanger, whose practical and theoretical work has been explored extensively by Jocelyn Szczepaniak-Gillece.[63] During the 1930s, Schlanger promoted a systematic removal of the décor and props of the theater, which he saw as a source of distraction, and the creation of spaces that were totally functional in creating an immersive experience. To reach this goal, he suggested innovative solutions such as inverting the slope of the floor, no longer sloping down to, but raised toward the screen so as to fill the entire spectators' field of vision,[64] and forms of transition between the screen's illuminated surface and the theater's darkness that created a homogenous environment. Though not always successful, these innovations marked a new stage in the history of movie attendance, a stage in which the comfort of the eyes was prioritized.

Within this history, an episode that deserves attention is the creation of the Film Guild Cinema. Designed by the architect Frederick Kiesler[65] and aimed at improving spectators' viewing experiences, the theater opened in New York on February 1, 1929. The project of this innovative film theater generated significant press coverage. Journals and magazines extensively anticipated the two major elements that distinguished this theater: the fact that spectators would be able to watch a movie without distractions and that they would enjoy a spectacle that exploits the whole space of the theater. The former aspect is at the center of the *New York Herald Tribune* report: "All lines [of the theater] converge [to the screen]. The walls, sloping ceiling and stadium floor incline to the screen. The interior coloring of black, blue, and silver intensifies the shadows on the white curtain, and the elimination of all lighting from the auditorium provides for concentration on the part of the audience."[66] The latter aspect is underlined by *Film Weekly*: "The interior of the theater will resemble inside of the camera with the bellows extended. The ordinary screen will occupy the place of the lens of the camera, and black screens will run along each side of the auditorium and the ceiling, converging at the round white screen on the stage. The arrangement will thus give four screens upon which pictures may been screened, three black and one white" (fig. 3.5a).[67] As combined effect, "the spectators themselves are suddenly and literally 'immersed' in the drama that is being played," as *The New York Times* comments.[68] Despite the fact that the completed Film Guild Cinema did not exactly look the way these announcements describe (and Kiesler initially planned), it met expectations. The day after the opening, Kiesler summarized the ultimate reasons behind its creation in a text for the *New York Evening Post*: "In the cinema which I have designed for the Film Arts Guild is this most important quality of the auditorium its power to suggest concentrated attention and at the same time to destroy the sensation of confinement that may occur easily when the spectator concentrates on the screen. The spectator must be able to lose himself in an imaginary, endless space even though the screen implies the opposite" (fig. 3.5b).[69]

Exoneration, Compensation

Revisiting the golden age of movie theaters allows us to capture the range and the aims of the comforts of cinema. While targeting the ambiance of film theaters, the habits of filmgoers, and the ways of screening a movie, these comforts implied an intense, but discreet use of technology, forms of regulation of bodies and images, and the creation of a refuge from an uncertain exterior. The result was an alternative environment that replaced the reality spectators left behind and at the same time offered them the opportunity to reestablish a safer contact with the world by other means. Such a result echoed the task of the projection/protection complex, whose imperative is to substitute for a risky and fearsome exposure to the world new and safer forms of mediation with it. This put comforts at the very core of cinema. While bolstering its attractiveness, they were the best way to instantiate the complex that ideally underpinned its emergence.

CINEMA "REVOLUTION" COMING?

Showing Films on Walls and Ceiling

"COMPLETE ILLUSION OF REALITY"

"FILM WEEKLY" SPECIAL

*D*ETAILS *transmitted by our New York corre-*
spondent of a new theatre to be opened
in that city by the Film Arts Guild fore-
shadow a period when, in every cinema, pictures
will be projected on the walls and ceiling, as well
as on the screen, giving every spectator the sensa-
tion that he or she is actually participating in the
events reproduced.

"A complete illusion of reality" is promised by
this new invention, the principles of which can
be deduced from our illustration and the details
published below.

A FILM WEEKLY artist's idea of the new-style theatre, illustrating the
extent to which the spectator is taken into the midst of the action.

THEATRE LIKE CAMERA BELLOWS

THE Film Arts Guild, which is sponsoring the new "four screen" theory, is a body of "advanced" persons interested in the art of the film, and it is believed in New York that they will certainly open an actual theatre embodying their ideas in the near future.

Inside a Camera!

The interior of the theatre will resemble the inside of a camera with the bellows extended. The ordinary screen will occupy the place of the lens of the camera, and black screens will run along each side of the auditorium and the ceiling, converging at the round white screen on the stage.

The arrangement will thus give four screens upon which pictures may be shown—three black and one white.

In the showing of a picture such as "The Big Parade," a projection machine may throw scenes on the sides showing soldiers marching and army trucks advancing, while on the ceiling airplanes may be shown flying toward the screen, while the real story is being shown in the white screen.

"Atmosphere"

Another claim for the four screens is that during the showing of a picture the interior of the theatre may be arranged to correspond with the theme of the picture by merely throwing "still" slides on the walls. Thus the effect of a cathedral or night club might be intimated at practically no cost.

In that sense the theory, if it ever finds general acceptance, will have almost as revolutionary an effect in a structural sense as it will dramatically. It will tend to make the "atmospheric" theatre unnecessary. Every cinema will be able to change its architecture with its pictures on Monday and Thursday, if its owners so desire.

The prospect of abolishing expensive architects' fees, to say nothing of sweeping the huge outlay for decoration necessary in the modern super-cinema, is one which would certainly appeal to cinema owners—if they did not think it "too good to be true" to believe that in the future it will only be necessary to build their theatres with inexpensive flat walls and ceilings.

Getting into the Picture

Leaving that side of the matter alone, there is much in the Guild's suggestion to appeal to—or to appal, according to temperament—the average picture-goer.

We all like to feel ourselves "part" of the film we are witnessing, but realism may be going just a little far if we are to sit through a war picture in which the guns, fired at our rear or over our heads!

Again, a picture of the Coliseum at Rome, with the spectator given the impression that he is actually one of the thousands howling for blood from the safety of the great tiers of seats may appeal to some and may tend to frighten others.

But the "Four Square" theatre is at present "in the air." Nervous patrons, like architects and builders, need have no apprehensions for a year or two, at any rate. Much depends on the reception accorded the Film Guild's experiment.

NOEL COWARD ACTS FOR THE FILMS

To Make a "Talkie"

TESTED IN ENGLAND

NOEL COWARD, the famous young playwright and actor, who is probably most popularly known as the author of C. B. Cochran's "This Year of Grace," has apparently succumbed to talking pictures in America.

Our New York Correspondent cables that Coward has associated himself with Paramount, and will make a "talkie" for release in the spring. No story has as yet been selected.

"Tested" in London

Coward, whose artistic interests are varied, was first an actor and then a playwright.

He wrote several plays for the London stage, including "The Vortex," "Easy Virtue," and "The Queen was in the Parlour," and at the age of twenty-five or so was one of the most discussed of the younger dramatists.

His work was highly sophisticated in character, depicting modern life as seen by a modern young man. Some people thought his work a mirror of the age, some were merely bored. He was always witty.

Besides writing plays, he has written revues and composed music for them; but never, so FILM WEEKLY is informed by a personal friend of his, has he thought seriously about adopting films work.

He has, however, had some of his plays adapted for the films. Two of these were "The Vortex" and "Easy Virtue." Unfortunately, the film versions of Coward's work hold little of the appeal of his plays.

The "Vortex," which was produced by Adrian Brunel, has been said to be one of the worst films ever made. It was certainly not a success. "Easy Virtue" was of better quality; but not comparable with the play of the same name.

British Associations

Clever British stars played in these films. Julie Suedo and Walter Butler both played in "The Vortex," and were little known to the public. Julie Suedo is now a clever player of "vamp" roles.

Coward's plays were adapted by British film concerns, and it is to be regretted that he has not decided to make his film debut in a British film. It may be that the superiority of American production in the field of the full-length "talkie"—British has not yet made one—has caused him to contract with an American company.

The Dramatic Prodigy

Some time ago, when Coward was visiting Gainsborough studios, he was invited, half humorously, to undergo a camera test. He agreed to this, and a few shots were taken.

It is said that he made a remarkably good screen subject; but at the time he did not think seriously of breaking into films.

When told that Coward was to make a talking picture, a Gainsborough official expressed great surprise, and said that it was certainly only during his visit to America that he could have changed his ideas in regard to films.

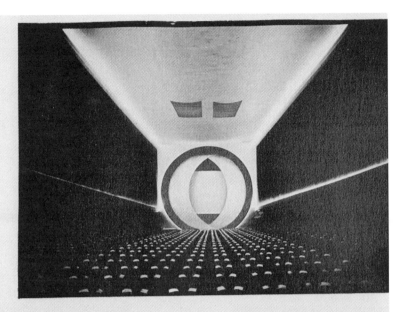

To concentrate the public's attention on the screen moving diaphragms were installed in front of it. These were called the "screeno-scope." The diaphragms give to the curved screen behind them any shape and size.
FILM GUILD CINEMA, New York
F. KIESLER, architect (New York)

Transforming the sidewalls of the Film Guild Cinema into black screen on which the motion picture or any other projected picture may be extended throughout the whole auditorium.
ELEVATION OF A SIDE WALL OF THE FILM GUILD CINEMA
FREDERICK KIESLER, architect

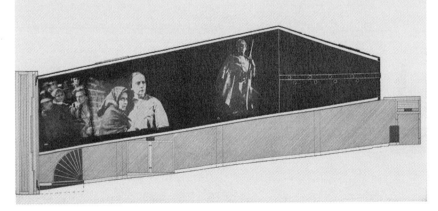

But what is "comfort," in the end, and what are its intimate dynamics? In his monumental treatise *Mechanization Takes Command*, the historian of architecture Sigfried Giedion recalls that the word "comfort" has its Latin root in the idea of "strengthening."[70] Comforts (plural) must be intended primarily as supports against the difficulties of the daily life. While offering forms of relaxation, they induce a sense of relief. In architecture, this function is clearly present in environments such as home interiors and in objects such as chairs, which put bodies—and souls—at ease and offer forms of repose. Likewise, the "modern comforts" of cinema that allow restful postures, a clean and temperate atmosphere, amiable regulations, safe interactions, and clear vision are forms of alleviation, not mere luxuries. Patrons enjoy a setting that minimizes effort and curtails potential risks. Consequently, they can lower their guard and indulge in the pleasures that the setting and the show have to offer. What they experience is something more than a simple escape from everyday hassle. It is an *exoneration* from the constant challenges that direct exposure to the world requires. Daily struggles subside; the ceaseless effort to manage often unpredictable situations finds a break; life becomes lighter.

The praise of cinema as a form of exoneration was a leitmotif in the discourse of the film industry during the 1920s and 1930s. While displaying a social commitment as a rationale for the entertainment business, this discourse implicitly recognized the difficulties that patrons met in their everyday milieu. Comforts were offered precisely as countermeasures to these difficulties. As we have seen, air-conditioning was motivated by the presence of an unhealthy climate, clean toilets responded to the risk of germs, and ushers prevented the interpersonal conflicts so common in social environments. Exoneration was thus first and foremost a way to dispel the permanent threats that patrons faced in their everyday lives—or at least a way to pause patrons' exposure to the world. Hence the need to separate the theater from its immediate reality.[71] There is no exoneration without retreat. It is not only the mental detachment discussed by Stanley Cavell, when he notes that at the movies, the spectators are "screened" from reality and reality from the spectators.[72] It is also a physical partition. The theater provides an enclosure and the screen a filter that together keep external reality at a distance. In exchange, on screen and in front of the screen, an alternate world takes shape. In this new environment — artificial yet friendly, temporary yet effective — patrons regain a safe way to cope with reality.

On the other hand, the idea of comfort suggests the presence of a *compensation*. The amenities of the theater, the support from ushers, and the accessibility of images offer not only a pause in spectators' struggle against the risks inherent to their milieu, but also a reward for spectators' diminished ability to manage existences marred by modern living conditions — a diminished ability that the loss of contact with the external world imposed by cinema may even exacerbate.

The presence of compensations finds a perfect illustration in a 1927 essay penned by the critic Seymour Stern.[73] A strong advocate of more functional film theaters and consequently a sort of predecessor of Schlanger and Kiesler, Stern justifies the need of a "complete focalization" on the screen by spectators as a form of "artistic compensation" for the loss of our grasp on reality due to the advent of a technological, destructive, and antihumanistic society. The "mechanist existence" that we live no longer allows us to enjoy nature. "We need something to take the place of the bridged rivers, the dying forests, the disappearing species, the evanescent romance which was Nature's. We need something to compensate us for the annihilation of our romantic heritage, a heritage which automatically and all too obviously is destroyed in proportion as science and the scientific spirit advance."[74] Stern is aware that a movie, with its silent and black-and-white images, is unable to restore the lost reality. In exchange, and due to its own limitations, a movie can offer a picture of the world that, while lowering the pressure of what usually surrounds us, allows us to see it again and differently. "The function of the cinema-house, the reason we shall attend there, is *emotional experience*. . . . It must show us the way to freedom by making its two hours, or three hours, of presentation a moment of license in a day of repression; by consistently stimulating the emotional system in ever-fresh ways and from constantly unique angles."[75]

Stern is concerned with a comfortable vision, yet his suggestions can be rephrased for the comfortable environment and the comfortable hospitality that cinema offers. Think of the courtesy and attention granted by ushers: it is a form of compensation for the hostile milieu that new living and working conditions have developed. Ushers embody the type of organization for which patrons usually work and that produces in them a sense of fatigue and alienation. The very fact that in the evening, when they fill the movie theaters, patrons find a similar organization available to them represents a reward for what their lives and labor have cost them during the day. What they serve is now at their service. To paraphrase Benjamin, in their workdays, patrons have relinquished their humanity in face of the apparatus. In the movie theater, they take revenge on the same apparatus — or they believe they take revenge on it — due to the ushers' work.[76] Care is not only a distinction. It is a reparation.

The same can be said of the comfortable atmosphere of the theater. Speaking of the "liveability" of domestic spaces, the theorist and architect Thomas Maldonado underscores the strict complicity of the idea of comfort with the capitalistic dynamics of supply and demand, the liberal cult of privacy, the techniques of the body developed by modern subjects, the confidence in machines typical of industrial society, and the nineteenth-century obsession with discipline.[77] Against this backdrop, home comforts, including interior layouts, functional furniture, and cleaned rooms, appear as "a procedure with a *compensatory function*, that is, a procedure seeking to restore — as much physically as psychologically — the energies consumed in the hostile external world of work."[78] The statement equally applies to the comforts of movie theater, a space that Rothafel repeatedly associated with a domestic environment.[79] In a movie theater, patrons find not only pleasures that they can enjoy — cooler air, cool water, clean restrooms, relaxing seats — but also a reward for the hard physical, climatic, and social conditions of the "outside." While providing a recess that shelters from the daily struggle, movie theaters also award a prize to those who survive in this struggle.

This link between comfort and stress may seem paradoxical, but it is intrinsic to both exoneration and compensation. Philosophical anthropology explored it, showing the dark side of the two concepts. Let's start with the exemption. The German scholar Arnold Gehlen underscored how human beings systematically try to create alternative environments that allow them to avoid direct exposure to reality.[80] Humans do it because they do not possess the strength that let other animals survive in their natural environments. They are deficient entities, and therefore more exposed to the risks that come from the surrounding reality. Alternative environments are an answer to these risks. Thanks to them, human beings can slow down their reactions; relieved of the obligations of direct interaction with the world and supported by tools that are an integral part of the new environments, they become able to manage reality more effectively and safely. Modernity accentuates this circuit of risk and protection.[81] Cinema is part of this circuit: as other media do,[82] it relies on the need to find a break from the pressures of a too intense life.

Even more revealing is the analysis of the concept of compensation offered in the same philosophical context by the German scholar Odo Marquard.[83] Starting from its original emergence in eighteenth-century theodicy, the idea of compensation implies the fact that a good is granted in reparation for the evil to which human beings are exposed. This definition lends itself to two possible interpretations. In the first, good is granted *despite* the evil, as a sort of benevolent gift; in the second, "good comes into being only through evil" and consequently depends on evil. Marquard speaks of "weak [and] strong form of the idea of compensation."[84] In the latter, a compensation literally needs damage to occur before it is granted and therefore shares its logic, rather than countering it. If we choose this strong form, the comforts of cinema come into view in a more dramatic light.

Far from mending the poverty of modern experience with temporary pleasures, they need this poverty to justify themselves, and consequently they reinforce the poverty's presence. Their relief perpetuates the illness. Take the images on the screen: while trying to offer a remedy to the fact that spectators no longer enjoy full contact with the world, these images rely on a physical and symbolic distance from actual reality. Or take the ushers' courtesy: aimed at healing the sense of anonymity suffered by patrons in factories and offices, it is imparted with the same rules that yield the anonymity. Or take the comfortable atmosphere inside the theater: the production of breathable air increases the pollution that makes normal air unbreathable. The reward for what Stern called a "mechanist existence" is a sophisticated machine that belongs to the same logic that elicited this existence.

While offering an undoubted relief from the pressures and burdens of everyday existence, cinema keeps spectators in a loop in which pressures and burdens are only reshaped and relocated. Hence new fears — including the fear of cinema itself as a deceiving machine — in which the delights of cinema appear ultimately poisonous. A concluding detour on a late novel by Roth — the same author from which I started — will bear witness to this aspect of the role of cinema and the doubts that it raised.

The Devil, Finally

Roth's *Der Antichrist*, originally published in 1934,[85] is a novel in the form of essay — or vice versa — that is pervaded by an almost unbearable sense of pessimism. While revisiting the great events that followed the end of First World War, Roth complains of a threefold loss: the loss of meaning (words are no longer tied to univocal references),[86] the loss of truth (our tongues are unable to express a common assessment),[87] and the loss of our own existence (life has become a shadow of life).[88] This threefold loss is directly caused by the Antichrist, who wants to destroy mankind and to take possession of the world. His action is unstoppable — and his main weapon is cinema.

During the 1920s, Roth loved cinema, though with a streak of detachment and irony. Then he is suspicious of it. In two chapters that are a monument of cinephobic literature, "Hollywood, the Hades of Modern Man" and "The Home of the Shadows," Roth dissects film's ability to make actual reality just a semblance of reality. A joyous sequence of young girls in swimsuits bears witness that what matters is no longer the human body, but how the body can be represented on the screen. In a newsreel, a parade of soldiers sent to the front makes clear that they became ghosts even before the battle in which they would die. Due to movies, actors are converted into alter egos of themselves not only on the screen but wherever they show themselves. Since what matters is not what one is, but how one appears, even ordinary people are now reduced to their own alter ego. Film enthusiasts imitate the postures and the clothing of their favorite stars, and in this way, they become not only alter egos of themselves, but also alter egos of somebody else. Once captured in a picture, nature dissolves into a shadow. Props are shadows. And shadows of dealers buy, sell, and exchange shadows of commodities.

In a spectacular anticipation of Baudrillard's simulacra, Roth sees the whole world as pure appearance with a residual reality that either is expelled from social circles or forced to follow what simulacra are. Such is the case of infants. Since they possess a glimmer of life, they are delivered in places severed from life, in hospitals; once they grow up and are part of the alleged social life, they become shadows. Against this backdrop, what can the comforts of theater be? And what kind of comfort can the amenities of cinema give?

Roth's protagonist now has no more words of appreciation for movie theaters, with their lavish interiors, cleaned restrooms, efficient ushers, and shining screens. They now appear to him just a shadow of an environment. Once, theaters were shelters in which spectators were "protected from all sides against all the evils of nature,"[89] and their comforts not only offered a pleasurable and safe harbor, but also a reward for giving up contact with the world. Now this challenging but solid world has evaporated. It "melted into the air," to borrow a sentence from Marx and Engels.[90] People no longer cope with reality, but only with appearances of reality. In the framework of a general loss of experience,[91] the comforts provided by cinema are no longer beneficial. They are as insubstantial as the world they are expected to reward. Instead of satisfying the needs of spectators, they respond to the design of the Antichrist, or, more simply, to the practices of expropriation of a technocapitalistic society.

Roth's novel ends in an emblematic way. The character who told the story — a first-person voice that openly reflects the writer's thoughts and that throughout the entire book tries to fight against the Antichrist while bearing witness of his advent — has a dense and oppositional conversation with a representative of Hollywood industry, after which he goes to the movies. "I saw my own shadow in a cinema. [The Hollywood representative] had taken it while he was speaking with me, who was the enemy of Antichrist. Among the shadows of skiers, rowers, tennis players, boxers, actors, politicians, and criminals he showed my shadow too. He had robbed me of my shadow. I left the theater."[92]

Somewhere, Not Too Far Away

Upset by his lackluster social life and troubled family, 1990s high schooler David spends most of his time watching *Pleasantville*, a 1950s TV sitcom set in an imaginary Midwest town where everything is perfect. One night, after a TV repairman replaces a broken remote control, David and his sister Jennifer are transported to the black-and-white world of the imaginary town. Now converted into Bud and Mary Sue, the son and daughter of the Parker family, the two siblings must face a harmless, comfortable world that is also totally repetitive and conventional. David/Bud and Jennifer/Mary Sue try to create new situations, and they find allies in their endeavors. Any time something new happens, a part of Pleasantville changes from black and white to color. Many citizens are scared by these trans-formations, and the mayor issues an edict that obliges everybody to follow the usual plot. Resistance ensues, and David/Bud finds new courage in carrying out the necessary changes. Novelties cannot be stopped, and Pleasantville turns completely into color—just as new color TV sets make their debut. David returns to his family and advises his recently divorced mother to find a new partner.

By telling a story that wants to be a true portrait of American society, *Pleasantville* (Gary Ross, 1998), whose title echoes the name of the imaginary town, brings to center stage another instantiation of the projection/protection complex: television. Indeed, television may be rightly considered a link between two of my main examples, cinema and electronic screen-based bubbles. While reiterating the basic arrangement of the complex — the possibility of a retreat from the usual milieu without the loss of contact with the world — television moves from the collective enclosure typical of film theaters to a space of domestic intimacy and from the reiterated presentation of a movie to a flow of disparate images and sounds. In this way, it paves the way for personal immersion into the laptop or smartphone typical of screen-based bubbles and for gestures such as surfing the internet or chatting/meeting online with a small group of interlocutors on the other side of the screen. Television belongs to the same lineage as my other examples: I mention it here for its transitional role from the early stages to the more recent forms of the complex.

This affiliation makes television a protective medium. While it seems to promise spectators contact with the whole world, it does this only after granting them a safe distance from the same world. In her extended exploration of the American television, Lynn Spigel has fully uncovered this characteristic of the medium.[1] In the United States during the 1950s, to sit in front of a TV screen in a newly built suburb meant to create an "antiseptic electrical space"[2] that offered safety and relief to those living in a no longer familiar environment in a nation economically, culturally, and racially stratified. In other national contexts, the pressures were different, but no less relevant. In postwar Europe, the medium acted as a positive force against the risks of social disruption, the sudden introduction of not yet digested habits, and the decline of the sense of family. Despite the fact of being part of the process of modernization there, its contents and forms of consumption integrated well with more traditional values.[3] On both sides of the ocean, television was a protective shield against a reality that in *Pleasantville* David/ Bud describes to his friend Margaret as "different . . . louder . . . and scarier . . . and a lot more dangerous."

The protection was accorded both by the physical retreat into a domestic space and by the constant filtering of the external world.

On the TV screen, spectators enjoyed a "desaturated" version of the world in which the unpredictable and conflicting elements that characterize human existence found an order and a motivation that made them tolerable. This strategy, however, was not without flaws — flaws that *Pleasantville*, the film, mercilessly analyses. In fact, a desaturated world represents a fictitious reality, intentionally reduced to mere representation. It is no coincidence that the inhabitants of Pleasantville, the city, are all unwitting actors forced to repeat their parts. It is true that in life, individuals always find themselves doing a bit acting, as Erving Goffmann demonstrated in the 1950s,[4] but the recitation of the inhabitants of Pleasantville appears completely cloying. As in a classic soap opera or sitcom, individuals are reduced to caricatures. All the schematic and repetitive universes offer a reassuring image of reality,[5] but the artificiality of the world filtered by television poses a problem. What is produced, in fact, is the *séparation achevée* between life and its representation that during these same years Guy Debord denounced incessantly.[6] Screened images are divorced from reality and in this way offer an escapist version of the world, instead of a picture that enables viewers to distance themselves from their milieu so that they can approach it again from a safe position.

In *Pleasantville*, David's and Jennifer's attempts to introduce new elements in the too-flat life of the town embody the necessity to overcome this radical separation. If they return its colors to the town, it is not because they want to make the plot of the sitcom more attractive, but because they want its narrative to perform its double function: to be reassuring for spectators who want to retreat from the world and also to be a conduit that brings back them to reality. This goal has a cost: the schematic life of Pleasantville faces unprecedented disruptions and dilemmas. For the first time, not only does the basketball team lose a game, but also men and women begin to express their doubts and desires. Yet the attempt is worthwhile. Due to David's and Jennifer's actions, the fictional world acquires a complexity that makes it more dense without losing its sense of safety, and the real world finally emerges — no longer spoiled by unsolvable problems — as a space of negotiation. Jennifer decides to restart a new life in Pleasantville, instead of going back to her former, broken home, and David returns to his previous family without the sense of discomfort that previously plagued him. He is now able to navigate the difficulty of his environment with an unprecedented wisdom.

Spigel offers abundant examples of this process of disconnection/reconnection with reality. According to her, postwar television "held out a new possibility for being alone in the home, away from the troublesome busybody neighbors in the next house," but at the same time, "it also maintained ideals of community togetherness and social interconnection by placing the community *at a fictional distance.*"[7] A happily structured universe, broadcast daily or weekly, favored the paradox of a safe exposure to the world.

Spigel also uncovers the risks of this process of disconnection/reconnection. When the purpose of maintaining a link with reality brings the screened universe too close to the actual world, the screened universe is perceived as just as threatening as the universe that spectators left behind. She writes: "The inclusion of public spectacles in domestic space always carried with it the unpleasant possibility that the social ills of the outside world would invade the private home."[8] This was the case with the dramatic events that burst onto American screens in the 1960s, particularly the Vietnam War, with the blood of victims now in color. Protection was not enough, and the audience experienced the shock of reality in a medium that they expected would relieve them from all anxieties.

Along with the fear of being trapped inside one's retreat, the fear of having to deal with an unpleasant reality, despite the filter provided by images, is now a constant attribute of TV spectatorship. It would return with other electronic media at the beginning of the twenty-first century. Cyberspace, initially conceived as a safe arena for mutual encounters, would increasingly become a place where individuals were exposed to any number of challenges, including aggressions and derision, just as in physical public spaces. Hence the need of further forms of defense, including the creation of a myriad little new Pleasantvilles, each politically and culturally uniform and devoted to a specific typology of users. Cyberspace would be progressively filled by these virtual towns without colors — just one tint for each — and digital users would increasingly flock into these monochrome spaces that provide them with a plot — a Qplot? — that they know well in advance. But this, as David and Jennifer would say, is another story.[9]

CHAPTER FOUR

Digitally Networked Bubbles:

Distance and Closeness

So Close, So Far

Mobile screens triumph. Our smartphones, tablets, and laptops follow us in our daily peregrinations. They travel with us, commute with us, accompany us as we reach one place or another. To peek at a screen while in motion is a typical gesture of our times and characterizes a wandering subject. While on the move, whether bored by familiar city settings or surprised by new landscapes, this subject does not stop checking emails, following maps, scrolling social media feeds, and retrieving data. Yet mobility can become virtual: the dispositifs that we take with us are equally ready to exonerate us from the need of physical movement and let us reach what we want, however far away, while staying in place. The smartphone that we keep in our pocket when we visit a museum abroad allows us to visit the same museum through a virtual tour while having breakfast at home. In the digital age, as Nanna Verhoeff suggests in her book *Mobile Screens*,[1] the word "navigation" is ambivalent. It can designate either actual travel from place to place or the possibility of exploring the world virtually, putting the body at rest. When the first meaning turns upside down, and the physical transference becomes a stillness full of curiosity, not only do the spatial vectors change direction—things come to us, instead of us going to them, and an hypertopic space replaces the heterotopic one[2]—but also the senses of distance and proximity change their balance. We no longer reach the world, but, on the contrary, we retreat from it; we sever our connection with the outside instead of crossing thresholds. At the same time, we remediate this regressive move due to virtual connections that allow us to project ourselves beyond the ideal enclosure in which we have found refuge. The severance is thus broken thanks to a screen.

The situation I have just described is not unprecedented. It emerges when we stop what we are doing to immerse ourselves in a page of a book or in a phone conversation, when we wear headphones to concentrate on music, or when we divert our attention from what is happening around to read breaking news on the front page of a newspaper. In these examples, we put our immediate environment into parentheses, we find refuge in a sort of imaginary bubble, and we reconnect with external realities through a different communication channel, a channel that is often more attractive than the usual reality. When the reconnection is provided by screened images or visual data, this overlapping of spatial deprivation and sensorial excitation is striking. Screen-based bubbles create a safe zone in which we can stay fully tuned into the outside world without exposing ourselves to it directly. This peculiar condition makes them a perfect instantiation of what I call the projection/protection complex, also exemplified by the Phantasmagoria and cinema. Screen-based bubbles, too, rely on an enclosure — no longer as material as in the two other dispositifs, but equally as effective — and on images that reestablish a connection with what we have left behind or are unable to reach.

In the next pages I explore these bubbles and their mode of working as instantiations of the projection/protection complex. An analysis of the ways in which distance and closeness interfere and overlap will introduce us to their logic. A brief description of the peripersonal space that develops around our body will bring us to the core of this logic. The peripersonal space includes what we can reach with our limbs, in particular, our hands, but when improved with tools that extend our senses, it ends up encompassing elements that are otherwise beyond reach. In the bubble, the screened images englobe portions of the external world into our zone of intimacy. Finally, the enclosure that screen-based bubbles create will be compared with the physical enclosures of the Phantasmagoria and cinema. In the bubble, the concrete walls of the theater give way to almost imperceptible thresholds, defined by the way in which a sensorium reacts to a flow of data. This apparent immateriality of the bubble is not a symptom of weakness. On the contrary, while revitalizing the fear of direct exposure to the world that undergirds the projection/protection complex, screen-based bubbles bear witness to the emergence of new ways of interacting with the world in which cognitive processes and technological practices, environmental affordances and bodily performances, and ultimately actual and virtual realities coalesce and shape unprecedented sensibilities.

The Screen and the Mask

Let's focus on a situation that the pandemic that began in 2020 made so familiar[3] and that has apparently lasted beyond the emergency: a conversation or a meeting online due to communication platforms such as Skype, Zoom, and Microsoft Teams. In this kind of encounter, we interact with individuals who are physically absent. They show themselves in full view, and we react to their presence as if they were just in front of us, yet as a matter of fact, they are far from us. If we carry on our conversation or meeting, it is because their space, to which we do not belong, merges with our space, eliciting what Shaun Moores appropriately calls the "doubling of place."[4] In this twofold place we can perform actions as if we were face to face with our interlocutors, and the screen summons what is elsewhere and brings it "here." The remoteness of interlocutors does not disappear; nevertheless, the screen does not work as a barrier, but as a filter that allows an external element to penetrate inside partially and safely, again in accord with the original meaning of the word "screen" as a protective device or a temporary partition. Interlocutors appear "here" from "there," where they still reside. This is why, while interacting with those on the screen, we experience a *closeness within a distance.*

This feeling is the opposite of that aroused by another dispositif that the pandemic made familiar: the mask. By containing the dangerous droplets and in this way by purifying the air that we breathe, masks allow individuals to meet face to face with others. Yet these actual encounters are felt as largely imperfect and even disappointing. By obscuring our expressions and muffling the sound of our words, masks subtract something that is essential. They take part of us from others and part of others from us. Consequently, meeting someone while wearing a facial cover detracts from the sense of "being together." Despite physical proximity, there is a sort of barrier between interlocutors. We are together, but split. Then, what we experience is a *distance within a closeness.*[5]

So screen and mask apparently create a perturbation in space that insists on opposite ends: the former elicits a bridge with what is distant, the latter a barrier against what is close. During the pandemic, this inversion favored a complementarity between the two dispositifs: thanks to a screen, we were able to drop the mask and look at each other's faces naked, and thanks to a mask, we were able to move around safely and experience in person what on screen we experienced only by proxy. Lockdowns became less onerous. However, the complementarity of the two devices did not cancel their specificity: the mask kept distant what was close, and the screen kept close what was distant.

The design becomes more complicated if we consider that a conversation or a meeting online not only implies the proximity with distant interlocutors, it also elicits a sort of detachment from one's immediate surroundings. While approaching on screen those that are far, we concentrate our attention on them, and we put into parentheses what happens around us. In a certain sense, we create a distance with what is close, just as we do when we wear a mask. Such exclusion of the immediate surroundings finds its iconic equivalent in the way these communication platforms frame our faces. We appear on the screen—ours and others'—in a more or less radical close-up, with the background only partially visible and often replaced by an image of esoteric places. The small vignettes isolate our faces, and by doing this, they bear witness to our severance from the reality around us.

So, in our online conversations or meetings, we experience both the detachment from the immediate surroundings and the reconnection with those who are absent, and the sense of distance within closeness merges with the sense of closeness within distance. Indeed, there is a border that excludes what is outside and, at the same time, there is the inclusion of a piece of remote world into this space of intimacy. What emerges then is a sort of *bubble* in which individuals engaged in a conversation or a meeting find shelter by withdrawing from their own milieu and in which at the same time they enter remote realities thanks to new forms of contact. We find in these bubbles a dynamic that we already encountered in other instantiations of the projection/protection complex—a dynamic that screen-based bubbles develop in an original way.

Bubbles
Bubbles are notoriously strange objects. In a proper sense, they designate a small body of gas within a liquid or a thin film of liquid inflated with air or gas: whatever their state, they imply a hollow space separated from an outside by fragile walls. In the first decades of the twentieth century, the biologist Jacob von Uexküll used the word to designate the "piece cut out of surroundings" that living creatures elect as their immediate space of action.[6] Today, in a world dominated by media, "bubble" has come to denote an enclosed sphere of experience in which people isolate themselves from the wider external world, either to reinforce the opinions that they share with a homogenous community or to find a space of intimacy while engaged in an immersive activity. In this new meaning, we create our own bubble when we rely only on a very few sources

of information—the ones that reinforce our beliefs—instead of opening up to a wider set of ideas, or when we wear headphones and abandon ourselves to a world of sounds while navigating a public space.[7] In both cases, we sever ourselves from the external world, and we find shelter in a more limited space.

In his monumental trilogy devoted to the idea of the sphere, Peter Sloterdijk expanded the term "bubble" to describe a wide array of situations that engage some sort of shell, wrap, or case, from domestic spaces to the great ideologies that enclose individuals into a set of certainties.[8] More modestly, I will focus on the spaces of retreat and communication created by screens. While centering my analysis on online conversations and meetings on Zoom, Teams, or Skype, I will also have in mind the bubbles that take shape when we text with a friend on our smartphone, when we surf the internet on our laptop and direct all our attention toward what we are discovering, or when we watch a TV show or movie video on our tablet while commuting by train.[9] The increasing ubiquity of the screen in the current media landscape makes these bubbles proliferate. The interconnected isolation that we experience when wearing a VR headset and immersing ourselves in virtual reality would be the last instantiation of this series. But to what extent is the screen-based bubble a bubble?

First, in bubbles composed of liquid and gas, inside and outside are split by a fragile, but well-defined divide. Screen-based bubbles inherit both this fragility and this definite character. On the one hand, in screen-based bubbles, the divide between inside and outside is immediately recognizable. Individuals frame their own space of intimacy and send signals to the immediate others about their unwillingness to pay attention to what happens around them. If in a public space, they divert their gaze from the setting, adopt specific postures, and make explicit their concentration on the screen. If at home, and when it is possible, they create a clear separation between the domestic space and the spot from which they engage in online conversations or meetings. Online, we find frequent comments that praise the clear-cut separation between digital users and their immediate surroundings.[10] Bubbles are always perceptible. On the other hand, the divide that isloates indiviuals immersed in their laptops, tablets, or smartphones from their immediate surroundings depend on the situation. When the visual content on the screen is highly attractive and the context in which users attends their device offers assets such as a private space at home, an individual seat on a train, and an uncrowded spot in a square, the boundaries that envelop a screen-based bubble appear stable, yet every change in these elements put this stability at risk. Many online remarks underscore these risks and try to prevent them.[11] The invisible walls of the bubble can easily dissolve.

Second, while ordinary bubbles are inflated with ethereal elements like air or gas, screen-based bubbles are filled with more complex and solid elements: we have a user, one or more surfaces on which visual data materialize, one or more technical devices of which the screen is a part, physical elements such as a desk, and a flow of data, potentially including the face and the voice of an interlocutor who thanks to the communication platform is "present" to the user. Such a set of components makes the tension between inside and outside more dramatic. The outside is our usual milieu, which we share with others and which we suddenly keep at a distance; the inside is a piece of this milieu that we cut away, transform into a space of intimacy, and fill with elements some of which are not within reach, but become available due to devices that establish a channel of communication. Screen-based bubbles rely on a game centered on the refusal of the world and its recuperation by other means.

Third, the ordinary bubbles rely on a sort of equilibrium between inside and outside. Indeed, they float suspended in the air. The screen-based bubbles reinforce and reshape this equilibrium. They englobe what is external and make it immaterial, and they create a space of intimacy that arises from a space of exclusion. The effect is to establish stronger forms of exchange between inside and outside: what is close and what is distant interpenetrate. This condition allows the screen-based bubbles to dot the social space. Like the real bubbles, they too are suspended in the environment in which we live. There is no lack of online comments about how crucial and spread the presence of screen-based bubbles is in our everyday.[12]

Finally, just as ordinary bubbles rely on sophisticated dynamics of physical forces, screen-based bubbles host a rich set of social, psychological, and symbolic processes. In a conversation on Skype or Zoom, interlocutors share the same focus; they take their turn in speaking; they negotiate the meaning of their exchanges; they tap on the keyboard or move a finger on the screen; they turn on or off the camera; they choose the configuration of images on the screen; and so on. In short, they activate their sight, hearing, and hands in a coordinated interaction. Karin Knorr Cetina provides a detailed analysis of the ways in which screen-based encounters — which she calls "synthetic situations" due to their mixing of actual and virtual elements — borrow and sometimes adapt the set of actions that underpin the face-to-face encounters studied by sociologist Erving Goffman.[13] Our bubbles absorb many of the processes that characterize our everyday life and perform them in a restricted space. The consequence is the emergence of extremely dynamic situations.

The existence of a boundary, the balanced yet dynamic inclusion of external elements, and the creation of a field of action make the bubble a true spatial entity. We accommodate ourselves into our bubbles. Now it is time to detect the nature of this space, its similarities to and differences from other forms of enclosure, such as the ones created by the Phantasmagoria and cinema, and eventually the motivations that undergird this space's peculiar configuration.

The Space around Us

Screen-based bubbles take up a thin space around us — a space that develops right around our body and whose limits coincide with the sphere of our active attention and the field of our immediate action. This space largely corresponds to what neuroscientists call the *peripersonal space*. As Vittorio Gallese and Michele Guerra sum-marize it, the peripersonal space "is multisensorial (based on the integration of visual, tactile, acoustic, and proprioceptive informa-tion), centered on the body (controlled by a system of coordinates that are anchored to the various body parts not to the position of the eye), and motor in nature."[14] It is defined by its extension around our head and our limbs, by its connection with our immedi-ate action, by its dependence on the multimodal integration of our senses, and by its plasticity, since it is remapped by our brain as the action unfolds.[15]

The peripersonal space is at once exclusive and inclusive. On the one hand, our brain makes a clear distinction between what is near to us and easily handled and what is far from us and out of reach. The two spaces are processed by different cortical regions of our brain. This distinction allows the peripersonal space to exclude what is not immediately accessible, because it falls beyond the range of our immediate action. From this point of view, the peripersonal space is something that surrounds individuals without encompassing their wider surroundings. On the other hand, the perimeter around our body is influenced by multiple factors and implies several degrees of distance.[16] It does not respond so much to the specific positions of the objects around us as to the situation in which we find our-selves.[17] This flexibility allows the peripersonal space to include not only what is ready at hand, but also what is pertinent to an ongoing action. In particular, the space can extend to what we can reach by using tools and even to what is summoned through memory, rep-resentations, and imagination. Experiments in neuroscience show that the neurons that manage the peripersonal space can also fire when stimulated by objects that we just assume to be near to us or by actions that we perform only virtually.[18] According to Gallese, this mechanism leads us to simulate within our body what we see done by others or what we believe could happen.[19] Gallese's notion of *embodied simulation* explains why, physiologically, we make present and ready at hand what is not actually within our reach.

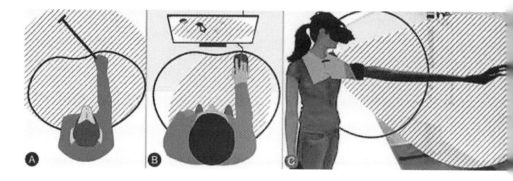

Figure 4.1. Peripersonal space remapped, as a consequence of (virtual) tool use, in Sofia Seinfeld et al., "User Representations in Human-Computer Interaction," *Human–Computer Interaction* 36.5–6 (2021), fig. 5, doi.org/10.1080/07370024.2020.1724790.

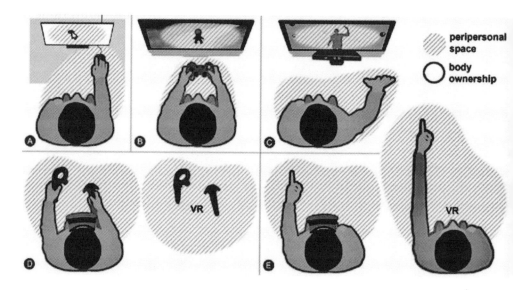

Figure 4.2. Changes in peripersonal space, body ownership, and visual perspective, depending on the interface and input devices used, in Sofia Seinfeld et al., "User Representations in Human-Computer Interaction," *Human-Computer Interaction* 36.5–6 (2021), fig. 9.

Personal screen-based bubbles reiterate these dynamics (fig. 4.1). They develop around our body when we focus on our laptop or smartphone, yet they can also encompass further slices of reality. This happens when we extend our action to the space represented on the screen of our device.

This extension becomes particularly clear when we introduce into this space a trace of our action on it — be it the cursor that signals the movements of our mouse or an avatar that embodies the ways in which we explore the virtual domain on the screen. These "User Representations," as Sofia Seinfeld and her collaborators call them,[20] testify to our involvement into the represented space: different User Representations bear witness to diverse forms of appropriation of this space and consequently to diverse forms that our bubble can take (fig. 4.2).[21]

Yet the extension of our bubble is also made possible by the simple idea of the presence of the user within this space. To make the screened space our space, it suffices that we project ourselves into it as implied observers; even more, it suffices that we transform it into the space of our virtual or imagined action. Our bubble englobes this screened reality, though with different degrees of implication. Of course, this situation lasts only as long as we turn our attention to a screen and dive into the displayed content. Once this content is no longer attractive, or, more radically, once we turn off our device, the displayed reality ceases to be "present."

The parallel I draw between the peripersonal space and the screen-based bubble shows that the two realities are largely overlapping. The bubble is our peripersonal space when we attend to a screen-based dispositive. Nevertheless, there is one crucial difference between the peripersonal space in our everyday life and the bubble that englobes us when engaged with digital media. Indeed, while in the peripersonal space the evocation of distant realities relies on mental images, in the screen-based bubbles, the summoning is made possible by the exhibition of physical images, either online or taped. In the screen-based bubbles, a technological dispositif performs a process similar to what the body and mind usually do via a psychophysiological process. The psychophysiological process through which we appropriate the external world due to mental images of it has been forged during our long evolution as *Homo sapiens* through a constant engagement with our environment. We have learned how to summon external realities thanks to an act of imagination, and we have progressively incorporated this capacity into our cognitive skills to the point that it has become one of our major assets. Now we transfer this ability to imagine to external tools, and screened images now do what we once learned to do in our own mind. Hence a sort of inversion: we *externalize* what was an internalized process. Consequently, images, either online or taped, become a cognitive extension of our body and mind.[22] In the end, such an externalization is the premise of an integration: in bubbles, the body and technology coordinate their actions and complement each other. The outcome is the progressive emergence of a new kind of *technosensibility*.[23]

Close-Ups

The mix of closeness and distance that characterizes the screen-based bubbles recalls not only the mechanism undergirding the peripersonal space, but also the dynamics elicited by cinematic close-ups. In a movie — and the same can be said for television programs, still photography, and graphic novels — a close-up denotes a shot in which a face or an object fills the entire frame and, by extension, all shots in which the represented reality is offered in a relevant scale and consequently appears near to the observer, despite its actual absence.[24] Early film theorists were fascinated by close-ups because of their unprecedented capacity to transform our sense of space. Among these theorists, Jean Epstein offered a suggestive first-person depiction of the effect that close-ups had on spectators in his 1921 essay "Magnification."[25]

The opening of the essay is stunning: "I will never find the way to say how I love American close-ups. Point blank. A head suddenly appears on screen and drama, now face to face, seems to address me personally and swells with an extraordinary intensity. I am hypnotized."[26] Such an intense implication of spectators is elicited by the apparent abolition of any distance: "The close-up modifies the drama by the impact of proximity. Pain is within reach. If I stretch out my arm, I touch you, and that is intimacy."[27] A particularly intense relationship is established between the screen and the auditorium: "The close-up is an intensifying agent because of its size alone."[28] What emerges is a sort of a communion with what is represented on the screen: "Never before has a face turned to mine in that way. . . . It is in me like a sacrament."[29] Yet while filling the gap between the screen and spectators, close-ups also put spectators in a state of isolation. "Wrapped in darkness, ranged in the cell-like seats, directed toward the source of emotion by their softer side, the sensibilities of the entire auditorium converge, as if in a funnel, toward the film. Everything else is barred, excluded, no longer valid."[30] Spectators are at once fused with the images, which work as a proxy for objects still distant, and severed from the world, which retreats from the spectators' attention.

Epstein was not the only one to explore the nature of close-ups. In 1916, Hugo Münsterberg suggested a parallel between the dynamics of the close-up and the mechanism of attention in which we focus on a detail at the expense of its context,[31] and in 1924 Béla Balázs praised the close-up's ability to put spectators in contact with the otherwise mysterious "face of things" while suspending their interest in the entirety of a situation.[32] Despite some difference in what they accent, theorists of the time converged around the idea that close-ups are able to create a space of intimacy in which spectators experience an absent object as if it were present and ready at hand and at the same time create a sense of detachment from their immediate surroundings.[33] This is exactly what happens with the screen-based bubbles: they, too, make distant objects close and immediate surroundings distant. Such a parallelism brings to the fore two facts.

First, it is not by chance that contemporary digital bubbles often emerge in coincidence with the display of images in close-up. It is the case of our conversations on Zoom or Teams, in which we exchange words with faces that generally fill the entire frame, either on the full screen or lined up in a grid that also includes ourselves. When in full screen, these vignettes reiterate the idea of intimacy heralded by Epstein. When in a grid, they add to this intimacy the effects of the split screen[34] — a split screen in which we can at once check the others and monitor ourselves. In both examples, these vignettes not only accentuate the sense of presence of our interlocutors, but also convey the idea that these interlocutors are part of the same sphere in which we are immersed, at the expenses of the reality that encircles us, which on the contrary withdraws.[35] Close-ups accelerate the creation of a bubble.

Second, the imbrication of close-ups and bubbles bears witness that we organize the space around us via both our immediate senses and the images that we are enjoying. Put another way, when we are sitting in front of our laptop, the sense of the space in which we are immersed depends both on an orientation of our body within this specific situation and on the input from the representations we are dealing with. The screen-based bubbles respond simultaneously to the existence of a peripersonal space and to the spatial configuration implied by the image in front of us. The medium, its content, and its users work together. Once again, Gallese's idea of embodied simulation offers a rationale for this convergence.

From Physical Walls to Immaterial Borders

The recurring presence of close-ups in digitally networked bubbles — a characteristic feature in film, and, albeit in a different form, in the Phantasmagoria — calls for a deeper comparison between these three dispositifs. Indeed, screen-based bubbles, cinema, and the Phantasmagoria not only share the same inclination for privileging close-ups, but also accommodate their spectators and users in a space that mirrors the ideal space suggested by close-ups: a space of intimacy at the expense of interest in context. Indeed, all three kinds of media are based on an enclosure that keeps the immediate surroundings out of reach and images that reestablish an even more strict contact with things. Yet if the spatial arrangement of bubbles recalls the enclosures of cinema and the Phantasmagoria, at least in its more general aspects, there are also crucial differences between the bubble and the other two dispositifs — differences that reveal new trends in our forms of mediation with reality.

In cinema and the Phantasmagoria, the closed space gathers a crowd, and the screen-based bubbles create a space that generally includes a single individual. While the former were social sites, the latter is a personal space. While hosting social interactions at a distance, bubbles are mainly centered on a platform's user. This implies an accentuated alienation from one's everyday context. After all, theaters were portions of world in which part of customary habits and behaviors were still actively shared, as Julian Hanich persuasively proves;[36] when engaged in a conversation online or when watching a movie on a tablet, individuals curtail this sense of sharing. Bubbles tend to convey a sense of isolation, responding to a subtle desire to avoid every form of direct exposure to real others, including exposure to the selected crowd of an in-person audience.

On the other hand, the setting of cinema and the Phantasmagoria were quite stable, both because they were clearly and permanently separated from the outside and because the events they hosted were well delimited and well regulated; the bubble, instead, is not a steady space but can change in size and structure, depending on the course of the action. For example, it expands when new objects of interest are included, and it shrinks when some of the elements that are already included are kept in reserve. Take the bubble that we occupy while watching a movie on our laptop at home. It can create isolation, but it also may aggregate some members of the family when they are interested in sharing the movie and lose them when they move away, sometimes only temporarily. Bubbles are circumstantial, and they respond to contingencies. These same

contingencies can lead them to dissolve, either because what is displayed on the screen comes to an end, as is the case of a conversation
online or a movie enjoyed on a laptop, or because something in the
surrounding environment diverts the attention of the individual at
the center of the bubble, as is the case when a domestic emergency
requires one to leave a meeting or to stop a movie. Online, we find
several remarks about the way in which contingencies can change
the arrangement of a screen-based bubble to the point of ending it.[37]

Finally, the bubble does not have the physical walls of the cinema or the Phantasmagoria. There may be physical elements that
contribute to bubble's emergence. (I think of the room in which an
individual finds shelter during a sensitive conversation on a smartphone.) Yet these elements are nonessential. What matters is a
diversion of the attention from the outside world to a specific media
content.[38] Bubbles' borders are immaterial. Such an immateriality
has a double consequence. It further favors the absence of a clear-cut
distinction between the inside and the outside of a bubble: if there
are boundaries, such as they are, they appear like a *modulation* of the
whole territory, more than like a tangible partition.[39] And, more
importantly, it changes our relationship with space; no longer physical stakes on our way, boundaries become an *internalized* reality.

I have already noted that screen-based bubbles summon distant
elements and make them present due to concrete representations
conveyed by a technological device, instead of mental images as
in the peripersonal space. Bubbles engage images that possess a
tangibility, even that of a digital picture. The availability of such
images allows the bubbles to *externalize* a process that in the peripersonal space is performed through internal means. In bubbles, we
expand our sphere of action thanks to concrete objects instead of
our mere faculties. Yet bubbles also do the opposite: they *internalize*
processes that we are used to performing via elements "outside" us.
This is the case of bubble's borders. Indeed, they no longer depend
on tangible entities, such as the walls of cinema and the Phantasmagoria, but rather on a set of sensorial cues that are generated by

the situation and that individuals collect and use to map the space around them. What becomes crucial, then, is the ability of the individuals' sensory apparatuses to capture these cues and process them in a way that mirrors goals and procedures previously supported by tangible entities. By engaging material walls, we have learned how to recognize perimeters. In the bubble, we must apply this lesson to a situation that has no walls. The data provided by the context and a sensorium that has memory of previous operations and adapts them to the new situation are enough. Thanks to them, we are able to draw the bubble's borders, despite the absence of external landmarks. Simply, we do this through "internal" operations instead of conferring this task on props that are outside us. This process of internalization relies on a broad set of skills. It mobilizes cognitive, neurophysiological, and informational procedures. At the same time, internalization constantly plays in combination with its apparent opposite, the processes of externalization. If we are able to deal with the world, it is precisely because we both perform "inside us" what pertains to external tools and let these tools perform "outside us" what we usually do due to our internal faculties.[40]

Zeitgeist

So, unlike the physical enclosures of the Phantasmagoria and cinema, screen-based bubbles are individual, contingent, and immaterial. They support a space that is modular and internalized. These characteristics reflect some of the recurring features that have been introduced by the so-called digital revolution. Think of the way in which new digital media promote dematerialization thanks to miniaturized and almost imperceptible devices (EarPods) and favor contingency thanks to multipurpose tools that respond to a situation (the smartphone and its different functions, from connecting by voice to communicating by texts or locating the user). Similarly, think of the extent to which the new digital media are directly connected to the user's body, both because they are designed to be worn (Google Glass) and because they are aimed at constantly monitoring vital signs (smart watches).[41] Finally, think of the structure of the internet, where boundaries are impalpable and whose nodes are reachable either directly or with a simple password. Screen-based bubbles mirror these trends, to the point that we can apply to them what Virilio notes about the massive bunkers of World War II: in an age of hypercommunication, these bunkers are now replaced by a constant flow of data that keeps the environment in which we live under control.[42]

Such a correspondence between the spirit of the times and the bubbles' configuration allows us to revisit a "prophecy" made by Jean Baudrillard in the 1980s.[43] Baudrillard envisioned the entire world becoming a set of networked bubbles, with individuals "isolated in a position of perfect sovereignty, at an infinite distance from [their] original universe," like an "astronaut in his bubble," and yet fully interconnected through a ceaseless circulation of data. Reachable from every point, reality would appear more and more transparent, and consequently obscene.[44] Individuals would be forced to enjoy it — or to protect themselves from it — by staying in orbit, at a distance, in a capsule. Baudrillard was a controversial scholar, yet his portrait of a world transformed into immaterial data and organized into individual bubbles maintains its strength.

The peculiar actuality of screen-based bubbles might imply a discontinuity with the Phantasmagoria and cinema. There is no doubt that the enclosure of the bubble is physically different from that of the other two dispositifs, though there are intermediate steps between the two poles; in a movie theater, for instance, the dimming of the lights produces an isolation of each spectator from the rest of the audience that prefigures the screen-based bubbles.[45] Nevertheless, despite their differences, the spatial arrangement of the three dispositifs remains structurally the same in that there is a separation from one's immediate surroundings and a connection with distant realities. This allows us to see in the screen-based bubbles a new instantiation of the projection/protection complex rather than the emergence of an unprecedented way of working.

While reiterating a previous optical-spatial arrangement, bubbles adapt it to a new technological phase. This idea of update
finds further evidence in the role that images play in the bubble.
In the Phantasmagoria and cinema, images supported by sound
made present what the enclosure seemed to exclude. They visually restored the reality that was out of sight. In the bubble, images
are not necessarily mimetic. Quite often, they simply attest the
presence of a link, as in a conversation on Zoom or Skype, when
interlocutors signal their attendance through an anagram or a logo.
In other words, the images in the bubble ensure an opening to the
world without the obligation of portraying it. What they grant is a
relationship, more than a presence. Such an inclination echoes the
emphasis that digital culture puts on the connection itself rather
than on the substance of what is connected. Digital images are not
necessarily representations in the traditional sense, but they are
very often *an-icons*, as Andrea Pinotti calls them.[46] Yet they create
references. Screen-based bubbles, similarly, do not necessarily represent something or someone, but persist in making present what is
distant or lost. They use different means than the Phantasmagoria
and film — ultimately, what they offer are connections instead of
depictions — but this difference is just another way, adapted to the
present moment, to perform the same task.

Bubbles and Cells

But why withdraw from the immediate surroundings and look for
contact with distant realities? Why find shelter in a bubble and then
include elements from which we have alienated ourselves? If bubbles
are a new instantiation of the projection/protection complex, the
answer lies in fears. On the one hand, once again, the first source of
anxiety lies in direct contact with the world. Our milieus, including
the everyday milieu, are at once aggressive and unpredictable and
consequently potentially dangerous. Screen-based bubbles prevent us
from feeling that we stand on open ground, prey to dangerous events
and people, and they create a refuge that protects us both from

unwanted confrontations and from a threatening environment. Pandemics amplify the dangers of the situation by adding physical infection to the risks posed by our environment and those who inhabit it. Yet menaces are endemic, intimately tied to our exposure to the world—to our being-there, as Heidegger would say.[47]

While protecting us from the external world, screen-based bubbles project us into cyberspace. Cyberspace is far from being the safe space that in its early stages it promised to be—or that Mark Zuckerberg's promotion of a "metaverse" makes us believe that it is.[48] Its uncontrolled expansion, based on the aggregation of myriad sites, applications, and voices, makes it as dangerous as the physical and social milieu from which we seek shelter. Consequently, to retreat into a screen-based bubble often means to be exposed to an equally risky reality: the virtual universe.

A series of specific protective actions try to avert this possibility. For example, bubbles help to filter what we want to show of ourselves and shield us from what others might want to make transpire of them. In an online meeting, choices such as limiting the vision of the environment in which we live, excluding our family members from view,[49] and defining the duration of the meeting go precisely in this direction. Bubbles equally help to avoid unwanted intrusion in the bordered world to which they give us access. Passwords halt strangers who want to "Zoombomb" our conversations, and firewalls and antivirus software defends against the actions of hackers. The ritual nature of online encounters,[50] the notices with which they take place, and the existence of waiting rooms—all forms of nonspatial but discursive enclosure—do the rest.

On the other hand, protection itself produce fears. While finding shelter in a bubble, we can feel trapped. It happens when bubbles shrink, stiffen, and become *cells*.[51] It is worth noting that Epstein, in his comments on the close-up, speaks of the "cell-like seats"—in the original, "les alvéoles des fauteuils"—in which spectators sit.[52] The word is undoubtedly suggestive. It underscores the minimal space in which the face-to-face encounter with the screen takes place. It could also apply to some of our current bubbles in which, on behalf of the effectiveness of communication, almost all components of the situation are removed from the screen and implicitly from the attention of participants.

To feel trapped in a cell means first to experience a radical reduction of the range of our action. While committing ourselves to a space of intimacy, we find ourselves restricted in our gestures and sight. This is the case of those communication platforms whose default layout organizes participants in a hivelike grid of vignettes centered on their face; these vignettes force users to adopt a limited number of postures, if only to avoid "improper" behavior during their interaction with others. The constraints of online communication come to the fore.

Cell-like bubbles also affect subjectivity. Mirrored in their vignettes, participants in an online conversation feel also forced into a constant self-monitoring that works as a double-edged sword. If, on the one hand, everyone is engaged in the permanent control of their own actions,[53] on the other hand, one also becomes aware that their own actions are under scrutiny of the entire group. An online meeting implies the fact that one looks at and is looked at. The effect of this accented bouncing off looks is a sense of either petrification or alienation: participants are often prey respectively to the fear that they will no longer feel any pleasure in what they are doing[54] and of the fear of becoming other than oneself.[55]

Finally, the cell-like bubble also implies the fear of being isolated.[56] While meeting friends or colleagues online or while streaming a movie on our laptop, we are constantly worried about losing our connection. Recurring disturbances come not only from power outages, absence of cell service, and lack of hotspots, but also from momentary delays in transmission of signals, as Neta Alexander has underscored in her analysis of different forms of buffering,[57] and more radically, from a systematic "discorrelation" between images and their perception due to microtemporal intervals of algorithmic processing, as Shane Denson has extensively highlighted.[58] Compressed bubbles convey a sense of exclusion, rather than protection.

So, not a single fear, but a multilayered anxiety. While screen-based bubbles emerge because of our caution toward our immediate surroundings, they also trigger the panic of being exposed to cyberspace, the concern that unknown people will enter our conversations, the distress for being compressed into a narrow space, and finally the apprehension of losing contact with reality, especially when included into a cell-like bubble. Anthony Vidler would say that we move from agoraphobia to claustrophobia.[59]

How to fix this multilayered anxiety? The idea of the cell helps us. Cells not only imply a space of constraints, alienation, and isolation, as is the case of the cells of a prison;[60] cells are also the smallest unit in which life expresses itself, the basic element of a living organism. If we keep these two meanings together, combining the disciplinary and the biological sides, what emerges is an entity that separates but does not isolate, and that safeguards but does not suffocate. When working correctly, the screen-based bubbles display these qualities. They offer a shelter from the everyday milieu, and at the same time, they let external reality infiltrate into this shelter. It is what happens in many of our online conversations: the participants who dismiss their immediate surroundings and become simple vignettes on a screen let the same surroundings insinuate into their conversation. While speaking, they pet puppies, instruct kids, handle a domestic emergency, and allow their partner to appear in the same frame. At the same time, they also often appear as they are, imperfectly dressed and not well combed. The everyday, put into parentheses, takes its revenge.

Ultimately, this tension between enclosure and openness defines the core of the projection/protection complex. Suspended as it is between the need to avoid a direct confrontation with a challenging and elusive reality and the risk of building permanent barriers, the projection/protection complex aims to produce shelters that do not trap and filters that do not halt. If it does not always succeed in achieving this goal, it nevertheless constantly tries to find a balance between its two constitutive elements. No less than the Phantasmagoria and cinema, screen-based bubbles contribute to this balance. With their invisible walls that allow us at once to dissociate from our immediate surroundings thanks to a change in attention and to stay in contact with distant realities thanks to channels that prompt an extraordinary sense of immediateness, they integrate enclosure and openness through means that are the epitome of the times.

Frames and Folds

The *Screen Tests* are a series of short, silent, black-and-white film portraits made by Andy Warhol between 1964 and 1966. They mostly depict Warhol's friends and accomplices, the Factory's superstars, personalities of art and fashion, and celebrities of the New York cultural scene. Each *Test* lasts around three minutes — the time allowed by a 100-foot roll of sixteen-millimeter film stock in a Bolex camera. Subjects are shown from the neck up and against neutral backdrops: they do nothing but minimal actions, such as looking into the camera (Edie Sedgwick), bowing her head and peeking at a review (Nico), trying different postures (Bob Dylan), or remaining motionless except for blinking their eyelashes (Ann Buchanan). The most sensational actions consist of drinking a bottle of Coca-Cola (Lou Reed) or brushing their teeth (Baby Jane Holzer). The camera hardly ever moves, except to make minor adjustments in the front shot. Exceptions are extremely rare: in the first *Screen Test* that featured Salvador Dali, he is recorded with the camera upside down; in the second, he vanishes from the screen during the test. Despite these random irregularities, the format is strongly repetitive: individuals are captured in close-up, the camera is stationary, and the only recurring performance by those in the close-up is to point their eyes toward the spectators.

The *Screen Tests*, of which 472 out of more than five hundred

survive, offer an extraordinary testimony to the feverish atmosphere of the mid-1960s, as well as Warhol's artistic evolution. Not
by chance, they can be seen as the point of convergence between
Warhol's experimentation with slow cinema (*Sleep, Empire*) and his
iconic silk-screen prints—Marilyn, Elvis, Jackie.[1] I am interested
in something else, though, something that the individuals filmed
by Warhol share with the ghosts of the Phantasmagoria, with many
other movie characters, and even with the participants of an online
meeting: a certain way of *being on the screen*.

Shot in a rigorous close-up, the protagonists of *Screen Tests* are
framed in a space that excludes them from their usual context.
While celebrating their appearance, their image on the screen dras-
tically reduces their space for action. This is certainly not new. As
Simmel famously noted, the frame of the painting not only circum-
scribes a representation, but also invites us to ignore everything
that lies beyond the edges of this representation. It is this act of
exclusion that ultimately gives representation its autonomy and its
unity.[2] To depict something within a frame means to enhance its
presence by insulating it. At the movies, screened images follow the
same path. They detach a piece of world from the whole to which it
belongs, and in exchange, they give to this piece of world a meaning
and a substance. Reality on screen triumphs at the cost of a clear
separation. However, unlike in painting, cinema has two means to
mitigate this separation: movement and editing. The movements
of the camera make the borders less dramatic because what is off
screen can easily be retrieved by a pan, by a tilt, by tracking. Editing fills with a new shot the spaces left empty by the previous shot,
and in this way, it conveys a more complete picture of the world.
These two means create an alternative to the closure that even
the cinematic image suffers from. The frame that surrounds this
image does not necessarily appear as a barrier that excludes the
off-screen reality; on the contrary, it becomes a mask that con-
ceals a reality temporarily invisible but ready to appear.[3] Although
camera movements or editing are an opportunity to mitigate the

sense of separation, Warhol's *Screen Tests* employ neither of them; the characters are included in a preassigned space forever. They are confined rather than comprised. Consequently, these screened images do not find any kind of opening. More than containers, they are a sort of containment.

This confinement seems even more radical because of the duration of these cinematic portraits. While in a painting, sitters are captured in a posture that freezes them and gives them immortality. Here, sitters literally relinquish three minutes of their lives. They give us not only a pose, but also a small slice of their time. During these three minutes, they could have performed different kinds of actions, but caged in a limited and limiting space, they can make only tiny gestures—and not by chance, they often end up with an almost perfect immobility. Confinement becomes even more constrictive.

What increases in return is the spectacular nature of *Screen Tests*. The restricted space in which sitters are located makes explicit that their presence is deeply staged, and their reaction to the constraints they face transforms their gestures into a performance. Yet if Warhol's *Screen Tests* are a spectacle, it is not only due to these characteristics. As Guy Debord wrote in the same years, a spectacle emerges when there is a hiatus from life: "Separation is alpha and omega of the spectacle."[4] Rigidly framed within an image that exposes them to the spectator's gaze, Warhol's sitters testify to this separation.

But are these sitters really separate from the flow of life? First, their persistent look into the camera implies an address to spectators and consequently a sort of line of communication between them and an audience. If the people depicted in *Screen Tests* perform a mini spectacle, it is on behalf of those who watch it. Second, the static camera and the minimal amount of action increase one's attention to the filmed characters, and spectators enjoy an image that discloses its entire content. Their relationship with filmed reality is marked by a sense of transparency. So, an address and a disclosure: in Warhol's *Screen Tests*, images lose contact with the world that surrounds them, but in exchange, they regain a connection with what lies in front of them. Blocked horizontally in two dimensions, they move perpendicularly in the third, outward. Hence the emergence of a space that literally envelops observer and observed. It opens to the onlooker images that otherwise are closed in on themselves. Indeed, this space no longer relies on a *frame* that isolates the interior from the exterior of a representation; on the contrary, it is a sort of *fold* that wraps the representation and its beholder. The frame does not disappear; it still borders the screened images. The fold comes over the frame and gives the space of representation a new inflection[5] due to the presence of an observer, which acts as a point of attraction.

This interplay of frame and folds recalls not only dynamics that are recurring in cinema, but also a situation that characterizes the apparitions in the Phantasmagoria and the participants in an online meeting on platforms such as Zoom or Webex. Despite an apparent freedom tied to their alleged ability to fly through the air, the ghosts of the Phantasmagoria enjoyed a limited space of action: they came from nowhere, and nothing and nobody on the screen complemented their appearance. In exchange, the ghosts approached the audience in an unprecedented effect of proximity, to the point that spectators often reacted to their presence by trying to fend them off with their canes. The isolation of the apparitions was compensated for by their strong interaction with the public. Likewise, the participants in an online meeting are confined to small vignettes that isolate them from their context, an isolation that is often broken by cats, kids, and unaware partners but that nevertheless works as a form of spatial deprivation. In exchange, these vignettes convey a sense of intimacy that englobes all the participants in the meeting and projects them in a sort of communal space. Close-ups at the movies elicit the same double effect: a sense of isolation and a sense of communion. The prominence of the characters in close-up, as well as the coming forward of the ghosts and the ideal protrusion of the participants of the online meeting, mobilize a haptic dimension. We can almost touch those who are on the screen, as we can almost touch Lou Reed who drinks a bottle of Coca-Cola or Baby Jane Holzer who brushes her teeth in Warhol's *Screen Tests*. Yet distance is maintained, and nobody can really touch or be touched. What emerges instead is a participation that allows framed bodies to occupy an encompassing fold of space.

The sense of seclusion and proximity that affects ghosts in the Phantasmagoria, the fictional characters in cinema, and the images of participants attending online meetings mirrors the physical situation that the three media create for their spectators and users. Indeed, the frame evokes the physical walls of the theater or the imaginary boundaries around the bubble, which sever the inside from the outside, and the fold reminds us of the ideal window of the screen that reconnects images and spectators with the world that has been left behind. In a way, the functioning of frame and fold epitomizes the inner configuration of the projection/protection complex of which the Phantasmagoria, cinema, and bubbles are instantiations. This finally reinforces the exemplarity of Warhol's *Screen Tests*: while mimicking through their name the cinematic practice of testing actors for a future movie, they speak dramatically of the convergence of spatial deprivation and reconnection with the world that we experience in front of a screen. Warhol's sitters are not only siblings of the free-floating ghosts of the Phantasmagoria, of cinematic heroes in close-up, and of the teleconference participants compressed in a small vignette. They stand there also for us, split from our surroundings and in search of new ties.

CHAPTER FIVE

Strategies of Mitigation

Facing Fears

The COVID-19 pandemic that hit the world at the beginning of 2020 brought to the fore something that in allegedly normal times is implicit: exposure to the world is often threatening. The space "out there" is potentially dangerous. In the midst of an emergency, we had to find an alternative: with the help of computer or a smartphone, we attended classes, we chose items on display in the department store, we raised a glass in company, and we even performed our professional duties, and with the help of a wide screen and an internet connection, we enjoyed a movie almost as if we were in a movie theater, a football game as if we were in a stadium, or a religious service as if we were in a place of worship. Echoing other forms of defense against the virus—the plastic shields in restaurants or offices, the six-foot distance between individuals, and masks to be worn in public spaces—the computer, smartphone, and TV set offered protection, and we were able to isolate ourselves at home, in a safer space, without losing our contacts with the world. Of course, these countermeasures were as disruptive as the viruses that made them necessary. We needed to go back to "normal" as soon as possible. Yet we must not let our guard down: space "out there" continues to convey a sense of danger.

This mindset that I summarize with a bit of irony—if we can

make irony out of tragedy — is paradoxically present in many situations that have nothing to do with the pandemic. It is what convinces us to buy an alarm system that safeguards our house from intrusions, to download an app that screens undesired calls to our phone, and to use GPS to drive safely in an unfamiliar region. Many contemporary media are protective tools rather than "extension[s] of man," as Marshall McLuhan famously called them.[1] They filter external data rather than accumulate them, and they control external space, rather than penetrate it. Such a propensity is not exclusive to our times. It was present also in the past, including the historical instantiations of the projection/protection complex. Cinema, in particular, offers a strong and in some ways surprising example.

There is no doubt that the first feeling that cinema raised was the astonishment at its capacity to reproduce reality. Spectators were amazed by the ability to see on the screen what usually did not amaze them.[2] Consequently, many critics of the time saw cinema as a non-art that was lacking the stylization common to all the arts and ultimately made of the very same stuff as the world. The influential French critic Louis Delluc was adamant: "Cinema is precisely a route toward the suppression of art — a route that goes beyond art, since it belongs to life. . . . A movie is no longer a movie. It is natural truth."[3] And moreover: "[Cinema] is pure life."[4] Delluc's stance was well received and inspired similar responses from other critics.[5] Yet film's capitulation to reality elicited a clear paradox: if on the screen there is reality as such, spectators are as exposed to the world as those who experience direct contact with it — and sometimes even more, given the strength of images. The German critic Walter Serner fully captured this short circuit in his radical essay "Cinema and Visual Pleasure."[6] According to him, the deepest human desire is to be a direct witness to the most terrible events, despite their potential danger,[7] and cinema fulfills this desire thanks to pitiless images. We go to the movies because we love to take risks.

Serner, a militant surrealist, praised the taking of risks; fundamentalist militants, aware of the same short circuit, condemned cinema. This was the case of the French right-wing critic Édouard Poulain. In a virulent book published in the same year of Delluc's statements,[8] Poulain claimed that the ultrarealistic representations on the screen required countermeasures: they needed to be either censored by public authorities or radically transformed into pedagogical tools.[9] In the 1910s and 1920s, almost every European country had its cinephobic voices—psychologists, educators, attorneys, and clergymen—who while chastising cinema for exposing spectators to the same bad influences as the actual milieu, drew up plans for limiting or transforming it.[10] Common-sense critics—not by chance derided by Benjamin a few years later for their conservatism[11]—played a similar game. Since art is by definition a means of elevation and education, they asked filmmakers to pursue a cinematic art instead of supporting the mimetic vocation of film, as if the beauty were the last veil of crude reality.[12] Cinema was called upon to protect itself from its own impulses in order to protect its audiences.

A reconciliation of mimetic attitudes and protective potentialities in cinema came with Kracauer. In the last pages of his *Theory of Film*—a book published in 1960, but largely conceived in the late 1930s[13]—Kracauer offers a brillian metaphor. After pages and pages that praise the "redemption of physical reality" bolstered by movies, and after a mention of the Holocaust as an example of an event that is ultimately unbearable to witness, Kracauer recollects the myth of Perseus, who approached the petrifier Gorgon through her image reflected on the shield lent him by Athena. Kracauer's comment is stunning:

> The moral of the myth is, of course, that we do not, and cannot, see actual horrors because they paralyze us with blinding fear; and that we shall know what they look like only by watching images of them which reproduce their true appearance.... Now of all the existing media the cinema alone holds up a mirror to nature. Hence our dependence on it for the reflection of happenings which would petrify us were we to encounter them in real life. The film screen is Athena's polished shield.[14]

So if it is true that film "holds up a mirror to nature" that allows it to reflect reality in all its aspects, it is also true that it provides a sort of distance from reality — a distance that is crucial when we face unbearable events. Cinema does not obscure anything, but at the same time, it defends us from the threats tied to direct exposure to reality. Thanks to the movies, we can enjoy a "mediated immediacy" in our approach to the world.

Thirty years earlier, Kracauer had also highlighted the protective nature of the theater, and not just of the screen, using another metaphor. In his 1928–29 inquiry about the living conditions of salaried employees in post–World War I Germany, published in the *Frankfurter Zeitung* between December 1929 and January 1930, Kracauer calls these employees "spiritually homeless."[15] Because of the war, they have lost their old world, and now, "they live in fear of looking up and asking their way to the destination."[16] Hence the need for spaces of distraction that protect them from their frustrations — spaces that literally work as *shelters for the homeless*.[17] Kracauer has in mind Haus Faterland, at the time the most famous pleasure palace in Berlin, with its lavish interior and its relaxed atmosphere, but — as he openly claims[18] — his description also applies to the film palaces, with their lights, their magnificent decorations, their spectacles, and their movies. What these places provide is a "world vibrant with color. The world not as it is, but as it appears in popular hits. A world every last corner of which is cleansed, as though with a vacuum cleaner, of the dust of the everyday existence."[19] Severed from their usual milieu, spectators encounter an illusory reality that is like a balm for their wounds, yet the show they enjoy — full of excitation, but empty, spectacular, but chaotic — is equally able to offer a full testimony to the meaningless and stressful milieu in which they live. This revealing aspect of the realty on the screen puts filmgoers in a unique position: secluded in film theaters supposedly meant to provide distraction, they ultimately "are so close to the truth."[20]

So, a screen that *shields* spectators from the horror of events and a theater that *shelters* them from the distress elicited by a turbulent world. Kracauer provides strong reasons for a definition of cinema as a protective medium, and he does this by reconciling this sense of protection with the ability of images to give back a full picture of reality and of the theater to balance a closure with new forms of opening to the world. The cinema was not the only medium to display a protective nature. As we have seen in the previous chapters, the Phantasmagoria was largely imbued with the same spirit, as, more recently, are the digital bubbles in which individuals find refuge when engaged in an online conversation. Not by chance the first announcement of Filidor's phantasmagoric show included the clarification that "the performance has no dangerous influence on the organs, no unpleasant odor, and persons of all ages and sexes may view it without inconvenience."[21] Not by chance internet users adopt supplemental strategies of isolation (for example, they create a dedicated spot within their domestic space) while engaged in online conversations or surfing the web. But what kind of protection have the Phantasmagoria, cinema, and digital screen-based bubbles offered? And at what cost?

Disciplinary Spaces
A first answer comes from Michel Foucault's analysis of the disciplinary practices that from eighteenth century onward have deeply marked Western history. Protective spaces can be considered counterparts and even byproducts of procedures aimed at forging an obedient, productive, and governable mass of individuals. Several scholars have already underscored the complicity of media in forging submissive individuals. It suffices to recall Max Horkheimer and Theodor W. Adorno's claim that the culture industry makes impossible for the individuals to escape the role of consumers that a capitalistic society assigns to them.[22] I am interested in correspondences, rather than in inevitable destinies, and my reference to Foucault is led by a convergence. According to Foucault, discipline is largely based on a spatial arrangement that assigns specific places

to specific individuals or groups of individuals in relations to their functions, potential mobility, and multiplicity of relationships. Such an arrangement increases efficiency and allows control on external and internal factors. Foucault writes, "disciplines create complex spaces that are at once architectural, functional and hierarchical. It is spaces that provide fixed positions and permit circulation; they carve out individual segments and establish operational links; they mark places and indicate values; they guarantee the obedience of individuals, but also a better economy of time and gesture."[23] By creating dedicated spaces, discipline removes individuals from the risks of conflicts, accidents, and unpredictability. They are no longer exposed to contingency and chance. Instead, they become part of an ordered system. This is precisely what happens with the instantiations of the projection/protection complex. The Phantasmagoria, cinema, and digital screen-based bubbles design spaces that soften the pressure of surrounding reality. In these spaces, individuals feel protected. At the same time, they become "docile bodies" that follow rules and fill functions.

The first of the disciplinary spaces investigated by Foucault is the enclosure. It is where a multitude can easily be gathered, organized, and controlled. In the enclosure, protection and discipline overlap. As Foucault ironically notes, "a place heterogeneous to all others and closed in upon itself . . . is the protected place of disciplinary monotony."[24] Yet to be effective, an enclosure must be wrought further, and the space needs to be partitioned, to become useful, and to create forms of ranking. Although the Phantasmagoria, cinema, and digital bubbles share the presence of an enclosure, they sometimes interpret these other processes in more individual ways.

Let's think of the partitioning of the space. It is the procedure through which a place is divided into parts to host distinct functions and distinct group of individuals.[25] Modern societies deal with a multiplicity of operations and operators, which must be located and coordinated in a well-designed environment. Our three media reflect such a need. For the Phantasmagoria, the partitioning of space entailed a linearization of the spectator's path. In the 1799 version of the show by Robertson, patrons had to linger in the passage called the Galerie de la Femme Invisible or in a vestibule called premier Salon de Physique, filled by scientific wonders, before being admitted to the "Salle de la Fantasmagorie," where apparitions occurred. Chaussard, in a first-hand account, speaks of a setting "divided into two parts, one bright and the other dark. The first displays all the luxury of physical science," while the second is more esoteric.[26] This split highlighted the presence of different objects of interest and consequently of different forms of enjoyment. The passage from one space to the other, marked by the address of the conjurer, coincided with the regulated passage from one form of spectatorship to the public, to another.

Cinema mobilized a different subdivision of space. Although the opulent picture palaces built in the 1920s were characterized by a variety of spaces, the general trend was toward a more homogeneous and compact theater design. From the beginning, the theater was largely considered a "democratic space" in which spectators enjoyed a shared experience. Of course, this was not true, due to the presence of racially segregated spaces in countries such as the United States. Nevertheless, the idea of democracy elicited a more opaque theatrical partition in which, as spectators, participants shared the same status.

Finally, the networked bubble in which we find refuge when engaged in an online meeting mobilizes an assembly of individuals, rather than a collectivity. The ideal space of communication is then subdivided into a set of small cells visible on the screen with the vignette of each participant. This set of vignettes, which recalls a Panopticon-like arrangement, says that every participant has their own space equal to that of the others and that every participant is at once supervisor and prisoner.

We witness the same kind of differences from one dispositive to another when we analyze the other spatial procedures mentioned by

Foucault. Take the process of functionalization: as Foucault states, "particular places were defined to correspond not only to the need to supervise, to break dangerous communications, but also to create a useful space."[27] The Phantasmagoria setting was an adapted old building, previously conceived as a site of a religious cult. At least in the golden era, cinema's setting was a dedicated space, built on purpose. Today, the setting of an online meeting is a coalescence of different spaces that find their unity only in the ideal space of communication. Or take the process of ranking, which builds spaces in which individuals are identified for the position they occupy in a network of relations.[28] The Phantasmagoria and cinema ranked their spectators by the price paid for the ticket — and by their race, as in the case of film theaters in the Unites States — but not necessarily by their gender and age, as other coeval institutions did. In our online meetings, the ranking of the participants — once again epitomized by the grid of vignettes on the screen — is paradoxically more accentuated, where the position of each participant depends on who is speaking, who has the camera on, and what device is used, and it changes when these parameters change.

Discipline does not limit its work to space. As Foucault recalls, in addition to assigning places, functions, and ranks, discipline also "prescribes movements, imposes exercises, [and] arranges tactics."[29] Yet spatial practices are foundational. Despite individual variations, in the Phantasmagoria, cinema, and digital bubbles, these practices converge in creating both protection and order. Spectators are sheltered from potential risks and in exchange must adhere to a set of rules. They can enjoy a safe haven, and at the same time, they become part of a well-structured social organization.

This twofold process brings to the fore the recurring need to build "good audiences." The 1917 report released by the English National Council of Public Morals and entitled *The Cinema: Its Present Position and Future Possibilities*[30] provides a useful example. The report has an extended section dedicated to film theaters in which the report's recurring concern is avoiding inconveniences that are typical of the external milieu and that inappropriate settings risk multiplying. To control the improper conduct that the liminal space of theater can favor, the report recommends "more adequate supervision and lighting, the provision of a seat for every person admitted, the abolition of standing room and boxes where they exist, and the provision of a special attendant to look after the children."[31] To prevent the potential multiplication of germs favored by the gathering in an enclosed space, the report suggests this is "a serious danger" and that it "should receive attention and be remedied, if at all possible, in the public interest." To these countermeasures the report adds other recommendations: if the projection is too intense, to the point of causing glares, flickers, and a lack of concentration,[32] spectators are invited to wear "green-tinted glasses,"[33] and finally, when cinematic representations raise incorrect ideas about social and sexual behavior,[34] public authorities must exert forms of censorship.[35] What must be pursued is "the hygiene of the mind" because "some of the films . . . are very suggestive and can only have a harmful influence."[36] All these recommendations are motivated by the need to make filmgoing a safe experience; as a matter of fact, they also result in a greater control of filmgoers and ultimately in their transformation into a "good" public.[37] Again, the cinematic experience will never be entirely safe, and the public will never be fully "good."[38] Yet this ideal will accompany the progressive institutionalization of cinema

We can detect the same need for "good" spectators/users in the Phantasmagoria and in the digital screen-based bubbles. In the Phantasmagoria, the creation of a "docile" audience began with a precise strategy of marketing and advertising in which spaces of the show and spectators' appropriate behavior were anticipated in detail.[39] The conjurer's address to the audience, full of suggestions about how to interpret apparitions, completed this process.[40] In the digital screen-based bubbles, especially those supported by platforms such as Zoom or Microsoft Teams, the creation of "docile" users is tied to forms of politeness that everyone must follow. It suffices to think of the backgrounds of the vignettes portraying each participant of an online meeting, and despite the fact that these backgrounds frequently show domestic spaces, they must avoid overly personal elements. Or think of the shift from one speaker to another: quite often the system automatically mutes participants to avoid unexpected voices and sounds. In all our cases, safety becomes the complement of an ordered distribution of bodies and operations that ultimately transforms an accidental group of people into a cohesive assembly. Its price is the acceptance of a directed and controlled existence.

Immunity

Disciplinary interpretations do not consider the fact that the projection/protection complex tries to balance the spectators' deprivations with a reconnection with the world, though in a different, less exposed way. The removal of contingencies and the imposition of rules are only the first half of the operations performed by the complex. The second half consists of summoning a milder version of what spectators have left behind. Indeed, the images on the screen and the arrangement of the setting create a world that recalls the reality that spectators have escaped, yet this new world is no longer as dangerous as the external world, and it can be enjoyed without the risks involved in directly facing events. This status allows it to prevent the perils of the external world, since it suggests and at the same time tests possible responses to these perils. Protection, then, becomes preemptive, and the replacement of lost reality offers not only a compensation for what has been removed, but also a prophylaxis for what could have occurred. Once diluted, the poison is no longer deadly; on the contrary, it works as a vaccine. What emerges, then, is an immune practice.

In his extended analysis of immunity, the Italian philosopher Roberto Esposito[41] notes that the concept crosses different fields: biological, political, juridical, communicative, and so on. What unifies these different applications is the idea of exemption; immune are those who, unlike others, do not fall prey to an illness or are not subject to the effects of the law. At the first stage, what matters is a difference, a separation. Yet to keep danger, and others, at a distance is not enough. Immunity implies more than a mere passive defense; it relies on the ability actively to confront an enemy. Typically, this is what antibodies do with a virus when they respond to aggression with a counterattack. And the stronger the aggression, the stronger the response. As Esposito notes, the preservation of life is inseparable from a constant taste of death. The administration of the vaccine bolsters and uncovers this mechanism, and the virus is weakened, injected, and used against itself. The outside is internalized in order to arouse the response against the outside. Esposito sees in this circuit a perfect example of including exclusion or of exclusion due to inclusion in that the summoning of what is kept distant both makes it harmless and confirms its distance. In short, the "other" is embodied in the "self" on the latter's behalf in a process that ultimately transforms the very nature of both "other" and "self."

Esposito's book makes room for an interpretation of media in terms of immunity. Nevertheless, this interpretation is not unprecedented; for example, it surfaces in Kracauer's reference to Athena's shield. As I already mentioned, Kracauer claims that images on the screen perfectly mirror the physical world, though they are not as effectual as reality as such. In this capacity, they can offer a detailed but harmless representation of what is otherwise unbearable. When this happens, spectators confront evil without facing consequences; on the contrary, they acquire the knowledge and the sensibility to fight against it.[42] These elements allow Kracauer to sketch an immune mechanism in which the screened images work as a sort of vaccine against the aggression of the external reality. This idea finds an even more effective illustration, in two different tones, by two scholars as different as Benjamin and McLuhan.

Benjamin addresses the model of immunity in a synthetic passage of the second version of his essay on the work of art. The passage deserves a full quotation:

If one considers the dangerous tensions which technology and its consequences have engendered in the masses at large—tendencies which at
critical stages take on a psychotic character—one also has to recognize
that the same technologization [*Technisierung*] has created the possibility of
psychic immunization against such mass psychoses. It does so by means of
certain films in which the forced development of sadistic fantasies or mas-
ochistic delusions can prevent their natural and dangerous maturation in
the masses.[43]

The passage continues by identifying a good example of this
process in American cinema: "The countless and grotesque events
consumed in films are a graphic indication of the dangers threatening mankind from the repression implicit in civilisation. American
slapstick comedies and Disney films trigger a therapeutic release
of unconscious energies."[44] A long footnote that details how Mickey
Mouse films reveal "the cozy acceptance of bestiality and violence
as inevitable concomitants of existence" brings Benjamin's argument to its conclusion.[45]

Benjamin's argument is illuminating. It does not target natural
reality, as Kracauer's does, but a modern reality imbued with technology—a reality that is at once exciting, since it enhances human
sensibility, and threatening, since it puts individuals at risk of psychotic reactions. Cinema is an accomplice of this reality. Indeed, in
line with the other instantiations of the projection/protection complex, it is a technical dispositif that associates an artificial enclosure
and mechanically produced and reproduced images and sounds. As
such, it is part of a process of "technologization" of society that
potentially elicits disorder and imbalance. Yet this very fact helps
cinema to work as a perfect vaccine. Its spectators are exposed not
only to scenes that are graphic, but harmless, but also to images and
sounds that are rooted in technology, but safe. Consequently, spectators absorb a mild version of what otherwise constitutes a danger for "civilized" societies. This mild version—the comedic violence of slapstick and Disney movies—prompts the antibodies—"a

therapeutic release of unconscious energies" — that would preserve spectators from contagion. A modern technical medium, cinema fights the effects of modern technologies with its own presence. Its very nature allows it to immunize its audiences.

Benjamin captures a process that affects a mediatized society and indirectly illuminates the kind of response that the projection/protection complex performs. In a different theoretical framework, McLuhan extends a similar notion far beyond cinema. He resurfaces the immune metaphor at the end of the first part of his influential and controversial book *Understanding Media*.[46] After a widespread praise of media, McLuhan is seized by a doubt: what if media, while providing prostheses that enhance our performances, also cause diseases? What if "the technologies by which we amplify and extend ourselves constitute huge collective surgery"[47] that exposes the social body to possible infections? The answer comes in the form of an appeal to art: "No society has ever known enough about its actions to have developed immunity to its new extension or technologies. Today we have begun to sense that art may be able to provide such immunity."[48] By "art," McLuhan does not mean a special field in human activity, separated from our constant effort to deal with the world. On the contrary, what he has in mind is the ability of any medium, from painting to television, to explore new forms of sensibility that keep us vigilant and active. It is not by chance his references largely go to works that are at once experimental and reflexive. Such an ability enables media "to cope with the psychic and social consequences of the next technology."[49] If used in an artistic mode, media can anticipate and prevent the future. They can provide the antibodies needed to combat the effects of their own growth.

McLuhan further expands the range of immune strategies. The vaccine is not exclusive to a single medium, but is provided by all dispositifs that undertake forms of experimentation, or at least those that work consciously on the forefront of technological development. When exploring their own role, media always help resist possible negative consequences. In this framework, the engagement of the dispositifs that I have associated with the projection/protection complex becomes even more cogent. Each of them, in its own time, represented a terrain of experimentation—each of them was or still is a sort of test for the media system. Consequently, they appear well suited to provide a vaccine that protects us from the threats intrinsic to modern reality. The individual's safety depends on this vaccine.

Government Technologies

The disciplinary and the immune paradigms highlight two different kinds of fears, to which they respond with two different kinds of strategy. Discipline speaks of an unpredictable, excessive world that elicits distress and confusion, immunity of a filthy, viral world that contaminates even the healthiest organism. The former reconfigures the situation to keep it under control; the latter creates antibodies that reinforce internal defences. By defining spaces and functions, discipline offers sociopolitical answers; by protecting lives from deadly events, immunity triggers biopolitical actions. These traits make disciplinary and immune practices the two paramount ways in which modern societies face the threats to their own existence. One replaces a tumultuous reality with a well-arranged universe, the other weakens a hostile milieu and transforms it into a palatable background. Both are aimed at containing and managing a world that appears challenging and aggressive. Modern governmentality[50] largely relies on the techniques displayed by the two paradigms: to assign, to distribute, to prevent, to strengthen, and to control.

The complicity of the projection/protection complex with disciplinary and immune practices not only confirms the complex's attention to its historical context, but also displays its ties with modern forms of government. The Phantasmagoria, cinema, and the digital screen-based bubble are tools for administering the social body, either through an imposed order or through forms of experience that prevent potential threats. Disciplinary techniques

were dominant during the nineteenth century, while immune procedures have come to the fore in the twentieth century. Nevertheless, the two paradigms frequently overlap. Take the Phantasmagoria: there is no doubt that it was part of the disciplinary answer to
an overexcited age, as Crary has underscored.[51] At the same time,
though, the laughter of the audience that contemporary chronicles
report[52] is a sign of the therapeutic effect of the show.[53] Or take cinema: as Boris Groys ironically notes, at the movies, the paradoxical
coexistence of images that display a world full of action and spectators that are literally immobilized in their seats is instrumental
to an ordered and peaceful assembly, and consequently to a disciplinary paradigm.[54] At the same time, cinema appears to Benjamin
as the great healer of the century thanks to its nature of vaccine.
Finally, take the screen-based bubbles, in which we find a retreat
from a milieu that demands 24/7 engagement.[55] There is no doubt
that the voluntary lockdown elicited by bubbles mirrors forms of
enforced confinement. Nevertheless, this confinement is also a preemptive attempt to avoid forms of "contamination" from the external environment.

This tendency of the disciplinary and immune paradigms to provide tools for governance means they are far from being innocent.
To give stable order to a society or to immunize it against viruses
involves measures that deeply affect individuals and their milieus.
What comes to the fore are forms of constriction, new cautious
habits, a new order of things, and new forms of subjectivity. Disciplinary and immune practices imply some sort of violence — and a
violence that often is no less intense than the one that characterizes
the impending dangers that must be defused. The Phantasmagoria subjected its spectators to a test that triggered their emotional
reactions. The cinema forced its audience to behave appropriately
and expelled those who infringed its norms. The bubbles created
by the screens induce forms of fatigue and exhaustion, of which
"Zoom fatigue" is just one example. Such an inclusion of the evil in
the practices that are aimed at fighting it casts a strange light on

the instantiations of the projection/protection complex. They, too, possess an aggressive penchant; they, too, are poised to use violence if the danger that they face requires it. Seen in this perspective, protection appears in its full ambiguity. It is a salvific act that keeps threats at a distance or neutralizes their effects. At the same time, is an act of force that builds an alternative environment in which individuals can better cope with reality. Protection transforms the world and even builds a new one. In doing this, it imposes its rationale over the whole situation. This inevitable implication, which undergirds protection's meritorious deeds, is also a sign of contradiction and ultimately an element of internal weakness.

On the other hand, the containment and submission of the world is not and cannot be the ultimate answer to a challenging reality. On the contrary, the more domesticated the world appears, the more challenging it becomes. To grasp this paradox, it suffices to consider the progressive steps taken by the instantiations of the projection/protection complex. The Phantasmagoria harnesses three liminal universes: capricious ghosts intervene on command; a tumultuous nature reveals its own laws; and spectators are able, in turn, to look within themselves. Cinema widens its action, and it tackles everyday life, which finds a new and better version in the images and sounds on the screen and in the setting in front of the screen. Finally, personal screen-based bubbles summon everything that users need and, in so doing, they structure a space that eventually coincides with the whole universe. In this progression, from a limited multiverse that reveals its docility to a cyberspace that contains everything, we not only deal with processes of homogenization and standardization that reorganize reality into established formats, we also deal with the construction of a progressively inclusive and open arena in which the exchange of material and immaterial commodities, including personal experiences, acquires an unprecedented range.[56] This arena, which ultimately is an extensive space of communication, increases our sphere of action, where we can always reach new portions of the world. This is what happened with our three examples: while the Phantasmagoria offered a limited terrain of manoeuvre in which spectators shared their reactions only with other spectators in the theater, cinema created a diffused horizon in which spectators were ideally connected to everyone else who enjoyed a movie, and the digital bubbles give substance to an integrated world in which all users are able to interact with one another.[57] Yet such an increase in our sphere of action has a counterpart. As the arena becomes bigger, we become increasingly subjected to the gaze of a global audience. The climax is represented by users who navigate the internet from their bubbles, where their retreat results in a broader exposure — and an exposure that sometimes is worrisome, due the unpredictable nature of a cyberspace that, by encompassing everything, is no longer fully controllable.

This impending reversal of a world that was intended to be risk free and that, once it becomes a wider space of exchange, is no longer necessarily under control reveals that replacing a challenging reality with a harmless one is neither easy nor without cost. The projection/protection complex incessantly tries to create a safe environment for mediation. This effort implies a parallel attempt to expand the range of such a safe zone, and due to this expansion, the complex confronts the necessity to discipline and immunize the whole universe; yet the same expansion reintroduces the presence of contingencies, adversities, and threats that the complex initially tried to expel. Hence a constant circularity, where safety must be always increased, but its increase is a potential risk. We cannot avoid confronting reality.

The Protective Shield
In his crucial work *Beyond the Pleasure Principle*,[58] Sigmund Freud envisions the existence of a specific organ whose function is to protect living organisms from stimuli that can be harmful. The "protective shield," as Freud calls it, is a sort of callous membrane that has been created by external blows and that now stops them from penetrating the deeper layers of our psyche at full force.

Impacted by the stimuli, the membrane has become inorganic, yet this transformation, which represents a form of death, preserves the inner layers from following the same fate and allows them to perform their duties. The protective shield is crucial for the preservation of living organisms: if they are impacted by too-strong stimuli, they may succumb. From this point of view, with a lapidary sentence, Freud states: "*Protection against* stimuli is an almost more important function for the living organism than *reception of* stimuli."[59]

Walter Benjamin[60] and then Wolfgang Schivelbusch[61] have underscored the relevance of Freud's hypothesis for understanding the traumatic effect of the hyperexcitation of modernity. For my part, despite the clear differences between Freud's hypothetical organ and the mechanism underlying the projection/protection complex, I would like to emphasize the presence of recurring elements that connect the two. First, in the Freudian hypothesis, there is an intensity of external stimuli that is frightening: any excess represents a threat. The projection/protection complex is activated to counteract the intensity of the world. It is not by chance that the Phantasmagoria, cinema, and digital screen-based bubbles emerged during "excessive" times. These have been times that have seen a transition from a society based on restrictions to a society that exerts forms of control on individuals that are apparently free.[62] They have seen the passage from an early modern culture fascinated by the exploration of the world to an age of incertitude and indetermination. And they have seen the shift from concrete fears tied to political and economic transformations — the "revolutions" of the eighteenth and nineteenth centuries — to more impalpable anxieties elicited by ubiquitous media. These changes are peculiarly demanding. Some form of defense is necessary.

Second, Freud's protective shield responds to external stimuli in a flexible way: it halts them, but it also absorbs them, channels them, and redirects them.[63] By combining discipline and immunity, the projection/protection complex displays the same flexibility.

While its main actions are to order and to prevent, its more refined techniques include suspending and delaying, repositioning and redesigning, replacing and simulating.

Third, Freud's protective shield is based on sacrifice: some layers become inorganic in order to create a barrier against external stimuli. Similarly, the projection/protection complex requires spatial deprivation in order to preserve individuals from direct exposure to the world. In a physical or mental enclosure, we lose connection with external reality. In exchange, we not only protect ourselves from the dangers of immediate encounters with threatening entities, but we also become aware of the need of overcoming the distance that we have created. Screened images and sounds allow us to reappropriate what we have left behind or what we never had in first place. Yet this reappropriation implies new dangers, and when reexposed, individuals face new threats. Hence the need of further protection — and consequently further sacrifices. As with Freud's shield, in which the callous membrane must become thicker and thicker, in the instantiations of the projection/protection complex, the means of defense must be ceaselessly improved.

Finally, both Freud's shield and the instantiations of the complex change the ways in which we acquire information from the world. Indeed, while offering a protection, both transform the *reception* of the stimuli and adapt it to new circumstances. In this framework, too, we can look at the Phantasmagoria, cinema, and screen-based bubbles as *sensoriums* that are the epitome of their times. In an age of discoveries and unexpectedness, with its optical and sound devices, the Phantasmagoria allowed the exploration of liminal realities that together formed a primal multiverse. In an age of machines, cinema's comforts helped viewers to regain confidence in a rapidly changing world. In the age of networks and pandemics, digital screen-based bubbles offered, and continue to offer, a space of intimacy from which we may stay in touch with others. In all these cases, the same basic structure — an enclosure and a screen — has responded to the pressures of the times through an advanced assemblage of technological means that modified the ways in which we have confronted the world. The result is the progressive emergence of a technosensibility that enables individuals to manage an increasing difficult reality, a reality that, permeated by the same technological means, requires this technosensibility in order to be apprehended. Ultimately, this technosensibility is the true asset of the projection/protection complex, something that explains its inner rationale and that enables it to face the transformations of the Anthropocene.

By comparing what Freud called a "far-fetched speculation"[64] and the projection/protection complex, I do not want to establish strict similarity. Yet the rich set of correspondences between the two mechanisms is illuminating. This allows me to conclude with a suggestion — or maybe a joke. If media are prostheses of human faculties, as McLuhan claims, may we say, with a bit of irony, that the projection/protection complex is a perfect prosthesis of Freud's hypothetical organ?

Protection, Overprotection,

and the Force of Screened Images

Protective Media

In the previous chapters, I discussed the Phantasmagoria, cinema, and the digital screen-based bubbles in which we retreat from our immediate surroundings to concentrate on a screen. I could just as well have analyzed other dispositifs that also instantiate what I call the projection/protection complex — television (to which I dedicated only a short "Intermezzo"), and virtual reality (which not by chance is increasingly used to heal the stress triggered by a demanding milieu with help from procedures of detachment and reconnection with the actual world).[1] Beyond these media, health devices such as facial covers during pandemics and warfare elements such as bunkers, which I also mentioned, equally perform some of the operations of the complex. Even storytelling implies protective and projective processes, as Michele Cometa has demonstrated,[2] and the walls that surround cities or states do the same, as Wendy Brown has argued.[3] If I focused on the three main examples, each analyzed in a specific phase of their life, it is because they provide an effective and comprehensive picture of the complex in its main articulations. In particular, they illustrate perfectly why and how the projection/protection complex intervenes in our process of mediation with reality and why and how it modulates its action.

The Phantasmagoria, cinema, and screen-based bubbles have

arisen in three distinctive intriguing situations. At the end of eighteenth century, the Phantasmagoria emerged in a context characterized by a double revolution, both political and social, and by an increased excitation of senses, to which expanding optical media both reacted and contributed.[4] One hundred years later, cinema appeared at a time when industrialization was at its peak and the masses had gained the center of social and political scene, changing the sense of the public sphere and the balance of political powers. A little more than another hundred years later, screen-based bubbles surfaced at the moment when a widespread process of digitalization was creating the conditions for what philosopher Luciano Floridi calls "onlife"[5]—a state of constant and extended interconnection that transforms the way in which we conceive of ourselves, our own modes of existence, and our grasp on the world. The defiant contexts in which the three dispositifs have appeared have made it difficult to cope with the world. As an answer to these difficulties, the three dispositifs have created a line of defense against exterior threats that allows individuals to reengage reality from a safe position. The usual milieu is put at a distance, and it becomes accessible thanks to sensorial cues that at once revamp its presence and filter it.

Quite paradoxically, this reengagement prompts an exploration of the world that is more extensive and more comprehensive than one elicited by a direct exposure to events. The initial limitation produced by the need for defense is an opportunity to go beyond it, the same means that protect individuals also expand their sensibility. In the Phantasmagoria, the rigid enclosure is ultimately a threshold that opens onto the kingdom of the dead, the secrets of nature, and the inner universe of the spectators—a sketch of what a multiverse will be. In the classical age of cinema, the theater is a microuniverse that compensates spectators for their miserable lives with a level of comfort to which they are not accustomed and that represents what life can be—even though this compensation ultimately reinforces the logic that undergirds spectators' distress.

In screen-based bubbles, the peripersonal space around the user's body becomes the position from which every corner of the world can be reached—if the connection does not fail. This expansion of the individual's horizons, however, relies on the presence of a defense; it comes after a safety is granted, and rather than an act of conquest, it is a counterattack based on the awareness that reality can be fearsome. This is why the Phantasmagoria, cinema, and digital bubbles, while belonging to the great family of media that supports an interaction with the world at a distance, maintain their special nature as *protective media*. They activate a spatial perimeter and a sensorial filter to make the world more manageable.

Overprotection

But what if the protection becomes an overprotection? What if the fear of exposure results in paralysis? We find an answer in a pitiless analysis of a "modern" country penned in 1930 by the renowned French author Georges Duhamel. *Scènes de la vie future*, which immediately was translated in English under the title of *America, the Menace*, is the chronicle of a trip to the United States. The book was quite successful, to the point of becoming a kind of manifesto against modernization.[6] Indeed, America is depicted as an example of how systematic mechanization, profound homogeneity, and a capitalistic economy improve the standards of life at the expense of individual freedom and creativity. At the same time, the country is plagued by recurring anxieties, in particular, the fear of threats from outside and inside. Duhamel records the obsessive control of foreigners who want to enter the country, the thorough disinfection of ships before they land, the constant attention to the safety of food, the antiseptic nostrums available almost everywhere, the ban on alcoholic beverages in an effort to preserve public health and order, the hygienic precautions imposed upon crowds, and the hotel room as a refuge from external pressures—in the face of constant surprises, threats, and shocks, the need of protection increases. Yet this protection encapsulates those who look for it. While reproducing the intensity that individuals want to escape — but cannot do without — dispositifs aimed at safeguarding citizens dull their senses and slow their reactions. Cinema epitomizes this state of numbness.

Duhamel hates cinema, which he defines as "a pastime for slaves, an amusement for the illiterate, for poor creatures stupefied by work and anxiety."[7] He hates it because while stealing the great artworks from literature, the theater, and music, cinema literally murders them[8] — a thought that later would attract Benjamin's harsh irony.[9] Yet what most surprises Duhamel is the state into which film reduces spectators. Under the pretext of distracting them from the pains of life, it turns off their sensitivity and replaces their feelings. Indeed, at the movies, spectators are in an "hypnotic condition . . . dull-eyed and patient," and when they leave the theater, they look "under the influence of an anesthetic" and prey to a "gloomy indifference."[10] Even he, Duhamel, is captured by this mechanism: "My thoughts where no longer under my control. The moving picture usurped the place of my ideas."[11] What comes to the fore is a totally fake world that denies any form of self-recognition: "Everything was false. The world was false. I myself was perhaps no longer anything but a simulacrum of a man, an imitation Duhamel."[12] Protection ensnares and destroys those in search of it.

Duhamel's arguments — which he also applies to other media, such as advertising[13] — would find an involuntary revival ninety years later in coincidence with the individual and collective forms of protection enforced by many countries against the spread of COVID-19. Approved by most citizens, these forms of protection also sparked criticism and resistance. To some, limitations of outdoor activities, travel, and contacts with others looked like a form of brutal sterilization of social life. Giorgio Agamben went even further. He spoke of a *state of exception* deceptively created by authorities in order to deprive citizens of the rights to which they are entitled.[14] Agamben's statement raised strong criticism in intellectual circles. Indeed, if on the one hand it captured the inner logic of protection, and more in general the logic underlying our mediation with the world, then it is on the other hand that it mistook its target. There is no doubt that mediation shapes the terms that are mediated. By establishing a relation, it defines a subject and an object, an agent and a target, a safe zone and a risky one, and so on. In this logic, the protection "produces" the threats that it is supposed to fight, and dangers consequently appear as an effect of the protection as much as their cause. Yet to assume that this process of retroaction is an intentional plot can be misleading. The emergence of threats is intrinsic to any form defense because to protect always and inevitably materializes a sense of danger, independently from human or institutional agency. Both the disciplinary and the immune interpretation of the protective media confirm this effect without the need to find a culprit.

An interesting first-hand testimony of the retroeffects intrinsically elicited by the protective measures against the pandemic is offered by a Reddit user who comments the state of lockdown experienced by those who find refuge in a screen-based digital bubble. The Reddit user states: "Zoom is all I have, and I do a lot of it, but you know what, I'm fucking sick of zoom."[15] Indeed, while online meetings are crucial to combat the pandemic, they also exhaust participants and void their existence. The Reddit user concludes: "Seriously, the quality of my life right now, I might as well just have someone put me into a medically induced coma until this whole thing is done." Protests against lockdowns were common on the net, yet the reference to the suspension of life—the "induced coma"—makes this comment particularly significant. The concern for citizens' safety intrinsic to protective measures can be deadly.

Apart, Together

So overprotection—to which media are so often prey, both now, as the screen-based bubbles testify, and in the past, as cinema demonstrated—creates more distress than healing. It strips individuals of their sensibility, putting them in a state of anesthesia, or it strips individuals of the fullness of their own existence, putting them in a state of suspension. In this framework, the projection/protection complex appears as something that, like Plato's *pharmakon*,[16] heals and poisons at once. While keeping danger at a distance, it threatens to disrupt the entity that it wants to preserve. This duplicity emerges with an extraordinary clarity when distance is converted into a form of suffocating isolation and the screened images are transformed into hallucinatory entities that simply echo spectators' and users' desires. How do we avoid these risks? How can we arrange forms of defense that do not trigger further pain?

Over the last few years, the disruptive effects of overprotection have attracted the interest of many scholars, who liken them to the effects of autoimmune diseases. When a living organism's self-defense is so heightened that it mistakes its own components for external enemies, it ends up killing itself. Likewise, human societies that increase their defenses beyond what is necessary create the conditions for their own collapse. In the aftermath of the terrorist attack of 9/11, Jacques Derrida developed this argument in a dialogue with Giovanna Borradori.[17] According to him, the "event," as he calls it, must be read as the symbolic suicide of a society that has internalized its fears and now fights against them.[18] More recently, while confirming that autoimmune responses are an impending risk for modern societies, philosophers Donna Haraway[19] and Roberto Esposito[20] have suggested possible remedies. A crucial step is to disentangle the idea of immunity from the idea of permanent war, as if the only response to threats is destruction. At the same time, there is no need to consider the environment in which we live as source of menace; on the contrary, a better embeddedness in this environment can unearth unthinkable resources. If we apply these suggestions to the field of media,[21] what emerges is the need for forms of protection in which fear and the fearsome, instead of being removed, are productively accepted and included in our ways of coping with reality. We can reach this goal along two paths: first, we must rethink the enclosure in a way that it is not limited to a sealed space; second, we must rely on the capacity of screened images to explore the possible beyond the actual.

Let's start from the first path. Enclosures are often thought as safe spaces because they keep the world at a distance. Yet distance does more than just protect us from external contaminations. Indeed, distance is what undergirds our negotiation with the world. In a sketch of the human evolution, Vilém Flusser claims that our early ancestors started to manage the natural world when they distanced themselves from it.[22] The musicologist and evolution scholar Gary Tomlinson adds that distancing allowed them to move from an action purely determined by circumstances—an indexical situation—to an action based on symbols.[23] Finally, the Italian philosopher Pietro Montani shows that distancing brought forward the possibility for our ancestors to become self-reflexive and consequently to be aware of their own mediation.[24] In a sense, distancing is at the origin of the human mediation. It allows us to face, to make sense of, and to cooperate with the world. The enclosure, based as it is on distance, can and must regain the plurality of distance's functions, where their full activation allows us to grasp the sense of protection as one of the components of a wider process of interaction with the world. Such a perspective opens up the possibility of recombining protection and hospitality, where the outside—the otherness—becomes something to be engaged rather than to be avoided. It must be regarded, understood, elaborated and not simply repressed. If it is true that it hurts, it can equally become a resource.

This reconsideration of enclosure as a space of dialogue also explains why isolation can generate a sense of collectivity. In an extraordinary chapter of *The Emancipated Spectator*, Rancière comments on Stéphane Mallarmé's idea that "apart, we are together"[25]—an idea that looks peculiarly problematic in our mediatic age, in which media users are frequently conceived as isolated, no matter the device with which they engage.[26] The fact of "being apart," with the struggles that this fact implies—Rancière has in mind artists tackling their work—favors the emergence of a set of "sensations" that ultimately represent a shared horizon. These sensations offer a common ground not because they reflect an agreement; on the contrary, they are prompted by dissent and disjunction, and the circumscribed location in which individuals isolate themselves gives evidence to this divisiveness. If these "sensations" represent a point of convergence, it is precisely because they embody an "openness despite the enclosure." Indeed, they are at once divisive and encompassing. While characterized by distinction, they offer themselves to everyone who knows what isolation and retreat mean, and consequently, they elicit inclusivity thanks to their exclusivity. It is their intrinsic qualities—spatial qualities, I would say—that confer to these "sensations" a power of aggregation.

The COVID-19 pandemic, with its forced lockdowns, prompted further elaborations of the idea of "apart, we are together." As Shane Denson notes, sitting alone in front of a computer undoubtedly implies an act of isolation, yet not only do networked images create new forms of connection, but autocorrect algorithms also trigger "future-oriented processes . . . that actively anticipate and thereby shape the subjectivity of the user."[27] The consequence is that an inert and dispersed mass of users benefits from present and future forms of synchrony. In front of our computer, we experience our becoming community.

So enclosures bolster the process of mediation thanks to the distance that they create and build a commonality, given the individuality they imply. Once we consider enclosures in these terms, the protection that they offer is no longer a form of anesthetization or, even worse, a loss of rights to which we are entitled. On the contrary, their borders become a threshold that invite us to a wider confrontation with the world.

The Force of Screened Images
The second path to mitigate the risks of overprotection is tied to the images that reconnect spectators and users to reality. The ubiquitous use of CGI technologies in recent years has prompted a

widespread disillusionment about images, to that degree that they are increasingly seen as deceptive tools, unable to grant the truth of what is represented. It is not an unprecedented feeling as images have always raised suspicion, either because they are only pale reproductions of existing things or because they exhibit things that do not exist. Yet as Emmanuel Alloa has persuasively demonstrated in an extensive revisitation of the Western philosophical tradition,[28] images can also be considered, and have been considered, forms of appearance of the world; as such they allow reality to become present to our senses and allow us to have some kind of hold on it. We can "grasp" the world, first of all, either because images unearth traces of reality or because they work as a sort of finger pointing to objects or events. Appearances mobilize both forms of indexicality: as record and as reference.[29] At the same time, images go beyond what they display; they redeem an absence, making present what is not actually there, and they offer a hypothesis about the world by configuring possible states of things. Such considerations restore the potentialities of images.

What is true for images in general is also the case for screened images — as well as for accompanying sounds. Their capacity to "envision" states of things beyond the mere reference to an actual reality gives them an extraordinary force. Images and sounds are not only memories of the past, but also imaginations of the future and the possible. The plasticity of the screen — a receptacle ready to host new configurations and in some way a sort of Platonic *chora* — bolsters this potential of the screened images. This allows them to adopt a fresh look on reality — a look that not only penetrates the world's depth and encompasses its breath, but also reveals new perspectives. In this sense, while unfolding aspects that transcend mere actuality, screened images can also anticipate the world, and they can "precede" or "premediate" what the world may become as well as their own action on it.[30] I mean the world as it might be, and not as we want it to be. In this sense, rewording the celebrated sentence about cinema that Jean Luc Godard put as epigraph at the beginning of *Contempt* (*Le mepris*, France, 1963), we can say that screened images do not have to "replace our gaze with a world in harmony with our desires," but "with a world in harmony with its — the world's — desires."[31] When following such a vocation, images become an extraordinary means of exploration. They do not erase what is still alien, but instead, they recognize and accept it. The terror elicited by an aggressive reality gives way to the wonder of an uncanny world that is ready to become familiar.

By tracking reality and unfolding its unexpected sides, analogic images already pursued this goal, as film theories have expansively stated. Digital images continue and even extend this path. According to Flusser, it is precisely the digital that allows technical images to maximize their ability to figure and prefigure possible realities.[32] Indeed, the fragmentation of the world implied in visual data makes it easier to produce recombinations that cast light on unprecedented states of things. Mark Hansen and Shane Denson have consolidated this suggestion through technical and physiological analyses of the digital. According to them, while challenging the users' perceptual faculties, contemporary digital media proactively expand the range of the sensibility in which we are immersed.[33]

This propensity of the screened image to point toward the possible finds a perfect testimony in an essay penned in 1912 by the now-forgotten Italian critic Fausto Maria Martini.[34] Martini starts from the ability of cinema to face a reality that is becoming more and more threatening: on the screen, "everything — human beings and things — is stirred up by an infernal wind. Existence jerks to a start: a step is a race; a race, a flight; the gaze, a furtive glance; laughter, a grimace; crying, a sob; a thought, a delirium; the human heartbeat, a fever. . . . It is a fantastic tumult: it is the mirror of the dreadful nervous disorder of our age."[35]

Yet screened images go beyond the description of existences "hounded by a nightmare." While reflecting the spirit of the times, they open new horizons that may be unexpected, but also equally real. In front of the screen, you may happen to see the unfolding of nature scenes, surprises in the most far-off regions: forests, mountains, lakes, seas, a ship, a desert, a glacier, a small village in a very distant, unfamiliar land, a city that you love only for the loveliness of its name, a center of life that awakened in you a tremendous curiosity when you were young, and a place to which you proposed to go, but to which you never will go.... [By doing this] the cinema satisfies a certain sentimental feeling which sleeps in all of our hearts—the nostalgia for those places that we have never seen, that we may never see, but where we almost seem to have lived in some previous life.[36]

Despite his focus on spectators' desires, Martini captures the screened images' ability to unfold potential realities. The world is ready to display itself in all its aspects, actual and possible.

Martini would have added that the look that these images offer is characterized by its technical nature as much as by its syntony with human perceptual and imaginative faculties. Screened images promote a technosensibility that increases their performance. In his writings of the 1920s, Epstein would make this addition: "The harmony of interlocking mechanisms: that is [film's] temperament. And nature is different too. [Film's] eye, remember, sees waves invisible to us, and the screen's creative passion contains what no other has ever had before: its proper share of ultraviolet."[37]

For my part, I add that Martini's comments on cinema equally recall the Phantasmagoria, with its confluence of fearsome apparitions and the chance to discover unknown sides of reality, just as they recall the far less dramatic online experiences in which there is a mix of suspicion and wonder for what the screen displays. What comes to the fore is not only something that belongs to cinema, but recurring characteristics of all the instantiations of the projection/protection complex.

Indeed, seen in its basic structure, the physical or attentional enclosure in which a screen is located, the projection/protection complex may appear quite banal. Its components have nothing special, and they activate obvious references—the maternal womb, the magic circle, and the religious retreat. However, the complex's ambitions — those of responding to the anxieties aroused either by a direct confrontation with reality or by an inappropriate detachment from it — place it at the center of the modern mediation process. What the complex discloses is that media, in working on and within a space, closely associate it with their action. This action consists not only in allowing individuals and human groups to expand the territory in which they move through an extension of their senses and their faculties, but also consists in providing them with some sort of shelter. This shelter, which maintains a connection with the exterior, elicits a safer and even more accurate exploration of the world, even if through processes that can in turn be insidious. The convergence of the optical and the spatial, as well as the parallel inclusion of fears and the potentialities of the world within the process of mediation ultimately guarantee the complex the exemplary position it deserves. Mediation makes room for the wider, contingent context and for a technosensibility tuned with our age. This ability helps us navigate a time characterized by deep transformations in familiar ideas such as perception, agency, experience, and nature. The world in which we live, and that includes the awareness of its and our own extinction, appears more bearable and manageable. It unfolds before us not because we seize it and submit it to our will, but because we can accept all aspects of it, including those that frighten us and those that speak of unexpressed possibilities. In this sense, in distancing us from reality, the projection/protection complex reconciles us with it: and it does so not "for" us, in support of our egoistic purposes or our desire for appropriation, but "with" us, starting from our availability to take the challenge and be part of the game.

Acknowledgments

This book is deeply indebted to my conversations over the years with Pietro Montani, Bernard Geoghegan, Mauro Carbone, Michele Cometa, and Gary Tomlinson. Its first design emerged in the framework of the Sawyer Seminar "Genealogies of the Excessive Screen," supported by the Mellon Foundation, which I coordinated with my friends and colleagues Craig Buckley and Rudiger Campe at Yale in 2016–2018. The book's main ideas were progressively shaped by lectures, conferences, and events organized by Weihong Bao, Andrea Pinotti, Vittorio Gallese, Peter Bloom, Errki Hutamo, Laurent Forestier, André Gaudreault, Gilles Mouilleic, Federica Villa, Francesco Vitale, and Claire Demoulin: I am grateful to the organizers and participants. For the archival research I found help in Marion Polirsztok (Chapter 2), Mal Ahern (Chapter 3), and Stefano Masserini (Chapter 4). Sections of the book were read by Pina De Luca, Julian Hanich, Ruggero Eugeni, Barbara Grespi, Marie Rebecchi, Sofia Seinfeld, Carmelo Marabello, Adriano D'Aloia, Morgan Ng, Jacopo Rasmi, Mariagrazia Fanchi, Richard Grusin, and Juliet Fleming: I thank them for their illuminating suggestions. Francesco Zucconi, Paul North, Emmanuel Alloa, Dudley Andrew, and Antonio Somaini read the manuscript at its different stages and helped to develop its rationale. Carolyn Jacobs and Bud Bynack exceeded the usual tasks of copyedit, providing substantial suggestions and help. Finally, my gratitude goes to Ramona Naddaff, Jonathan Crary, and Meighan Gale: at Zone Books I found a group of people characterized by intellectual enthusiasm and generosity.

Beyond the names of those who actively helped me with this book, I must also thank the many people I have met in recent years, in person, online, and by email — including my colleagues at Yale. Often, they have been unwitting sources of suggestions and advice. The fabric of these ongoing conversations is ultimately the pattern this book responds to.

Part of the Introduction appeared in the collective book *What Film is Good For*, edited by Julian Hanich and Martin Rossouw. Sections of Chapter One were also included in the essay "The Optical and the Environmental: From Screen to Screenscapes," published by *Critical Inquiry*. An early version of Chapter Two appeared as "Rethinking the Phantasmagoria: An Enclosure and Three Worlds" in the *Journal of Visual Culture*. Thanks to the publishers and to the journals for their permission to use this material.

Notes

INTRODUCTION: THE PROJECTION/ PROTECTION COMPLEX

1. Antonello Gerbi, "Iniziazione alle delizie del cinema," *Il Convegno* 7, nos. 11–12 (November 25, 1926), pp. 836–48. Republished in Antonello Gerbi, *Preferisco Charlot: Scritti sul cinema, 1926–1933*, ed. Gian Piero Brunetta and Sandro Gerbi (Savigliano: Aragno, 2011), pp. 35–49. Gerbi's essay is not published in English. I will quote here from a translation by Siobhan Quinlan, whom I thank.

2. Roland Barthes, "Leaving the Movie Theater," in *The Rustle of Language*, trans. Richard Howard (Berkeley: University of California Press, 1986), pp. 345–49.

3. The association can also be extended to another essay that is fundamental in understanding the classic filmic experience: Eric Feldmann, "Considérations sur la situation du spectateur au cinéma," *Revue Internationale de Filmologie* 26 (1956), pp. 83–97.

4. Gerbi, "Iniziazione alle delizie del cinema," p. 836.

5. Ibid., p. 841.

6. Ibid.

7. Ibid.

8. Ibid., p. 837.

9. Ibid., p. 838. Gerbi uses a verb, "swallow," which also recurs in the novel *Shoot* by Luigi Pirandello, who repeatedly states the film "swallow[s] the life." Luigi Pirandello, *Shoot!: The Notebooks of Serafino Gubbio Cinematograph Operator*, trans. C. K. Scott Moncrief (New York: E. P. Dutton, 1926).

10. Gerbi, "'Iniziazione alle delizie del cinema,'" p. 838

11. Ibid., p. 841.

12. Ibid., p. 840.

13. Ibid., p. 839.

14. Ibid. In a gendered prose, Gerbi describes the negative film stock as female: "The negative, which allows itself to leave its mark with the first ray of light that comes by, and then jealously always keeps the imprint of it, has something feminine about it." Ibid.

15. Ibid. We find the same sense of uselessness in Maxim Gorky's description of an early Lumière screening: "And suddenly [the image] disappears. Before your eyes there is simply a piece of with canvas in a wide black frame, and it seems there never was anything on it." Maxim Gorky, "Lumière's Cinematograph," trans. Richard Taylor, in Richard Taylor and Ian Christie, eds., *The Film Factory: Russian and Soviet Cinema in Documents 1896–1939* (Cambridge, MA: Harvard University Press, 1988), p. 26. Gorki's essay is dated 1896.

16. Gerbi, "Iniziazione alle delizie del cinema," p. 840.

17. Ibid., p. 841.

18. Ibid., p. 842. Gerbi also speaks of screen as "the bed of a river of images, the frigid mirror of the most passionate ghosts, of the most erotic dreams." Ibid.

19. Ibid., pp. 842–43

20. Ibid., pp. 840 and 842.

21. Ibid., p. 842.

22. Ibid., p. 845.

23. Ibid., p. 843.

24. Ibid.

25. Ibid., p. 845.

26. Ibid., p. 846.

27. In a silent parallel with Jean Epstein and Béla Balázs, Gerbi describes slow motion as able to capture bodies, things, and events with unprecedented precision: "A microscope applied not to points in space but to moments in time, slow motion examines the phases of each act with an equal love for all of them, and with an equal, very attentive zeal." Ibid., p. 844

28. Stanley Cavell captures this status of the screen when he writes: "The world of a moving picture is screened. The screen is not a support, not like a canvas.... A screen is a barrier. What does the silver screen screen? It screens me from the world it holds—that is, makes me invisible. And it screens that world from me—that is, screens its existence from me." Stanley Cavell, *The World Viewed, Enlarged Edition* (Cambridge,

MA: Harvard University Press, 1979), p. 24. The protective nature of screen has been explored also by Giorgio Avezzù, "The Deep Time of the Screen, and Its Forgotten Etymology," *Journal of Aesthetics and Culture* 11.1 (2019), pp. 1–15; Mauro Carbone and Graziano Lingua, "Being Screens, Making Screens: Functions and Technical Objects," *Screen Bodies*, 6.2 (Winter 2021), pp. 1–22; and Francesco Casetti, "Primal Screens," in Craig Buckley, Rüdiger Campe, and Francesco Casetti, eds., *Screen Genealogies: From Optical Device to Environmental Medium* (Amsterdam: Amsterdam University Press, 2019), pp. 27–50. On fears and protection related to cinema, see Sarah Keller, *Anxious Cinephilia: Pleasure and Perils at the Movies* (New York: Columbia University Press, 2020).

29. The idea of "representations taken for a perception" has been expansively explored by Jean-Louis Baudry, "The Apparatus: Metapsychological Approaches to the Impression of Reality in Cinema," in Philip Rosen, ed., *Narrative, Apparatus, Ideology* (New York: Columbia University Press, 1986), pp. 299–318.

30. Marshall McLuhan, *Understanding Media: The Extension of Man* (New York: McGraw Hill, 1964).

31. On the Phantasmagoria's history, see Laurent Mannoni, *The Great Art of Light and Shadow: Archaeology of Cinema* (Exeter: University of Exeter Press, 2000), and Mervyn Heard, *Phantasmagoria: The Secret Life of the Magic Lantern: A Full-Blooded Account of an Extraordinary Theatrical Ghost-Raising Entertainment of the Early Nineteenth-Century and the True Exploits of Its Mysterious Inventor, Paul de Philipsthal, in Britain and Abroad* (Hastings: Projection Box, 2006).

32. The bubble as a personal space in which an individual can take refuge is explored by Michael Bull, "To Each Their Own Bubble: Mobile Spaces of Sound in the City," in Nick Couldry and Anna McCarthy, eds., *Mediaspace: Place, Scale, and Culture in a Media Age* (New York: Routledge, 2004), pp. 275–93. For visual bubbles, see Francesco Casetti and Sara Sampietro, "With Eyes, with Hands: The Relocation of Cinema into iPhone," in Pelle Snikars and Patrick Vonderau, eds., *Moving Data: The iPhone and the Future of Media* (New York: Columbia University Press, 2012), pp. 19–32.

33. On immediacy and mediation, see Jay David Bolter and Richard Grusin, *Remediation: Understanding New Media* (Cambridge, MA: MIT Press, 1999), and Grusin, "Radical Mediation," *Critical Inquiry* 42.1 (Autumn 2015), pp. 124–48.

34. The postwar television was located in the living room, at the core of domestic space, and it reconnected the family to the social space momentarily left behind. On television as a domestic fixture, see Lynn Spigel, *Make Room for TV: Television and the*

Family Ideal in Postwar America (Chicago: University of Chicago Press, 1992).

35. See Sigmund Freud, *Beyond the Pleasure Principle*, trans. James Strachey (New York: Liveright, 1950), p. 9.

36. Such a perception of the modern world emerged in particular in the work of Georg Simmel, *Simmel on Culture: Selected Writings*, eds. David Frisby and Mike Featherstone (Thousand Oaks: Sage, 1997), and in particular "The Metropolis and Mental Life," pp. 174–85.

37. On the disciplinary practices of modern societies, see Michel Foucault, *Discipline and Punish: The Birth of the Prison* (New York: Random House, 1975). On the immune paradigm and the risks of overprotection, see Roberto Esposito, *Immunitas: Protection and Negation of Life*, trans. Zakiya Hanafi (London: Wiley, 2011), and Esposito, "The Immunization Paradigm," trans. Timothy Campbell, *Diacritics* 36.2 (2006), pp. 23–48. A recent discussion of the immune paradigm in cinema is Francesco Vitale, *La farmacia di Godard* (Naples: Orthotes Editrice, 2021).

38. The role of contingency and conjuncture in defining the territory has been recently underscored by Keller Easterling, *Medium Design* (London: Verso, 2021).

CHAPTER ONE: SCREENS, SPACE, FEARS

1. An accurate description of Phantasmagoria's show at the Couvent des Capucines is in Laurent Mannoni, *The Great Art of Light and Shadow: Archaeology of Cinema* (Exeter: University of Exeter Press, 2000), pp. 157–64.

2. A reconstruction of the early film séances is in Santiago Hidalgo and Louis Pelletier, "Le mystère du 'grand tableau gris': L'animation des images fixes dans les premières projections cinématographiques," *1895, Mille huit cent quatre-vingt-quinze, revue d'histoire du cinéma*, no. 82 (Spring 2017), pp. 87–106. See also Martin Loiperdinger, "Lumière's *Arrival of the Train*: Cinema's Founding Myth," *Moving Image* 4.1 (Spring 2004), pp. 89–118.

3. For a consideration of radar in the history of surveillance, see Jeremy Packer, "Screens in the Sky: SAGE, Surveillance, and the Automation of Perceptual, Mnemonic, and Epistemological Labor," *Social Semiotics* 23.2 (2013), pp. 173–95.

4. On TV in the 1950s, see Lynn Spiegel, *Make Room for TV: Television and the Family Ideal in Postwar America* (Chicago: University of Chicago Press, 1992).

5. On control rooms, see Cormac Deane, "The Control Room: A Media Archaeology," *Culture Machine* 16 (2015), pp. 1–34.

6. The difference between gaze and glance is underscored in visual media by John

Ellis in *Visible Fictions* (London: Routledge, 1982) and applied to painting by Norman Bryson in *Vision and Painting: The Logic of the Gaze* (London: Macmillan, 1983); the distinction between viewing and monitoring is advanced by Stanley Cavell in "The Fact of Television," *Daedalus* 111.4 (Fall 1982), pp. 75–96.

7. In the eighteenth century, the optical connotation of the word "screen" was relatively rare. An exception is Henry Baker, *The Microscope Made Easy*, 3rd ed. (London: Doldsley, 1744), pp. 23 and 25–26, who speaks of "screen" and "paper screen" for the surface on which the magnified image appeared. A turning point is offered by two notices that refer to the patent of the Phantasmagoria granted to de Philipsthal in London in early months of 1802 ("Specification of the Patent granted to M. Paul de Philipsthal," *The Repertory of Arts and Manufactures*, first series, 16 vols. (London: Nichols and son, 1802), vol. 16, pp. 303–305. The two notices, "M. de Philipsthal's Patent," in *Cobbett's Annual Register, Volume 2, from July to December, 1802* (London: Cox and Baylis, 1802), p. 1053, and "M. de Philipsthal's Patent (of the Lyceum, Strand) for the invention of representing in a dark scene human figures in various characters, size, etc.," in *Monthly Magazine*, vol. 13, pt. 1, no. 87, June 1802, p. 488, say "transparent screen" instead of "transparent body," which is the term employed by de Philipsthal in his patent. At the time, the word "screen" usually meant a "protection," "filter," or "divide." The substitution of the new term for the old—authorized by the fact that in the Phantasmagoria, the screen had to hide the projector before hosting the projected images—and the immediate success of the new term allow us to detect the time and context in which the visual connotations of "screen" started to become dominant.

8. See the entry s.v. "Screen," in James A. H. Murray, ed., *A New English Dictionary on Historical Principles* (Oxford: Clarendon Press of Oxford University Press, 1914). See also the entries s.v "Écran" in É. Littré, ed., *Dictionnaire de la langue française* (Paris: Librairie Hachette, 1873), and s.v. "Schirm," in Jacob Grimm and Wilhelm Grimm, *Deutsches Vörterbuch* (Leipzig: S. Hirzel, 1899).

9. Jinying Li, "Toward a Genealogy of the Wall-Screen," *differences: A Journal of Feminist Cultural Studies* 33.1 (2022), pp. 28–59.

10. This reconsideration of the screen echoes a wider environmental turn in media theories. See Sean Cubitt, *Eco Media* (Amsterdam: Rodopi, 2005), and Stephen Rust, Salma Monani, and Sean Cubitt, eds., *Ecocinema Theory and Practice* (New York: Routledge, 2012). A productive articulation of the field in Jacopo Rasmi, "Comment le cinéma atterrit-il?: Repérages cinématographiques au pays de la crise écologique," in Hélène

Schmutz, ed., *De la représentation de la crise à la crise de la représentation: Esthétique et politique de l'Anthropocène* (Chambery: Presses Université Savoie Mont Blanc, 2019), pp. 327–51. There are excellent case studies in Yuriko Furuhata, *Climatic Media: Transpacific Experiments in Atmospheric Control* (Durham: Duke University Press, 2022). An accurate historical analysis of the "environmental orientations" in media theories is Antonio Somaini, "Walter Benjamin's Media Theory: The Medium and the Apparat," *Grey Room*, no. 62 (Winter 2016), pp. 6–41.

11. Gilbert Simondon, *On the Mode of Existence of Technical Objects*, trans. Cécile Malaspina and John Rogove (Minneapolis: Univocal, 2017), pp. 25–26.

12. When compared with the idea of dispositif, the concept of assemblage underscores the coalescence of heterogeneous elements in what is becoming a functional complex. In this sense, it characterizes "dynamic relation rather than synthetic totality, organization rather than organism," as Bill Brown brilliantly states in "Re-Assemblage (Theory, Practice, Mode)," *Critical Inquiry* 46.2 (Winter 2020), p. 274. In the field of film and media, praise for the term "assemblage," as opposed to the problematic concept of an apparatus, can be found in Francesco Casetti, *The Lumiére Galaxy: Seven Key Words for the Cinema to Come* (New York: Columbia University Press, 2015), in particular, pp. 67–97.

13. "In a contemporary engine each important item is so well connected to the others . . . that *it cannot be other than what it is.*" Simondon, *On the Mode of Existence of Technical Objects*, p. 26; (emphasis mine). M. J. T Mitchell echoes this Simondon's passage when he writes: "Screens never appear by themselves, but only as relational component of a larger scene of projection or viewing, a theatrical structure of spectacle and image-making that may well include the other arts." M. J. T Mitchell, "Screening Nature (and the Nature of the Screen)," *New Review of Film and Television Studies* 13.3 (2015), p. 232.

14. Prior to the Phantasmagoria, the magic lantern did not include a proper screen. As Athanasius Kircher's description makes clear, the projection machine did not require a specific surface on which images were projected. The dispositif's specifications regarded the lamp, the concave mirror aimed at enhancing the lamp's light, the slides, the lenses and objectives (*tubus palmaris*), and finally the image that emerged in front of spectators. It is true that Kircher mentions the white wall (*muros candidus*) of the room (*cubiculum*) in which the projection took place, yet the wall is a preexisting element whose existence has to be taken for granted and whose function is merely accidental. See Athanasius Kircher, *Ars Magna Lucis et Umbrae* (Amsterdam: Joannis Janssonium, 1671), book 10, pp. 768–70. The wall would retrospectively become a screen only later, when the

screen is included within the essential components of the projection dispositifs: see an early handbook addressed to projectionists and theater owners, *Richardson's Handbook of Projection* (New York: Chalmers, 1923), pp. 226–33.

15. The idea of a screen in a magic lantern—in which the projector is not hidden—came quite soon. The *OED* signals an occurrence in 1846, when the word was now familiar. *Oxford English Dictionary,* s.v. "screen."

16. For the variety of materials and devices that can become a screen, each one responding to specific purposes of the ensemble, see, *Richardson's Handbook of Projection,* pp. 226–33.

17. On the temporal extension of a medium's emergence and on its deviation from an original project, see the remarks about the birth of cinema in André Gaudreault and Philippe Marion, "A Medium Is Always Born Twice," *Early Popular Visual Culture* 3.1 (May 2005), pp. 3–15. See also Benoît Turquety, *Inventer le cinéma. Épistémologie: Problèmes, machines* (Lausanne: L'Âge d'Homme, 2014).

18. Simondon, *On the Mode of Existence of Technical Objects,* p. 55

19. The associated milieu "is a certain regime of natural elements surrounding the technical being, linked to a certain regime of elements that constitute the technical being. The associated milieu mediates the relation between technical, fabricated elements and natural elements, at the heart of which the technical being functions." Ibid., p. 59.

20. Simondon's renowned example is the stream of water in the turbine invented by Jean Guimbal in which the device's environment was incorporated into its conception. On the associated milieu's role in bringing the technical object to its completion, see ibid., p. 59.

21. "It is that through which the technical object conditions itself in its functioning." Ibid., p. 59.

22. In *On the Mode of Existence of Technical Objects,* Simondon speaks of a process of *adaptation-concretization*; later, he will speak of *individuation*.

23. Delluc speaks of "the amphitheater of the whole world." Louis Delluc, "Le cinema, art populaire," *Le cinema au quotidien* (1921), now in Delluc, *Écrits cinématographiques,* 3 vols. in 4 (Paris: Cinémathèque Française, 1990), vol. 2, pp. 279–88.

24. For media as infrastructure, see Lisa Parks and Nicole Starosielski, eds, *Signal Traffic: Critical Studies of Media Infrastructures* (Champaign: University of Illinois Press, 2015).

25. "The show had to spread a sort of religious awe. Consequently, in choosing an abandoned chapel in the middle of the cloister I would not have made a better choice. The former destination of the building favored spectator's concentration. The memory of the graves located in the convent increased this feeling, in association with the fascination exerted by the shadows. Ghosts looked like they were getting out of the tombs, flying around the corpses that once they animated." Étienne Gaspard Robertson, *Mémoires récréatifs, scientifiques et anecdotiques du physicien-aéronaute E. G. Robertson: Connu par ses expériences de fantasmagorie, et par ses ascensions aérostatiques dans les principales villes de l'Europe*, 2 vols. (Paris: Chez l'auteur . . . et à la Libr. de Wurtz, 1831–1833), vol. 1, p. 276. The association of the show with its site was so strong that when Robertson ceased his activity six years later, another physicist-conjurer resumed the Phantasmagoria, choosing a similar location—no longer the Couvent des Capucines, but the old Abbey of Saint Germain. See the announcement of a "Cabinet de physique et fantasmagorie de M. Le Breton" in *Le Journal de l'Empire* (November 27, 1805), p. 1.

26. Jakob von Uexküll, *A Foray Into the Worlds of Animals and Humans: With a Theory of Meaning*, trans. Joseph D. O'Neil (Minneapolis: University of Minnesota Press, 2010). For a recent reconsideration of von Uexküll, see Gottfried Schnödl and Florian Sprenger, *Uexkülls Umgebungen: Umweltlehre und rechtes Denken* (Lüneburg: Meson, 2022).

27. Michel de Certeau, *The Practice of Everyday Life*, trans. Steven F. Rendall (Berkeley: University of California Press, 1984), in particular, part 3, "Spatial Practices," pp. 91–130.

28. Ibid., pp. 97–105.

29. Benjamin quotes Paul Valery on the "general infusion of energy" into the world by electricity in the age of Napoleon and compares it to the innervation of the world by Christianity during Tiberius's reign in terms of its ability to change the world: see Walter Benjamin, "Paul Valéry: On His Sixtieth Birthday," trans. Rodney Livingstone, in *Walter Benjamin Selected Writings, Volume 2, 1931–1934*, ed. Michael W. Jennings, Howard Eiland, and Gary Smith (Cambridge, MA: Belknap Press of Harvard University Press, 1999), p. 534, For Benjamin's idea of innervation, see in particular "One-Way Street," trans. Edmund Jephcott, in *Walter Benjamin: Selected Writings, Volume 1, 1913–1926*, ed. Marcus Bullock and Michael W. Jennings (Cambridge, MA: Belknap Press of Harvard University Press, 1996), pp. 444–87; "Surrealism: The Last Snapshot of the European Intelligentsia," trans. Edmund Jephcott, in *Walter Benjamin: Selected Writings*, Volume 2, Part 1, pp. 207–19; and "The Work of Art in the Age of Its Technological Reproducibility: Second Version," trans. Edmund Jephcott and Harry Zohn, in *Walter Benjamin Selected*

Writings, Volume 3, 1935–1938, ed. Howard Eiland and Michael W, Jennings (Cambridge, MA: Belknap Press of Harvard University Press, 2003), pp. 101–33. A wide exploration of Benjamin's concept of innervation in Miriam Bratu Hansen, *Cinema and Experience: Siegfried Kracauer, Walter Benjamin, and Theodor W. Adorno* (Berkeley: University of California Press, 2011).

30. "Revolutions are the innervation of the collective — or, more precisely, efforts at innervation on the part of the new, historically unique collective, which has its organs in the new technology." Benjamin, "The Work of Art in the Age of Its Technological Reproducibility," p. 124, n. 10.

31. "In technology a *physis* is being organized through which mankind's contact with the cosmos takes a new and different form from that which it had in nations [*Völkern*] and families." Benjamin, "One-Way Street," p. 487.

32. "Only when in technology body and image so interpenetrate that all revolutionary tension becomes bodily collective innervation, and all the bodily innervations of the collective become revolutionary discharge, has reality transcended itself to the extent demanded by the *Communist Manifesto*." Benjamin, "Surrealism," p. 218.

33. Lynn Spigel, *Make Room for TV: Television and Family Ideal in Postwar America* (Chicago: University of Chicago Press, 1992).

34. Anna McCarthy, *Ambient Television: Visual Culture and Public Space* (Durham: Duke University Press, 2001).

35. Against a tradition exclusively attentive to images on the screen, in the 1950s, the Filmology movement included the space of film theater into the crucial elements of what it called the "filmic situation." In particular, Filmology explored the "segregation of spaces," opposing the imaginary world of the movie and the real space of the theater, the effects due to the presence of a crowd in front of the screen and the influence of the milieu on the different phases of the spectator's experience. On the "segregation of spaces," see Albert Michotte, "Le caractère de 'réalité' des projections cinématographiques," *Revue Internationale de Filmologie* 3–4 (October 1948), pp. 249–61; on the "filmic situation" and the spectator's experience, see Eric Feldmann, "Considérations sur la situation du spectateur au cinéma," *Revue internationale de filmologie* 26 (1956), pp. 83–97. Recently, in a sort of neo-Filmology, film studies have challenged again the environmental nature of cinema. On the space of cinema theater and its different typologies, see Amir H. Ameri, "The Architecture of the Illusive Distance," *Screen* 54.4 (Winter 2013), pp. 439–62. An analysis of the different role of the screen in the

picture palaces and the more functional theaters of 1930s is Ariel Rogers, *On the Screen: Displaying the Moving Image in the Long 1930s* (New York: Columbia University Press, 2019). A reconstruction of the "revolution" represented by the more functional theaters of 1930s is Jocelyn Szczepaniak-Gillece, *The Optical Vacuum: Spectatorship and Modernized American Theater Architecture* (Oxford: Oxford University Press, 2018).

36. The invisibility of the practices in so called "operational images" has been underscored by Harun Farocki, "Phantom Images," *Public*, no. 29 (January 2004), pp. 12–22, and by Trevor Paglen, "Operational Images," *E-Flux*, no. 59 (November 2014), https://www.e-flux.com/journal/59/61130/operational-images, and Paglen, "Invisible Images (Your Pictures Are Looking at You)," *New Inquiry*, December 8, 2016, https://thenewinquiry.com/invisible-images-your-pictures-are-looking-at-you.

37. Bernard Dionysius Geoghegan, "An Ecology of Operations: Vigilance, Radar, and the Birth of the Computer Screen," *Representations* 147.1 (Summer 2019). In the following pages the word "operation" will refer to one or more actions as performed by an assemblage, while the word "practice" will refer to a set of operations as consolidated and recognized by a society.

38. Luciano Floridi "What the Near Future of Artificial Intelligence Could Be," *Philosophy & Technology* (2019) 32, pp. 1–15.

39. In order to underscore the technical objects' persistent genesis, Simondon speaks of "unit of coming-into-being" (or "unit of becoming"). In particular: "The technical object is that which is not anterior to its coming-into-being, but is present at every stage of its coming-into-being; the technical object in its oneness is a unit of coming-into-being [l'objet technique est unité de devenir]." Simondon, *On the Mode of Existence of Technical Objects*, p. 26.

40. Jacques Rancière, *The Politics of Aesthetics: The Distribution of the Sensible*, trans. Gabriel Rockhill (London: Continuum, 2004).

41. I reshape here Laura Mulvey's concept of "to-be-looked-at-ness," which defines the recurring situations in movies in which women are "spectacle" and men are "the bearer of the look," in order to characterize a gaze that aims at an object tendentially in a predatory way, independently of its bearer. Laura Mulvey, *Visual and Other Pleasures* (Bloomington: Indiana University Press, 1989).

42. Francesco Casetti, "A Countergenealogy of the Movie Screen; or, Film's Expansion Seen from the Past," in Richard Grusin and Jocelyn Szczepaniak-Gillece, eds., *Ends of Cinema* (Minneapolis: University of Minnesota Press, 2020), pp. 23–52.

43. See Wendy Brown, *Walled States, Waning Sovereignty* (New York: Zone Books, 2010).

44. Martin Heidegger, *Being and Time*, trans. John Macquarrie and Edward Robinson (Oxford: Blackwell, 1962). The section on fear is pp. 179–82; the section on anxiety is pp. 228–35.

45. Arnold Gehlen, *Man, His Nature and Place in the World*; trans. Clare McMillan and Karl Pillemer (New York: Columbia University Press, 1988). Michele Cometa acutely applied the approach of philosophical anthropology to a study about narrative as a tool for fighting our anxieties: *Perché le storie ci aiutano a vivere* (Milan: Cortina, 2017).

46. Georg Simmel, "The Metropolis and Mental Life," in *Simmel on Culture: Selected Writings*, eds. David Frisby and Mike Featherstone (Thousand Oaks: Sage, 1997), pp. 174–85.

47. Walter Benjamin, "Experience and Poverty," trans. Rodney Livingstone, in *Walter Benjamin: Selected Writings, Volume 2, Part 2, 1931–1934*, pp. 731–36. On modern shocks, see "On Some Motifs in Baudelaire," trans. Harry Zohn, in *Walter Benjamin: Selected Writings, Volume 4, 1938–1940*, ed. Marcus Bullock et al. (Cambridge, MA: Belknap Press of Harvard University Press, 2002), pp. 313–55. On the modern loss of experience, see "The Story-Teller: Reflections on the Works of Nicolai Leskov," trans. Harry Zohn, in *Walter Benjamin: Selected Writings, Volume 3, 1935–1938*, pp. 143–66.

48. Paul Virilio, *The Administration of Fear*, trans. Ames Hodges (Los Angeles: Semiotext(e), 2012).

49. Alexander Galloway, *The Interface Effect* (Cambridge: Polity, 2012). See also Seunghoon Jeong, *Cinematic Interfaces: Film Theory after New Media* (New York: Routledge, 2013), in particular chapter 1, "The Medium Interface," pp. 19–60.

50. Gary Tomlinson, *Culture and the Course of Human Evolution* (Chicago: University of Chicago Press, 2018).

51. "The pure technical schema defines a type of existence of the technical object, grasped in its ideal function, which is different from the reality of a historic type." Simondon, *On the Mode of Existence of Technical Objects*, p. 45.

52. Mauro Carbone has explored this overlapping of generality and specificity through his idea of *arche-screen*; see Mauro Carbone, "Thematizing the Arche-Screen through Its Variations," in *Screens*, ed. Dominique Chateau and José Moure (Amsterdam: Amsterdam University Press, 2016), pp. 62–69; and Carbone, *Filosofia-schermi: Dal cinema alla rivoluzione digitale* (Milan: Cortina, 2016).

53. Think of cinema in the open air, where the sense of a physical enclosure is strongly diminished and whose finality appears as the simple display of images and sounds.

54. Two good examples are the dispositifs that Rüdiger Campe describes in his accurate exploration of the meanings of the word *Schirm* in Germany between the second half of the seventeenth century and the first half of the nineteenth century. The *Jagd-Schirm* was a mobile shed in which the hunter hid from his prey so as to keep an eye on the hunting ground, but also to avoid the dangers of engagement in full view. In the legal domain, *Schutz und Schirm* indicated the request for and the granting of a protection that, without implying any sovereignty of the protector over the protégé, nevertheless entailed that the former "represented" (*Avocat*) the latter. In both cases, we have someone who faces the world, but who also tries to do this while sheltering himself from something or someone. See Rüdiger Campe, "'Schutz und Schirm': Screening in German during Early Modern Times," in Craig Buckley, Rüdiger Campe, and Francesco Casetti, eds., *Screen Genealogies: From Optical Device to Environmental Medium* (Amsterdam: Amsterdam University Press, 2019), pp. 51–72.

55. Martin Heidegger, "The Age of the World Picture," in *Off the Beaten Track*, ed. and trans. Julian Young and Kenneth Haynes (Cambridge: Cambridge University Press, 2002), pp. 57–85.

56. For an influential redefinition of mediation, see Richard Grusin, "Radical Mediation," *Critical Inquiry* 42.1 (Autumn 2015), pp. 124–48.

57. See John Durham Peters, *The Marvelous Clouds: Towards a Philosophy of Elemental Media* (Chicago: University of Chicago Press, 2015).

58. David Brewster, *Letters on Natural Magic* (New York: Harper and Brothers, 1836), p. 81.

59. On Zoom fatigue, see Geert Lovink, "The Anatomy of Zoom Fatigue," *Eurozine*, November 2, 2020, https://www.eurozine.com/the-anatomy-of-zoom-fatigue.

60. See Stanley Cavell: "Film takes our very distance and powerlessness over the world as the condition of the world's natural appearance." Cavell, *The World Viewed*, p. 119.

61. On the spectral nature of cinematic images, see "Cinema and Its Ghosts," an interview with Jacques Derrida by Antoine de Baecque and Thierry Jousse, trans. Peggy Kamuf, *Discourse*, 37.1–2 (Winter–Spring 2015), pp. 22–39. In the same issue of *Discourse*, see Leo Cahill and Timothy Holland, "Double Exposures: Derrida and Cinema, an Introductory Séance," pp. 3–21, and David Wills, "Screen Replays," pp. 74–86.

62. Marshall McLuhan, *Understanding Media: The Extension of Man* (New York: McGraw Hill, 1964).

63. Jennifer Lynn Peterson claims that climate change creates the condition for a new kind of spectatorship in which "a dominant culture comes to understand itself as imbricated within a previously concealed dynamic of threat and survival." See Jennifer Lynn Peterson, "An Anthropocene Viewing Condition," *Representations* 157.1 (2022), p. 19.

64. On the multiplicity of worlds tied to the screen, see Dan Yacavone, *Film Worlds: A Philosophical Aesthetics of Cinema* (New York: Columbia University Press, 2015).

65. As Richard Grusin claims, in the process of mediation, "being in the middle" is the only immediate element—everything else is mediated. Grusin, "Radical Mediation."

66. Tony Bennett, "The Exhibitionary Complex," *new formations*, no. 4 (Spring 1988), pp. 73–102, and Bennett, *The Birth of the Museum: History, Theory, Politics* (London: Routledge, 1995). The complex regards the urgency of displaying objects considered artistic in appropriate spaces for a new class of patrons.

67. Raymond Williams, *Television: Technology and Cultural Form* (New York: Schocken Books, 1974), pp. 13–16. I incline to date the emergence of the *communicative complex* to the end of eighteenth century, with the invention of the optical telegraph, created in 1792 by the French inventor Claude Chappe. The optical telegraph already responded to the need to "transmit specific information and maintain contact and control." Ibid., p. 13. On the birth of the optical telegraph, see Jean-Marie Dilhac, "The Telegraph of Claude Chappe—an Optical Telecommunication Network for the XVIIIth Century."

INTERMEZZO ONE: BUNKERS

1. "Since the arming of the jet, and especially since the arrival of artillery on the scene, warfare has not only created a landscape by defensive constructions, by the organization of fronts and frontiers, but it has also competed successfully with natural forces; firearms, explosives, screens, and gasses have contributed the creation of an artificial climate, reserved to the battleground or, more precisely, to the moment of combat." Paul Virilio, *Bunker Archeology*, trans. George Collins (New York: Princeton Architectural Press, 1994), p. 37.

2. "From then on, on, there was no more protective expanse or distance, all territory was totally accessible, everything was immediately exposed to the gaze and to destruction. This marked the disappearance of the battleground and of peripheral combat; the Fortress Europe was three dimensional, the casemates on the beaches complemented the antiaircrafts shelters of the cities, the submarine bases were but the counterpart of industry subterranean bases." Ibid, p. 40

3. The complicity of media with warfare has already been underscored by Friedrich Kittler, *Optical Media: Berlin Lectures 1999*, trans. Anthony Enns (Cambridge: Polity, 2010), and Paul Virilio, *War and Cinema: The Logistics of Perception* (London: Verso, 1989). Recent scholarly work has further developed this argument through a detailed reconsideration of military technologies and organization. See in particular Antoine Bousquet, *The Eye of War: Military Perception from the Telescope to the Drone* (Minneapolis: University of Minnesota Press, 2018). I contend here that this complicity implies not only a media performance aimed at striking the enemy, but also at protecting the troops; and moreover, that this complicity is not tied to a parallel development of media and warfare, but it is intrinsic to the process of mediation performed by media.

4. "Defense, in the course of the Second World War, switched from entrenchment to intelligence through the prodigious development of detection systems and telecommunication. In fact, while most of the means of acoustic detection had been created during the First World War with the improvement of optical telemetering, radiophony and radar stem from the Second World War." Virilio, *Bunker Archeology*, p. 30.

5. Christian Metz, "Mirror Construction in Fellini's 8½," in *Film Language: A Semiotics of Cinema*, trans. Michael Taylor (New York: Oxford University Press, 1974), pp. 228–34.

CHAPTER TWO: THE PHANTASMAGORIA

1. Étienne Gaspard Robertson, *Mémoires récréatifs, scientifiques et anecdotiques du physicien-aéronaute E.G. Robertson: connu par ses expériences de fantasmagorie, et par ses ascensions aérostatiques dans les principales villes de l'Europe*, 2 vols. (Paris: Chez l'auteur . . . et à la Libr. de Wurtz, 1831–1833), vol. 1, p. 156.

2. Ibid., p. 157.

3. Ibid., p. 162.

4. An accurate biography of Robertson is Françoise Levie, *Étienne-Gaspard Robertson: La vie d'un fantasmagore* (Brussels: Le Préamble, 1990).

5. Laurent Mannoni, "The Phantasmagoria," in *The Great Art of Light and Shadow: Archaeology of Cinema* (Exeter: University of Exeter Press, 2000), pp. 136–75.

6. Terry Castle, *The Female Thermometer: Eighteenth-Century Culture and the Invention of the Uncanny* (New York: Oxford University Press, 1995), in particular, the chapter "Phantasmagoria and the Metaphorics of the Modern Reverie," pp. 140–67.

7. Stefan Andriopoulos, *Ghostly Apparitions: German Idealism, the Gothic Novel, and Optical Media* (New York: Zone Books, 2013).

8. Tom Gunning, "Illusions Past and Future: The Phantasmagoria and its Specters" (2004), and Gunning, "Phantasmagoria and the Manufacturing of Illusions and Wonder: Towards a Cultural Optics of the Cinematic Apparatus," in Andre Gaudreault, Catherine Russell, and Pierre Veronneau, eds., *The Cinema: A New Technology for the 20th Century* (Lausanne: Éditions Payot, 2004), pp. 31–44.

9. Noam Elcott, "The Phantasmagoric *Dispositif*: An Assembly of Bodies and Images in Real Time and Space," *Grey Room*, no. 62 (Winter 2016), pp. 42–71.

10. Laurent Mannoni (*The Great Art of Light and Shadow*) and Deac Rossell ("The 19th Century German Origins of the Phantasmagoria Show," unpublished conference paper for the Lantern Projections Colloquium, London, February 2001), find an earlier instantiation of the Phantasmagoria in Johann Schröpfer's necromantic shows in Leipzig around 1774 — soon imitated by other German lanternists. The link between the first Parisian Phantasmagoria and German sources is openly evoked by a letter to *Magazin Encyclopèdique* that speaks of "a German by the name Philidor" who conjured up ghosts thanks to optical illusions in Vienna, and whose "Phantasmogorie" (sic) was soon to open in Paris (A.L.M., "Phantasmogorie: Lettre au rédacteur du Magazin Encyclopedique sur le phantômes, les apparitions des illuminès, et sur un physicien qui se propose de produire tous ces effets par une illusion optique," *Magazin Encyclopédique*, December 3, 1792, pp. 17–19; the acronym "A.L.M." likely stands for Aubin-Louis Millin de Grandmaison). The letter ends with an excerpt from the *Gazette de Vienne* — the *Wiener Zeitung* — dated 1790, which describes Philidor's performances in that city. There is no doubt that many of the Parisian features were already performed in Vienna; nevertheless, it is reasonable to say that the Phantasmagoria assembled all its components into a standard format in Paris.

11. *Affiches, annonces et avis divers, ou Journal Général de France*, no. 350, December 16, 1792, p. 5189. The same announcement appeared in in the same day in *Le journal de Paris*, no. 351, December 16, 1792, "Spectacles" section, p. 2. In the following days and months, announcements of the show regularly appeared in *Affiches, annonces et avis divers*; they ceased after August 8, when, in the full Age of Terror, the Phantasmagoric spectacle also ceased its run. The incident that caused the end to the show — a slide of Louis XVI was inadvertently managed in a way that the king seemingly was raised to the sky — is narrated in *Madame Tussaud's Memoirs and Reminiscences of France: Forming an Abridged*

History of the French Revolution (London: Saunders and Otley, 1838), pp. 249–51. Erkki Huhtamo offers a critical revision of the incident in "Ghost Notes: Reading Mervyn Heard's *Phantasmagoria: The Secret Life of the Magic Lantern*," *Magic Lantern Gazette* 18.4 (Winter 2006), pp. 11–12.

12. *Affiches, annonces, et avis divers*, no. 121, January 20, 1798, p. 2224. The actual opening is advertised three days later, in no. 124, January 23, 1798, pp. 2271–72; in the following months, *Affiches, annonces, et avis divers* would host regular announcements, including a special one detailing the content of the show and its main purposes, published on the issue 137, February 5, 1798, pp. 2495–96.

13. While referring to de Philipsthal's patent, *The Monthly Magazine* objected that it was too similar to Robertson's apparatus and that it did not include any reference to the invention's pedagogical purposes. "The Parisian invention was intended avowedly for the very useful purpose of dissipating all vulgar notions, prejudices and fears, respecting ghosts and apparitions. But at Lyceum no attempt has made to explain, to the less enlightened part of the audience, the principles upon which the delusions are founded, or the apparatus with which the exhibitions are made." *Monthly Magazine* 13, part 1, no. 87, June 1802 (London: Richard Philips), p. 488.

14. For a contemporary report about the English Phantasmagoria and its variations, see [Schirmer and Scholl], *Sketch of the Performances, at the Large Theatre, Lyceum; and a Short Account of the Origin, History, and Explanation of all the late Optical and Acoustic Discoveries, called the Phantasmagoria, Ergascopia, Phantascopia, Mesoscopia, &c. Together with the Invisible Girl* (London, 1805), available online as a Google Book. A good reconstruction of the Phantasmagoria in England is Mervyn Heard, *Phantasmagoria: The Secret Life of the Magic Lantern: A Full-Blooded Account of an Extraordinary Theatrical Ghost-Raising Entertainment of the Early Nineteenth-Century and the True Exploits of Its Mysterious Inventor, Paul de Philipsthal, in Britain and Abroad* (Hastings: Projection Box, 2006).

15. On the Phantasmagoria's later experiences, see the interesting documents in Francois Binetruy's collection in Versailles, https://www.collection-binetruy.com/7707.html.

16. On the expansion and improvement of the magic lantern, see Mannoni, *The Great Art of Light and Shadow*, in particular, pp. 136–41. On the "nebulous lantern," see Edmé-Gilles Guyot, *Nouvelles récréations physiques et mathématiques* (Paris: Gueffier, 1770). Guyot describes his lantern as able to project images onto curtains of smoke in *Tome troisième: Illusions de l'optique*, in particular, in the sections "Lanterne Magique sur la fumée,"

p. 185–86, and "Faire paroître un Fantôme sur le piédestal placé au milieu d'un table," pp.186–90. Robertson mentions the apparitions on the smoke in *Mémoires récréatifs*, vol. 1, p. 354, but no contemporary chronicle bears witness of this fact. The use of smoke as a screen in the Phantasmagoria is very likely a simple legend. Friedrich Schiller's novel *Der Geisterseher — Aus den Papieren des Grafen von O*** was firstly published in several install-ments on the journal *Thalia* from 1787 and 1789.

17. Francis William Blagdon, *Paris as it was and it is, or a Sketch of the French capital illustrative of the effects of the Revolution*, 2 vols. (London: C. and R. Baldwin, 1803), vol. 1, pp. 429–37. At the time, the "Phantasmagoria's secrets" were already in the public domain due to a trial that opposed Robertson to two former assistants, whom he sued for stealing his invention. The trial is documented by the "Acts du Tribunal de Cassation," *Journal du Palais* (Paris), no. 86, May 25, 1802, pp. 193–98. See also the sentence: "Jugement qui condamne les citoyens Clisorius et Martin Aubée, entrepreneurs de la Fantasmaparasta-sie, comme ayant porté atteinte au brevet accordé au cit. Robertson, physicien" (Paris: Boutonet, 24 Germinal, an 8 [1800]), Bibliothèque historique de la ville de Paris, classifica-tion number 2-AFF-005257. The "Playodoyer [plea] prononcé par le cit, Delahaye ... " is available at the Bibliothèque nationale de France, 8-FN-648. See also "Procès relatif à la Fantasmagorie," *L'observateur des spectacles, de la littérature et des arts*, May 31, 1802, p. 2, and a letter by Robertson sent to *L'observateur des spectacles*, June 7, 1802, p. 2.

18. "The illusion which leads us to imagine that an object which increases in all its parts, is advancing towards us, is the basis of the *Phantasmagoria*, and, in order to produce it ... you have only to withdraw slowly the lantern from the place on which the image is represented, by approaching the outer lens to that on which the object is traced: this is easily done, that glass being fixed in a moveable tube like that of an opera-glass." Blagdon, *Paris as it was and it is*, pp. 434–35.

19. Ibid., p. 435.

20. Robertson, *Mémoires*, vol. 1, pp. 313–14.

21. "La Phantasmagorie: Description d'un spectacle curieux, nouveau et instructif," *Feuille villageoise* 3.22, February 28, 1793, pp. 489–510.

22. "Well! I have really seen these simulacres of the dead, and everybody who wants to see them will be able to do it, just paying one *écu* or two, even in assignats." Ibid., p. 489.

23. Ibid., p. 490.

24. Ibid., p. 508.

25. Ibid., p. 508. A hallucination both visual and auditive is reported in G.D.L.A, "Au Rédacteur du Courrier des Spectacles," *Le Courrier des spectacles, ou Journal de théâtres*, no. 1092, March 7, 1800, p. 3: "What is certain, however, is that one of the objects was in relief; indeed, when a spectator touched it, the end of his cane made a noise, and the shadows, as we know, are always impalpable." The acronym G.D.L.A. stands for Grimod de la Reynière.

26. Jean-Baptiste Chaussard, *Le nouveau diable boiteux: Tableau philosophique et moral de Paris, au commencement du XIXe siècle*, 2 vols. (Paris: Barba, 1803), vol. 2, p. 188. Chaussard's memoir covers both Philidor's and Robertson's Phantasmagorias: according to him, Philidor was a "philosopher," while Robertson was more of a scientist—to be praised because "physics is the natural antidote to any superstition." Ibid., p. 183.

27. Ibid., p. 187.

28. Chaussard adds: "It's at the Phantasmagoria that appointments are made that cannot take place elsewhere. I do not know who is the one who said that women are bold in the dark, men are not timid there." Ibid., pp. 188–89. Mannoni, who does not mention Chaussard, mentions two other testimonies, both published by the *Courrier des spectacles* in 1800. See Mannoni, *The Great Art of Light and Shadow*, pp. 161–62.

29. *Les ombres, ou, Les vivans qui sont morts: Fantasmagorie littéraire* (Paris: Imprimerie de la rue Cassette, 1801), p. 129

30. The "lucrative idea" of which the almanac speaks: the tickets for Philidor's show (twice a day, initially at 5:30 p.m. and at 9:00 p.m., when the spectacles in the legitimate theaters ended, later at 5:00 p.m. and 9:45 p.m.) were three livres; the tickets for Robertson's show were six livres, likely for the better places, and three livres for the other places. See *Affiches, annonces, et avis divers*, December 16, 1792, January 6, 1793, and January 20, 1798.

31. *Les ombres*, pp. 129–30.

32. See Robertson, *Mémoires*, vol. 1, p. 325.

33. "Brevet d'invention du Fantascope—ou perfectionnement de la lanterne de Kircher—déposé par le citoyen Etienne Gaspard ROBERT, dit ROBERTSON le 27 ventôse l'an 7," p. 9, Archive of the Institut National de la Propriété Industrielle (Courbevoie), classification number 1BA99.

34. It's worth noting that neither Robertson's patent nor de Philipsthal's patent used the word "screen" (*écran*): they used respectively *cloison* (which means "partition": ibid., p. 10) and "transparent body" ("Specification of the Patent granted to M. Paul de

Philipsthal," *The Repertory of Arts and Manufactures*, first series, 16 vols. [London: Nichols and Son, 1794–1802], vol. 16, pp. 303–305).

35. *La feuille villageoise*, "La Phantasmagorie," p. 507.

36. As the anonymous reporter of *La feuille villageoise* noticed, "it is the wall that seems to open to allow [the ghosts] to come in." Ibid.

37. "Descriptive account of the Original Phantasmagoria of Philipsthal," *The Portfolio* 4.21, January 29, 1825, p. 329.

38. Chaussard, *Le nouveau diable boiteux*, p. 187.

39. Elcott, "The Phantasmagoric Dispositif."

40. Chaussard, *Le nouveau diable boiteux*, p. 179.

41. The option started with Filidor and was taken up by Robertson. For Filidor, see *Affiches, annonces et avis divers*, March 14, 1793, p. 1083, July, 31, 1793, and August 5, 1793.

42. *La feuille villageoise*, "La Phantasmagorie," p. 490.

43. See, in particular, Robertson, *Mémoires*, vol. 1, pp. 276ff.

44. The "Instructive Program" published by Robertson around 1800 as promotional leaflet is reproduced in Laurent Mannoni, Donata Pesenti Campagnoni, and David Robinson, *Light and Movement: Incunabula of the Motion Picture 1420–1896* (Pordenone: Le giornate del cinema muto / Cinémathèque francaise-Musée du Cinéma / Museo Nazionale del Cinema, 1995), pp. 118–19.

45. On the path that spectators were supposed to follow in order to reach the Phantasmagoria's site, see the reconstruction offered by Mannoni, *The Great Art of Light and Shadow*, pp. 159–60.

46. David Brewster, *Letters on Natural Magic* (New York: Harper and Brothers, 1836), p. 81. Brewster was among the first scientists to display an interest for the Phantasmagoria. See his accurate description of the dispositif in *Ferguson's Lectures*, 2 vols. (Edinburgh, Glasgow and London: Bell, Fairbain, Mundell, etc, 1806), vol. 1, pp. 264–65.

47. Robertson, *Mémoires*, vol. 1, pp. 358–60.

48. Ibid., p. 358

49. See for example *Phantasmagoria, or, Authentic relations of the most remarkable apparitions, visions and dreams* (London: M. Jones, 1805). The book contains some ninety stories related to premonitions, apparitions, or even simple dreams that happened both to ordinary people and historical figures, including Constantine's vision. In the preface, the anonymous author distances himself from the habits of an "enlightened age."

50. Jonathan Crary, "Géricault, the Panorama, and Sites of Reality in the Early Nineteenth Century," *Grey Room*, no. 9 (Autumn 2002), pp. 5–25.

51. See the aforementioned announcement by Filidor: the spectacle has "no dangerous influence on the organs, no unpleasant odor, and persons of all ages and sexes may view it without inconvenience." *Affiches, annonces et avis divers*, no. 350, December 16, 1792, p. 5189.

52. Mannoni, *The Great Art of Light and Shadow*, pp. 159–60.

53. For Filidor's opening address, see *La feuille villageoise*, "La Phantasmagorie," p. 490. For Robertson's opening address, see Robertson, *Mémoires*, vol. 1, pp. 204–205.

54. There is an extremely interesting—though highly gendered—a passage in Robertson's "Instructive Program": "The citizen Robertson believes that he must advise the Ladies that the Phantasmagoria's effects are based on felicitous optical combinations. Consequently, the Ladies have no longer to be afraid of them more than they are scared by the sometimes worrisome effects of the moon's light" (p. 7 of the leaflet).

55. For example, in a report dated "15 vendémiaire, an 9 de la République Française" (October 7, 1800), Antoine-Charles Aubert raised the question of an appropriate illumination "to avoid disorders in the premises of the Capucines." Hence the request to place at least fifteen lamps—each one with one to four burners—in points of passage or at the entrance of some of the apartments, laboratories, and shops hosted in the former convent. Quite interestingly, four of these lamps involved Robertson and the Phantasmagoria: the corridors and the stairs around the theater were too often left in the darkness, and the audience had to be channeled to the place of the show. Good illumination also avoided the presence of prostitutes, who hid themselves at the end of one of the stairs. Report 1313, Archives de Paris, Cote: DQ10258. Other reports involved the closure of some passages, the list of expenses and rents, the need of reparations, and the offenses committed by the inhabitants. For a description of the different spaces of the former convent, with an estimate of their commercial value, see the report dated 23 Thermidor, an 9 de la République Française. Archives de Paris, Cote: DQ10256.

56. See Babied de Mercenary's account, reported by Robertson, *Mémoires*, vol. 1, p. 209. De Mercenary states that a mass of people in a theater is able to cope with fears better than are isolated individuals.

57. A historical analysis of the idea of interiority is offered in Rüdiger Campe and Julia Weber, eds., *Rethinking Emotions: Interiority and Exteriority in Premodern, Modern, and Contemporary Thought* (Berlin: De Gruyter, 2014).

58. See, in particular, Bernhard Greiner: "'That until now, the inner world of man has been given . . . such unimaginative treatment': Constructions of Interiority around 1800," in ibid., pp. 137–71. It may be worth noticing that the first edition of the French dictionary *Littré* recorded the word *interiorité* with reference to Kant. See Émile Littré, ed., *Dictionnaire de la langue française* (Paris: Librarie Hachette, 1873), s.v. "interiorité."

59. On competing paradigms of the interiority of confessions and memoires, the interiority of the interiors in sixteenth-century Dutch paintings, the interiority of eighteenth-century and nineteenth-century domestic interiors, and the interiority of psychoanalysis, see Ewa Lajer-Burcharth and Beate Söntgen, introduction to Ewa Lajer-Burcharth and Beate Söntgen, eds., *Interiors and Interiority* (Berlin: De Gruyter, 2016), pp. 1–13.

60. Robertson, *Mémoires*, vol. 1, p. 222.

61. See Oliver Grau, *Virtual Art: From Illusion to Immersion* (Cambridge, MA: MIT Press, 2002).

62. Robertson, *Mémoires*, vol. 1, pp. 294–304.

63. *Courrier des spectacles*, no. 1086, February 23, 1800, p. 4.

64. The archives where the slides are available include the Museo del Cinema of Turin and the Cinémathèque Française in Paris. See Laurent Mannoni and Donata Pesenti Campagnoni, *Lanterne magique et film peint* (Paris: Éditions de la Martinière, 2009). The Richard Balzer Collection is partly documented in Richard Balzer, *Peepshows: A Visual History* (New York: Harry N. Abrams, 1998); it has been exhibited in 2018 at the Boston Museum of Fine Arts. The collection of the Hauch Physiske Cabinet, Denmark, is available online at https://en.awhauch.dk/instrument-catalogue/category/light/side/5.

65. The parallelism between fluidity, metamorphosis, and hysteria has been brilliantly explored by Alessandra Violi, *Il teatro dei nervi: Fantasmi del moderno da Mesmer a Charcot* (Milan: Bruno Mondadori, 2004). On the passage from visible and invisible, see Barbara Maria Stafford, *Body Criticism: Imaging the Unseen in Enlightenment Art and Medicine* (Cambridge, MA: MIT Press, 1991).

66. Edgar Morin, *The Cinema, or the Imaginary Man*, trans. Lorraine Mortimer (Minneapolis: University of Minnesota Press, 2005). On the concept of the imaginary, see the two foundational contributions, Jean-Paul Sartre, *The Imaginary: A Phenomenological Psychology of the Imagination*, trans. Jonathan Webber (London: Routledge, 2004), and Jacques Lacan, "The Mirror Stage as Formative of the Function of I as Revealed in Psychoanalytic Experience," in *Écrits: A Selection*, trans. Bruce Fink, with Héloïse Fink

and Russell Grigg (New York: W. W. Norton, 2002), pp. 3–9. The concept underwent different elaborations (including by Cornelius Castoriadis and Gilles Deleuze), yet it still defines the presence of expectations and interpretations within our direct approach to reality.

67. James W. Carey, "A Cultural Approach to Communication," in *Communication as Culture: Essays in Media and Society* (New York: Routledge, 1992), pp. 13–28, in particular, pp. 21–22.

68. Bruno Latour, "Visualization and Cognition: Thinking with Eyes and Hands," *Knowledge and Society* 6.6 (1986), pp. 1–40. Latour sees in the maps provided by La Pérouse between 1785 and 1788 an example of the process of "visualization": instead of a mere illustration of a territory, they recorded its characteristics according repetitive and controllable procedures in order to solve potential controversies and provide a set of reliable data. On the modern transformations of the relationship between map and territory and the emergence of postrepresentational geography, see William Rankin, *After the Map: Cartography, Navigation, and the Transformation of Territory in the Twentieth Century* (Chicago: University of Chicago Press, 2017).

69. Robertson, *Mémoires*, vol. 2, p. 15.

70. See the section "Expériences et observations aérostatiques faites à Hambourg, le 18 juillet 1803, par E. G. Robertson, membre de la Société Galvanique de Paris, et associé honoraire de celle des Encouragements des Arts et des Sciences de Hambourg," in ibid., pp. 65–83.

71. During the first decade of nineteenth century, the Phantasmagoria was regularly included as a must-see attraction in the early guides for visitors to Paris. See, for example, *Paris et ses curiosités, ou Nouveau guide du voyageur à Paris* (Paris: Marchand, 1802), pp. 103–104; L. Proudhomme, *Miroir de l'ancienne e du noveau Paris, avec treize voyages en vélocifères dans ses environs* (Paris: Proudhomme and Debray, 1804), p. 315; Jean-Baptiste de Bouge, *La boussole, ou La guide des étrangers dans Paris et ses faubourgs* (Brussels: Leduc, 1806), in particular, pp. 62–67; and the already mentioned *Paris as it was and it is* by the English journalist Blagdon. Advertisements and reviews bring further evidence to the interpretation I offered in the previous pages. For example, the relevance of the natural world is confirmed by the change in name of Robertson's show, which around 1806 was called "Cabinet de Physique" (see de Bouge, *La boussole*, p. 65), as well as by the proliferation of "experiments in physics" in several venues, such as the Théatre Pittoresque et Méchanique on Rue Neuve de la Fontaine (de Bouge, *La boussole*, p. 65, as well). On the

other hand, the relevance of the setting is confirmed by the location of a competitor's show in the former Abbey of Saint Germain in Rue Bonaparte—another abandoned convent. See, for example, *Le journal de l'empire*, August 21, 1805, p. 1.

72. See, for example, *Phantasmagoria; or The Development of Magical Deception*, third installment of *Marvellous Magazine and Compendium of Prodigies* (London: Tegg and Castleman, 1803).

73. See, for example, T. Dibdin, *Irish Phantasmagoria, sung by Mr Incledon in his new entertainment call'd Variety* (London, Goulding & Co., ca., 1801).

74. That is, any work of imagination that was not a vivid depiction of life, for example, in the series of sketches penned by Charles Robert Forrester in his *Phantasmagoria of Fun* (London: R. Bentley, 1843).

75. See Andriopoulos, *Ghostly Apparitions*, in particular, p. 53.

76. In *Kapital*, Marx speaks of the "phantasmogorische Form" taken by commodities after their exchange value has obliterated their real value. Karl Marx, *Das Kapital 1*, in *Marx-Engels Werke*, 42 vols. (Berlin: Dietz, 1957–), vol. 23. p. 86. It typically is translated as "fantastic form" in English translations. See, for example, Kark Marx, *Capital, Volume One*, trans Ben Fowkes (New York: Vintage, 197), p. 165.

77. The initial title of Benjamin's *Passagenwerke* was, not by chance, "A Dialectical Phantasmagoria."

78. Lewis Carroll, *Phantasmagoria and Other Poems* (London: Macmillan, 1869).

79. Tom Gunning, "The Cinema of Attractions: Early Film, Its Spectator, and the Avant-Garde," in Thomas Elsaesser, ed., *Early Cinema: Space, Frame, Narrative* (London: BFI, 1900), pp. 56–62.

80. On remediation, see Jay David Bolter and Richard Grusin, *Remediation: Understanding New Media* (Cambridge, MA: MIT Press, 1999).

81. Mark S. Weil, "The Devotion of the Forty Hours and Roman Baroque Illusions," *Journal of the Warburg and Courtauld Institutes* 37.1 (1974), pp. 218–48.

82. We can find a first-hand testimony of the ritual with the homilies in Alessandro Canobbio, *La divota oratione delle Quaranta Hore fatta nella città di Verona la settimana santa dell'anno MDLXXXVII* (Verona: Giovanni Discepolo, 1587), and in Canobbio, *La divota oratione delle XL Hore fatta da tutto il Popolo di Verona la Settimana Santa dell'anno 1604* (Verona: Giovanni Discepolo, 1604). I thank art historian Lorenzo A. Ratto for bringing these two documents to my attention. An extensive and accurate reconstruction of the ritual is in Carla Bino, "La predicazione cappuccina per le

Quarantore e un sermonario annotato della fine del Seicento," *Drammaturgia* 17.7 (2020), pp. 7–54.

83. James Chandler and Kevin Gilmartin, eds., *Romantic Metropolis: The Urban Scene of British Culture, 1780–1840* (Cambridge: Cambridge University Press, 2005).

84. On the Eidophusicon, invented in 1781 by the French painter Philippe Jacques de Loutherbourg, see Ian McCalman, "Mystagogues of Revolution: Cagliostro, Loutherbourg and Romantic London," in Chandler and Gilmartin, eds., *Romantic Metropolis*, pp. 177–203.

85. On the Panorama, invented in by Robert Barker in 1787, see Stephan Oettermann, *The Panorama: History of a Mass Medium*, trans. Deborah Lucas Schneider (New York: Zone Books, 1997). The Panorama's first steps in London are accurately described by Markman Ellis, "'Spectacles within doors': Panoramas of London in the 1790s," *Romanticism* 14.2 (2008), pp. 133–48.

86. Exhibited in London in 1802, *Eidometropolis* measured 18 feet high and 108 feet long; admission was one shilling. On *Eidometropolis*, see James Chandler and Kevin Gilmartin, "Introduction: Engaging the *Eidometropolis*," in Chandler and Gilmartin eds., *Romantic Metropolis*, pp. 1–41.

87. La Veillée was owned by the architect and real estate speculator Nicolas Lenoire, famous for his fashionable meeting places and sites of lavish entertainments. It included slopes that led through rocks, two orchestras, and two theaters. "It is believed to be in a site of enchantment," Jean-Baptiste de Bouge wrote in *La boussole*, p. 64. It is also described in Mercier de Compiègne, *Manuel du voyageur à Paris* (Paris: Favre, 1798), pp. 17–22.

88. In a more inclusive archeology—what I would call a *rhizomatic archeology*—it might be useful to recall also that the Phantasmagoria's connection is with the optical telegraph—a line of towers, each in view of two others and each able to relaunch to the next one a message encoded in conventional visual signs, created in 1792 by the French inventor Claude Chappe. In his *Mémoires*, Robertson pays a tribute to Chappe, a friend with whom he spent happy times, and he claims to have played a part in Chappe's invention. Though a boast, his assertion reveals an unexpected parallel. Indeed, Robertson's definition of the optical telegraph as "the art of traversing, through reciprocal communications, the largest country in a few minutes" (*Mémoires*, vol. 1, p. 199) equally applies to the Phantasmagoria. Both dispositifs are an attempt to connect spaces from which we are separated. Both display a content—messages and worlds—on behalf of a contact.

INTERMEZZO TWO: THE BALLISTICS OF PERCEPTION

1. Thierry Kuntzel, "Sight, Insight, and Power: Allegory of a Cave," *Camera Obscura* 2.6 (Fall 1980), pp. 91–110.

2. "The actors/stagehands have become spectators, sitting in darkness and watching the brightly-lit stage framed by the entrance to the cave: theater, cinema." Ibid., p. 95.

3. "Global apparatus: on a first stage (the space delimited by the trees and the entrance to the cave, the bed): actors who are seen but do not see (Zaroff, the parental couple); on a second stage, separated from the first by footlights (the threshold to the cave, the head of the bedstead): a spectator who watches-or attempts to watch-the "primal" scene (Rainsford and Eve, the younger brother) and who is himself watched by another spectator (. . . the spectator of *The Most Dangerous Game*). For this ultimate spectator, who sees both scenes at once — and often sees them better than the first spectator, who is caught up in the scene and must conceal himself — to see is to have divine (in)sight." Ibid., p. 109.

4. "Each apparatus has its regimen of light, the way it falls, softens and spreads, distributing the visible and the invisible, generating or eliminating an object, which cannot exist without it." Gilles Deleuze, "What Is a Dispositif?," in *Two Regimes of Madness: Texts and Interviews 1975–1995*, ed. David Lapoujade, trans. Ames Hodges and Mike Taormina (New York: Semiotext(e), 2006), p. 339.

5. Ruggero Eugeni, *Il capitale algoritmico: Cinque dispositivi postmediali (più uno)* (Brescia: Morcelliana, 2021), in particular, chapter 6, pp. 223–29.

6. See John Durham Peters, "The Charge of a Light Barricade: Optics and Ballistics in the Ambiguous Being of the Screen," in Craig Buckley, Rüdiger Campe, and Francesco Casetti, eds., *Screen Genealogies: From Optical Device to Environmental Medium* (Amsterdam: Amsterdam University Press, 2019), pp. 215–35.

7. See Walter Benjamin, "On Some Motifs in Baudelaire," trans. Harry Zohn, in *Walter Benjamin: Selected Writings, Volume 4, 1938–1940*, eds. Marcus Bullock et al. (Cambridge, MA: Belknap Press of Harvard University Press, 2002), pp. 313–55. On modernity as an age of shocks, see also David Frisby, *Fragments of Modernity* (Cambridge: Polity Press, 1985), and Leo Charney and Vanessa R. Schwartz, eds., *Cinema and the Invention of Modern Life* (Berkeley: University of California Press, 1995).

8. On tests as modern form of perception, see Walter Benjamin, "The Work of Art in the Age of Its Technological Reproducibility: Second Version," trans. Edmund Jephcott and Harry Zohn, in *Walter Benjamin: Selected Writings, Volume 3, 1935–1938*, ed. Howard

Eiland and Michael W. Jennings (Cambridge, MA: Belknap Press of Harvard University Press, 2003), pp. 101–33. In "On Some Motifs in Baudelaire" (p. 161), Benjamin quotes Sigmund Freud and his idea of a "protective shield" that helps the organism to endure the excess of stimulation and that in turn is improved by the same stimulation. Wolfgang Schivelbusch borrows Freud's idea and suggests that the creation of a "protective shield," at once against and thanks to the shocks that modern life inflicts to individuals occurs in wide array of experiences, including train journeys. For Sigmund Freud, see *Beyond the Pleasure Principle*, trans. James Strachey (New York: Liveright, 1950); for Wolfgang Schivelbusch, see *The Railway Journey: The Industrialization of Time and Space in the Nineteenth Century* (Berkeley: University of California Press, 1986).

CHAPTER THREE: CINEMA: A SPACE FOR COMFORT

1. The documentary was directed by Herbert Ponting and was based on material shot during Scott's tragic expedition of 1919–13. Part of Ponting's film was first included in the short *Captain Scott's South Pole Expedition*, released by Gaumont in 1912. An excellent analysis of the Gaumont's short is Jennifer Lynn Peterson, "An Anthropocene Viewing Condition," *Representations* 157.2 (2022), pp. 17–40. Peterson claims that this kind of movie elicits forms of spectatorship oriented toward the sense of loss implied by the current dramatic climate change.

2. Joseph Roth, "Filme," in *Drei Sensationen und zwei Katastrophen: Feuilletons zur Welt des Kinos*, ed. Helmut Peschina and Rainer-Joachim Siegel (Göttingen: Wallstein, 2014), p. 147; originally published in *Frankfurter Zeitung*, March 17, 1925.

3. William Troy, "Beauty and the Beast," *The Nation*, March 22, 1933, p. 326, reprinted in Stanley Kauffmann and Bruce Henstell, eds, *American Film Criticism: From the Beginnings to "Citizen Kane"* (New York: Liveright, 1972), pp. 281–82.

4. On alternative models of film exhibition, see Charles Acland and Haidee Wasson eds., *Useful Cinema* (Durham: Duke University Press, 2011); Haidee Wasson, "The Reel of the Month Club: 16mm Projectors, Home Theaters and Film Libraries in the 1920s," in Richard Maltby, Melvyn Stokes, and Robert C. Allen, eds., *Going to the Movies: Hollywood and the Social Experience of Cinema* (Exeter: University of Exeter Press, 2007), pp. 218–20; Wasson, *Museum Movies: The Museum of Modern Art and the Birth of Art Cinema* (Berkeley: University of California Press, 2005); Wasson, "Electric Homes! Automatic Movies! Efficient Entertainment!: 16mm and Cinema's Domestication in the 1920s," *Cinema Journal* 48.4 (Summer 2009), pp. 1–21. Outside the Western Hemisphere, for postwar China, see

Chenshu Zhou, *Cinema Off Screen: Moviegoing in Socialist China* (Berkeley: University of California Press, 2021).

5. For a historical approach to comfort, see Jean Fourastié and Françoise Fourastié, *Histoire du confort* (Paris: Presses Universitaires de France, 1962); John E. Crowley, *The Invention of Comfort: Sensibilities and Design in Early Modern Britain and Early America* (Baltimore: Johns Hopkins University Press, 2001); and part 5 of the monumental work of Sigfried Giedion, *Mechanization Takes Command: A Contribution to Anonymous History* (New York: Oxford University Press, 1948).

6. Recent research has started to underscore the connections between cinematic experience and comfort. See Jocelyn Szczepaniack-Gillece, "Revisiting the Apparatus: The Theatre Chair and Cinematic Spectatorship," *Screen* 57.3 (Autumn 2016), pp. 253–76, and Jocelyn Szczepaniak-Gillece and Stephen Groening, "Afterword: Objects in the Theater," *Film History: An International Journal* 28.3 (2016), pp. 139–42.

7. Film theories have already connected cinema to the process of projection—not only by exploring the role of projector within the apparatus, but by focusing on the way spectators psychologically "project" themselves into screened images. See, in particular, Edgar Morin, *The Cinema, or the Imaginary Man*, trans. Lorraine Mortimer (Minneapolis: University of Minnesota Press, 2005). Including cinema among the instantiations of the projection/protection complex adds attention to the protection and to the space in which images appear.

8. Douglas Gomery, *Shared Pleasures: A History of Movie Presentation in the United States* (Madison: University of Wisconsin Press, 1992).

9. These aspects recall the complex dynamics—implying innervation, test, and play—that Walter Benjamin recognized at the core of cinema. On these dynamics, and especially on what Benjamin calls *Spielraum* (room for play), see Miriam Bratu Hansen, "Room-for-Play: Benjamin's Gamble with Cinema," *October* 109 (Summer 2004), pp. 3–45, and more extensively, Hansen, *Cinema and Experience: Siegfried Kracauer, Walter Benjamin, and Theodor W. Adorno* (Berkeley: University of California Press, 2012).

10. "The 'Movie' Theater Up-To-Date: Many Modern Comforts Provided," *Scientific American* 137.6. December 1927, pp. 516–17.

11. On Rothafel, see Ross Melnick, *American Showman: Samuel "Roxy" Rothafel and the Birth of the Entertainment Industry, 1908–1935* (New York: Columbia University Press, 2012), in particular, chapter 6, pp. 251–305, on the building of the Roxy Theater.

12. The opening of the Roxy Theater was immediately and largely publicized. It

suffices to look at the *Exhibitors Herald World* 29.1. March 19, 1927, whose "Better Theater" section was almost entirely dedicated to the new movie palace.

13. "Mastbaum Theater, Philadelphia, Last Word in Elegance, Comfort," *Billboard* 41.9, March 2, 1929, pp. 4 and 89; "A Memorial to a Theatre Pioneer," *Exhibitors Herald World*, April 13, 1929, section 2, pp. 17–19.

14. *Billboard* remarks that in the lounge, "men and women may smoke"—an exception, since women were usually not allowed to do this. For the prohibition of smoking for women, see, for example, *Exhibitors Herald World* 28.6, January 22, 1927, section 2, p. 29.

15. An essential introduction is David Naylor, *American Picture Palaces: The Architecture of Fantasy* (New York: Prentice Hall, 1981).

16. "Universal to Build First Atmospheric House in New York," *Exhibitors Herald World* 26.12, September 4, 1926, section 2, pp. 31 and 34.

17. Barry H. Holquist, "Motion Picture Theatre Progress in the Smaller Cities," *Exhibitors Herald World* 25.9, May 15, 1926, section 2, pp. 9, 11, 43.

18. With the advent of 1930s, descriptions became less magniloquent, yet we still find almost all the items listed by Holquist. An interesting example is Gray Strider's review of the Cape Cinema. Located in Dennis on Cape Cod, and offering only 359 seats, the Cape Cinema is praised as "a monument to amusement, to progress, to art." It is characterized by a playful contrast between a simple exterior and a modernistic interior in which emerges a mural by the painter Rockwell Kent, who also exhibits a number of his works in the foyer. The individual chairs are specially designed by Frankl Galleries, and there is more room than usual between the rows. The curtain is governed by an electrical device. And the projection and acoustic systems, as well as the ventilation, are first-class. Gray Strider, "Screen Theater," *Screenland* 22.1, November 1930, pp. 61 and 120–21.

19. Siegfried Kracauer, "Cult of Distraction: On Berlin's Picture Palaces," in *The Mass Ornament: Weimar Essays*, ed. and trans. Thomas Y. Levin. (Cambridge, MA: Harvard University Press, 1995), pp. 323–28.

20. Kurt Pinthus, "Ufa Palace," in Anton Kaes, Nicholas Baer, and Michael Cowan eds., *The Promise of Cinema: German Film Theory, 1907–1933* (Berkeley: University of California Press, 2016), pp. 170–72. Unlike Kracauer, who sees in the "surface splendor" of cinema palaces an emblem of the externality and disorder of the Weimar age, Pinthus complains that in a such an environment, the movie did not receive its rightful place.

21. "No surface phenomenon was better suited to house and to project these collective fantasies than the grand film palaces, which were the most significant and most

numerous public building enterprises of the entire Weimar Republic, particularly during the relative prosperity of the stabilization period of 1924 to 1929. The façade of the building that housed the filmic product was promoted to the status of film itself." Janet Ward, *Weimar Surfaces: Urban Visual Culture in 1920s Germany* (Berkeley: University of California Press, 2001), p. 164. On Weimar film palaces, see Leonardo Quaresima, "Luoghi dello spettacolo e spazi della visione," *Cinema & Cinema*, no. 47 (December 1986), pp. 35–37. Quaresima highlights the process of "cinematization" of the urban spaces. On the historical and architectural aspects of German film palaces, see Peter Boeger, *Architektur der Lichtspieltheater in Berlin: Bauten und Projekte 1919–1930* (Berlin: Arenhövel, 1993); Rolf Peter Baacke, *Lichtspielhausarchitektur in Deutschland: Von der Schaubude bis zum Kinopalast* (Berlin: Fröhlich & Kaufmann, 1982); and Silvaine Hänsel and Angelika Schmitt, eds., *Kinoarchitektur in Berlin 1895–1995* (Berlin: Dietrich Reimer, 1995).

22. Joseph Roth, "Bekehrung eines Sünders im Berliner Ufa-Palast," *Frankfurter Zeitung*, November 19, 1925. See also "Amerikanisiertes Kino," *Frankfurter Zeitung*, October 4, 1923.

23. "Movie theaters . . . were the first large market for commercial comfort air-conditioning." Joseph M. Siry, *Air-Conditioning in Modern American Architecture, 1890–1970* (University Park: Pennsylvanis State University Press, 2020), p. 64.

24. Gail Cooper, *Air-Conditioning America: Engineers and the Controlled Environment, 1900–1960* (Baltimore: John Hopkins University Press, 1998), p. 88.

25. See Siry, *Air-Conditioning in Modern American Architecture*, p. 64. Siry quotes another statement, dated 1925, about Balaban and Katz's theatrical chain: "many physicians had advised that convalescent patients should spend as much time as possible in the theaters of this corporation, when the air is washed and cooled to the clarity and dryness of mountain zephyrs." Ibid.

26. The economic and health benefits of a cooling system are repletely discussed in *Exhibitors Herald*, which often gives voice to the owners or inventors of the most popular systems. See, for example, F. C. Largen, "Ventilation — Its Reactions on Audience and Box Office," *Exhibitors Herald* 25.5, April 17, 1926, pp. 50–51.

27. Carrier Engineering Corp., *Theatre Cooling by Carrier Centrifugal Refrigeration and Air Distribution: A Restful Refuge Summer & Winter* (New York: Carrier Engineering Corp., 1925). On the Carrier Company, see Carrier Engineering Corp., *The Story of Manufactured Weather, by The Mechanical Weather Man* (New York: Carrier Engineering Corp., 1919).

28. Carrier Engineering Corp., *Theatre Cooling by Carrier Centrifugal Refrigeration and Air Distribution*, p. 26.

29. Balaban and Katz Theater Corporation, *Theatre Employees for Balaban & Katz Service* (Chicago: Balaban & Katz, 1926), pp. 79–91.

30. Ibid., p. 90.

31. Ibid., p. 81.

32. One example: "Thousands and thousands of patrons during the hot summer months and especially during real hot spells seek shelter in your theater where they obtain temporary relief from the broiling sun and scorching heat on the streets." "Cooling System Trailers," *Motion Picture Herald*, June 25, 1932, p. 56. Another good example is the subtitle of the Carrier Company booklet, A *Restful Refuge Summer and Winter*.

33. See, in particular, Siegfried Kracauer, "Shelter for the Homeless," in *The Salaried Masses: Duty and Distraction in Weimar Germany*, trans. Quintin Hoare (London: Verso, 1998), pp. 88–95.

34. James A. H. Murray, ed., *A New English Dictionary on Historical Principles* (Oxford: Clarendon Press of Oxford University Press, 1914), s.v. "screen."

35. "Our Movie Ushers Prize Courtliness," *The New York Times*, December 26, 1928, p. 36.

36. "Try This on Your Ushers! — It's OK," *Motion Picture News* 41.23, June 7, 1930, p. 160.

37. Balaban and Katz Theater Corporation, *Theatre Employees for Balaban & Katz Service*, pp. 25–30.

38. On the dangers tied to film attendance, see Gary D. Rhodes, *The Perils of Moviegoing in America, 1896–1950* (New York: Continuum, 2011).

39. Balaban and Katz Theater Corporation, *Theatre Employees for Balaban & Katz Service*, p. 95.

40. Ibid., pp. 28–29.

41. In *Motion Picture News*, the top-of-the-list duties are: "1. Be on time. Do not chew gum and always be neat. 2. Be dignified in your behavior. No unnecessary talk. 3. Never give a short or 'smart' answer. Do not have a grouch on. 4. Always stand erect — walk snappy. 5. Never lose your temper — keep cool. 6. Never argue with a patron, if anything is beyond you, see your superior. 7. Remember — quietness must be always kept in the house. 8. Never be discourteous, even to grouchy people. 9. Try to please and satisfy every patron as if you owned the theatre." "Try This on Your Ushers! — It's OK," p. 160.

42. As Jack Knight, supervisor of theater management for the Balaban and Katz Theater Corporation, states, "the men and women of our service departments are trained to interpret and personify the ideals of standard of our service." Jack Knight, interviewed by Frank B. Archer, "The Welfare of Your Visitors," *Exhibitors Herald World* 30.12, September 3, 1927, p. 35.

43. "Sleek and Slim? Maybe He's an Usher," *The Baltimore Sun*, September 25, 1927, p. SOC2. *The New York Times* in "Our Movie Ushers Prize Courtliness" sketches an ideal profile: "The perfect usher is tall and slim, with clean-cut features. He is flute-voiced and velvet-handed. He acts with dignity, politeness, tact and dispatch. His attitude is of the 'firm but kind' variety, and his philosophy is that the customer is always right" (p. 36).

44. Samuel L. Rothafel, "What the Public Wants in the Picture Theatre," *Architectural Forum* 42.6, June 1925, p. 361. The Balaban and Katz manual presents an accurate model of how to schedule training courses for ushers, with a distinction between routine three-period training and emergency training to be imparted when ushers are under pressure by unusually large numbers of people attending the movies. Balaban and Katz Theater Corporation, *Theatre Employees for Balaban & Katz Service*, pp. 7–15.

45. An example thoroughly described by *Motion Picture News* in 1926 is the Saxe Wisconsin Theater in Milwaukee. Larry Lane, "Train Future Managers at Ushers' School," *Motion Picture News* 33.19, May 8, 1926, pp. 2279–80.

46. "Our Movie Ushers Prize Courtliness," p. 36.

47. Ibid.

48. Balaban and Katz Theater Corporation, *Theatre Employees for Balaban & Katz Service*, p. 25.

49. S[amuel] L. Rothafel, "The Welfare of Our Visitors," *Exhibitors Herald World* 30.12, September 3, 1927, p. 15.

50. For example: "Our young men are trained by an ex-sergeant of marines who puts them through their daily routine of setting-up exercises." Ibid., p. 15. Rothafel often underscores the military qualities of his organization: "To this end the house staff should be under strict training, of almost military character." Rothafel, "What the Public Wants in the Picture Theatre," p. 361.

51. The fact that movie theaters mimic the way offices and factories are organized and ruled finds a candid testimony in the Balaban and Katz manual. "This is an age of efficiency, and the business of this country today is spending large sums of money in

the study and the devising of efficient means of operation." Balaban and Katz Theater Corporation, *Theatre Employees for Balaban & Katz Service*, p. 23.

52. A foundational history of movie theaters in the United States in the framework of the wider history of film presentation is Gomery, *Shared Pleasures*. An analysis of the different role of the screen in the picture palaces and the more functional theaters of 1930s is Ariel Rogers, *On the Screen: Displaying the Moving Image in the Long 1930s* (New York: Columbia University Press, 2019). A reconstruction of the "revolution" represented by the more functional theaters of 1930s is Jocelyn Szczepaniak-Gillece, *The Optical Vacuum: Spectatorship and Modernized American Theater Architecture* (Oxford: Oxford University Press, 2018). A relevant historical document is George L. Rapp, "History of Cinema Theater Architecture," in Arthur Woltersdorf, ed., *Living Architecture* (Chicago: A. Kroch, 1930), pp. 58–59, which already foregrounds the presence of different models of movie theaters.

53. Developing the suggestive typology by Amir H. Ameri based on different ways of negotiating the "real" and the "imaginary" in "The Architecture of the Illusive Distance," *Screen* 54.4 (Winter 2013), pp. 439–62, we can say that in the nickelodeon, the "here" of the audience and the "elsewhere" of the fiction were two heterogeneous spaces simply juxtaposed, yet both included in a site whose façade represented a clear point of departure from the ordinary reality; in the cinema palaces, the "here" was a lavish place in competition with the "elsewhere"; in the more functional theaters of 1930s, the "here" was literally oriented toward the "elsewhere"; and in the multiscreen venues, Imax cinemas, and black box theaters, the "here" is just the site where the "elsewhere" is displayed.

54. *Billboard* ironically remarked in 1931 how in the movie palaces, the pleasure of watching risked becoming secondary to the pleasures of the place: "People today have gotten into the habit of the well-lighted, bright, clean atmosphere of the movie cathedrals, the consistent courtesy that is always present, and they like it, even if the picture is not so hot." "Lack of Customer Comfort, Another Item on List of Legit Ills," *Billboard*, 43.45, November 7, 1931, p. 38. The same feeling is expressed in the aforementioned article in *Scientific American*: "No longer is the theater a mere place in which to view a motion picture. Instead, it is more of a place of entertainment and a club combined." "The 'Movie' Theater Up-To-Date," p. 517.

55. On the transformations of movie theater between the 1920s and the 1930s, see Szczepaniak-Gillece, *The Optical Vacuum*), and Rogers, *On the Screen*, as well as interesting remarks in Melnick, *American Showman*.

56. John Belton, *Widescreen Cinema* (Cambridge, MA: Harvard University Press, 1992). A testimony of the debate around widescreen at the beginning of 1930s is Fred Westerberg, "Symposium on Wide Film Proportion," *Motion Picture Projectionist* 4.1, November 1930, p. 20–21.

57. F. H. Richardson, *Richardson's Handbook of Projection*, 5th ed., 3 vols. (New York: Chalmers, 1927), vol. 2, pp. 483–92. The fourth edition listed six kinds of surfaces that that could perform as screen, from glass to white walls and from translucent surfaces to canvases, already opting for kalsomine. F. H. Richardson, *Richardson's Handbook of Projection* (New York: Chalmers, 1922), pp. 226–33.

58. Rogers, *On the Screen*.

59. Alva Johnston, "3-Dimensional Film Made Like Stereopticons," *New York Herald Tribune*, February 24, 1929, p. 1.

60. Ibid. We find the same announcement in the *The Boston Daily Globe*, which nevertheless suggests that "spectators at the movies, by closing one eye, may get added realism in form of depth." "Closing one Eye Adds to Realism," *The Boston Daily Globe*, February 24, 1929, p. A16.

61. See, for example, Gabriel Costa's 'The Future of the Cinema," in the English magazine *Picture Show*, July 12, 1930, p. 10. Costa wonders: "After the talkies, the 'smellies?'" Such a development is by no means impossible: it would be on behalf of a more accurate realism. Yet what Costa really dreams of is the quest for a comfortable and glamourous experience in which patrons can regain the fullness of their life. Not by chance, Costa's article ends with an Edenic depiction of future movie theaters "with their flat roofs devoted to tennis and ice-skating; with their restaurants, gymnasiums, massage and beauty parlors, nurseries for the youngsters and fashion parades for the devotees of *la mode*. These gigantic haunts of pleasure will seat their ten thousand of fifteen thousand patrons with the utmost comfort — plus elegances and refinements unknown even to the sumptuous cinemas of our time."

62. Rogers, *On the Screen*, p. 7.

63. Szczepaniak-Gillece, *The Optical Vacuum*.

64. Ben Schlanger, "Reversing the Form and Inclination of the Motion Picture Theater Floor for Improving Vision," *Journal of the Society of Motion Picture Engineers* 17.2 (August 1931); Schlanger, "The floor and the Screen," *Motion Picture Projectionist*, December 1932, pp. 15–19.

65. In an extensive study of Frederick Kiesler's work, Stephen J. Phillips summarizes

the architect's main idea as follows: "Performing a restorative operation, Kiesler's continuous structures sought to smooth out disturbing differences, separation, and disjunction in both the *physis* and the *psyche* of the dweller by modulating architectural surfaces
in correlation to everyday human motions, with hopes to eliminating all nonessential
actions. Continuous architecture thus served as a strategy for naturalizing the harsh, jar-
ring, and discomforting effects of the twentieth-century technology in order to ensure,
for better or worse, more satisfyingly productive working lives; it creates spaces that
induce the perceiving body to move about more freely and habitually—if not autonomi-
cally—unobstructed by abrupt changes in the environment." Stephen J. Phillips, *Elastic
Architecture: Frederick Kiesler and Design Research in the First Age of Robotic Culture* (Cambridge, MA: MIT Press, 2017), pp. 7–8.

66. "New Film Theater Sponsored by Guild Opens Friday Night," *New York Herald
Tribune*, January 27, 1929, p. F3

67. "Cinema 'Revolution' Coming?," *Film Weekly*, no. 12, January 7, 1929, p. 5. *Film
Weekly* was an extremely popular British magazine.

68. "4-Screen Theatre Being Built Here," *The New York Times*, December 9, 1928,
p. N1.

69. Frederick Kiesler, "Building a Cinema Theatre," in *Selected Writings*, ed. Siegfried
Gohr and Gunda Luyken (Ostfieldern bei Stuttgart: Verlag Gerd Hatje, 1996), pp. 16–19.
Originally published in the *New York Evening Post*, February 2, 1929. See also the section
that Frederick Kiesler devoted to the Film Guild Cinema in his *Contemporary Art Applied
to the Store and Its Display* (New York: Brentano's, 1930), pp. 118–19.

70. Sigfried Giedion, *Mechanization Takes Command*, p. 260.

71. Quite paradoxically, the desire to separate the theater from its immediate reality
came from those who were more wary of the cinema: parental associations, religious
authorities, and educators were scared by the intrusion of the everyday reality, especially in its more brutal aspects, into theatrical space. An excellent testimony to these
fears comes from the Payne Fund Studies—twelve research projects between the late
1920s and the early 1930s. Here is the list of eight volumes that collect the twelve studies, all published by Macmillan in 1933. Volume 1, W. W. Charters, *Motion Pictures and
Youth: A Summary*, combined with P. W. Holaday and George D. Stoddard, *Getting Ideas
from the Movies*; volume 2, Ruth G. Peterson and L. L. Thurstone, *Motion Picture and the
Social Attitudes of Children*, combined with Frank Shuttleworth and Mark A. May, *Social
Conduct and Attitudes of Movie Fans*; volume 3, W. S. Dysinger and Christian A. Ruckmick,

The Emotional Responses of Children to the Motion Picture Situation, combined with Charles C. Peters, *Motion Pictures and Standards of Morality*; volume 4, Samuel Renshaw, Vernon L. Miller, and Dorothy Marquis, *Children's Sleep*; volume 5, Herbert Blumer, *Movies and Conduct*; volume 6, Edgar Dale, *The Content of Motion Pictures*, combined with Edgar Dale, *Children's Attendance at Motion Pictures*; volume 7, Herbert Blumer, *Movies, Delinquency, and Crime*; volume 8, Paul G. Cressey and Frederick M. Thrasher, *Boys, Movies, and City Streets*. To the eight volumes we can add the "manual of motion-picture criticism prepared for high-school students" by Edgar Dale, *How to Appreciate Motion Pictures* (New York: MacMillan, 1934): Dale's work makes direct reference to Payne Studies and appears one year later in the same book series.

72. Stanley Cavell, *The World Viewed: Enlarged Edition* (Cambridge, MA: Harvard University Press, 1979), p. 24 and p. 26.

73. Seymour Stern, "An Aesthetic of the Cinema House: A Statement of the Principles Which Constitute the Philosophy and the Format of the Ideal Film Theatre," *National Board of Review Magazine* 2.5, May 1927, pp. 7–10 and 19, republished in *Spectator— The University of Southern California Journal of Film and Television* 18.2 (Spring–Summer 1998), pp. 26–32. In the 1930s, Stern would be coeditor of *Experimental Cinema*.

74. Ibid., in *Spectator*, p. 27.

75. Ibid., p. 28.

76. I am paraphrasing—and reversing—a well-known passage in "The Work of Art in the Age of Its Technological Reproducibility": "For the majority of the city dwellers, throughout the workday in offices and factories, have to relinquish their humanity in the face of apparatus. In the evening these same masses fill the cinemas, to witness the film actor taking revenge on their behalf not only by asserting his humanity (or what appears to them as such) against the apparatus, but by placing that apparatus in the service of his triumph." Walter Benjamin, "The Work of Art in the Age of Its Technological Reproducibility: Second Version," trans. Edmund Jephcott and Harry Zohn, in *Walter Benjamin: Selected Writings, Volume 3, 1935–1938*, ed. Howard Eiland and Michael W. Jennings (Cambridge, MA: Belknap Press of Harvard University Press, 2003), p. 111.

77. Tomas Maldonado, "The Idea of Comfort," trans. John Cullars, *Design Issues* 8.1 (Autumn 1991), pp. 35–43. The essay is a section of Maldonado's book *Il futuro della Modernita* (Milan: Feltrinelli, 1987).

78. Ibid., p. 36.

79. See, for example, the principle that "happiness begins at home" that Rothafel

heralds in "The Welfare of our Visitors," p. 15. At the same time, Rothafel recognizes that theaters are "a living factor of local activities and a community center." Rothafel, "What the Public Wants in the Picture Theatre," p. 361.

80. Arnold Gehlen, *Man, His Nature and Place in the world*, trans. Clare McMillan and Karl Pillemer (New York: Columbia University Press, 1988).

81. Arnold Gehlen, *Man in the Age of Technology*, trans. Patricia Lipscomb (New York: Columbia University Press, 1980).

82. Michele Cometa provides a brilliant application of the idea of exoneration to storytelling. See Michele Cometa, *Perché le storie ci aiutano a vivere* (Milan: Raffaelo Cortina, 2017).

83. See Odo Marquard, "Indicted and Unburdened Man in Eighteen Century Philosophy," in *Farewell to Matters of Principle: Philosophical Studies* (New York: Oxford University Press, 1989), pp. 38–63; Marquard, *Krise der Erwartung—Stunde der Erfahrung: Zur aesthetische Kompensation des modernen Erfahrungenlustes* (Konstanz: Universitätsverlag Konstanz, 1982), pp. 15–37. See also Marquard, *In Defense of the Accidental: Philosophical Studies* (New York: Oxford University Press 1991). On Marquard, see Benjamin De Mesel, "Competence in Compensating for Incompetence: Odo Marquard on Philosophy," *Pluralist* 13.2 (Summer 2018), pp. 50–71.

84. Marquard, "Indicted and Unburdened Man in Eighteen Century Philosophy," p. 44.

85. Joseph Roth, *Antichrist*, trans. Moray Firth (New York: Viking Press, 1935).

86. "Empty words resound in our poor brain, and we no longer know exactly what these words signify." Ibid., p. 4.

87. "I soon perceived, however, that that which my tongue spoke was not only not the same as that which the other tongues spoke, but that all our thousand tongues were contradicting one another; and that even this contradiction was no immutable law, but that our tongues now agreed, now accused one another of lying—and this alternately from moment to moment." Ibid., p. 48.

88. "We have only given to our shadows the greater part of the short life which was granted to us. We have not engendered life but have lost it." Ibid., p. 24.

89. Roth, "Filme," p. 147.

90. The sentence in German: "Alles ständische und Stehende verdampft," is in the *Manifesto of the Communist Party*. Marshall Berman borrowed the sentence for his book *All That Is Solid Melts into Air: The Experience of Modernity* (New York: Simon & Schuster, 1982).

91. On the loss of experience, in a key different but parallel to Roth, see Walter Benjamin, "Experience and Poverty," trans. Rodney Livingstone, in *Walter Benjamin: Selected Writings, Volume 2, Part 2, 1931–1934*, eds. Michael W. Jennings, Howard Eiland, and Gary Smith (Cambridge, MA: Belknap Press of Harvard University Press, 1999), pp. 731–36.

92. Roth, *Antichrist*, p. 177.

INTERMEZZO THREE: SOMEWHERE, NOT TOO FAR

1. See, in particular, Lynn Spigel, *Make Room for TV: Television and the Family Ideal in Postwar America* (Chicago: University of Chicago Press, 1992) and *Welcome to the Dreamhouse: Popular Media and Postwar Suburbs* (Durham: Duke University Press, 2001).

2. Lynn Spigel, "The Suburban Home Companion: Television and the Neighborhood Ideal in Postwar America," in Beatriz Colomina, ed., *Sexuality and Space* (Princeton: Princeton Architectural Press, 1992), pp. 185–217.

3. On the social impact of television in postwar Italy, see the ethnographic research by Lidia De Rita, *I contadini e la televisione: Studio sull' influenza degli spettacoli televisivi in un gruppo di contadini lucani* (Bologna: Il Mulino, 1964); see also Peppino Ortoleva and Teresa Di Marco, *Luci del teleschermo* (Milan: Electa, 2004). On England, see Su Holmes, *Entertaining Television: BBC and Popular Television Culture in the 1950s* (Manchester: Manchester University Press, 2008); see also sections in John Corner, ed., *Popular Television in Britain: Studies in Cultural History* (London: BFI, 1991). For France, see suggestions in Monique Sauvage and Isabelle Veyrat-Masson, *Histoire de la télévision française de 1935 à nos jours* (Paris: Nouveau Monde, 2012).

4. The reference is to Erving Goffman, *The Presentation of Self in Everyday Life* (Edinburgh: University of Edinburgh, Social Sciences Research Centre, 1956). Spigel uses Goffman's contrast between front stage and back stage to underscore the creation of a retreat. Speaking of the "theatricalization of the home," she claims that it was instrumental "to draw a line between the public and the private sphere—or, in more theatrical terms, a line between the proscenium space where the spectacle took place and the reception space in which the audience observed the scene." Spigel, "The Suburban Home Companion," p. 199. My bet, in quoting Goffman, goes a little further: I suspect that television, with its representation of the everyday, offered a (un)conscious contribution to Goffman's understanding of the everyday as a stage for the (re)presentation of the self. Anyway, Spiegel speaks of the "theatricalization of the home" diffusely in her research, and she attaches to the concept a variety of functions.

5. Anthony Giddens, in *The Consequences of Modernity* (Stanford: Stanford University Press, 1990), speaks of "ontological security" as a sense of order and continuity in regard to an individual's experiences. He argues that this is reliant on people's ability to give meaning to their lives and to avoid a threatening sense of chaos and anxiety.

6. Guy Debord, *The Society of Spectacle*, trans. Donald Nicholson-Smith (New York: Zone, 1994).

7. Spigel, "The Suburban Home Companion," p. 205.

8. Ibid., p. 200.

9. A potential sequel of *Pleasantville* is *WandaVision*, a miniseries created in 2021 by Jac Shaeffer for the streaming service Disney+. The two main characters of the story live in a changing universe that recalls the different worlds that television created over the last decades.

CHAPTER FOUR: DIGITALLY NETWORKED BUBBLES

1. Nanna Verhoeff, *Mobile Screens: The Visual Regime of Navigation* (Amsterdam: Amsterdam University Press, 2012).

2. On the passage from a heterotopic regime to an hypertopic one, see Francesco Casetti, *The Lumiére Galaxy: Seven Key Words for the Cinema to Come* (New York: Columbia University Press, 2015), especially pp. 129–53.

3. On media and the pandemic, see Philipp Dominik Keidl, Laliv Melamed, Vinzenz Hediger, and Antonio Somaini, eds., *Pandemic Media: Preliminary Notes Toward an Inventory* (Lüneburg: Meson Press, 2020), and Roberto De Gaetano and Angela Maiello, eds., *Virale: Il presenta al tempo dell'epidemia* (Cosenza: Pellegrini Editore, 2020).

4. Shaun Moores, "The Doubling of Place: Electronic Media, Time-Space Arrangements and Social Relationships," in Nick Couldry and Anna McCarthy, eds., *MediaSpace: Place, Scale and Culture in a Media Age* (London: Routledge, 2004), pp. 21–37.

5. The reiterated protests against face covering not only raised a political question, but also echoed, often unconsciously, the difficulty of coping with a spatial contradiction. Among the vibrant protests against the obligations elicited by the pandemic, perceived as a unilateral limitation of our liberties, see Giorgio Agamben, "Lo stato d'eccezione provocato da un'emerganza immotivata," originally published as "L'invenzione di una epidemia," *Il Manifesto*, February 26, 2020, https://ilmanifesto.it/lo-stato-deccezione-provocato-da-unemergenza-immotivata.

6. Jakob von Uexküll, *A Foray into the Worlds of Animals and Humans: With a Theory of*

Meaning, trans. Joseph D. O'Neill (Minneapolis: University of Minnesota Press, 2010), pp. 43 and 53. The afterword by Geoffrey Winthrop-Young, "Bubbles and Webs: A Backdoor Stroll through the Readings of Uexküll," pp. 209–43, is illuminating.

7. See Michael Bull's analysis of the "mobile and privatized sphere of communication" that users of "mobile sound systems, mobile phones, and personal stereos" build around them while crossing the city. Michael Bull, "To Each Their Own Bubble: Mobile Spaces of Sound in the City," in Nick Couldry and Anne McCarthy, eds., *MediaSpace: Place, Scale and Culture in a Media Age* (London: Routledge, 2004), pp. 275–93

8. Peter Sloterdijk, *Spheres, Volume 1, Bubbles: Microspherology* (Los Angeles: Semiotext(e), 2011), *Spheres, Volume 2, Globes: Macrospherology* (Los Angeles: Semiotext(e), 2014), and *Spheres, Volume 3, Foams: Plural Spherology* (Los Angeles: Semiotext(e), 2016), all trans. Wieland Hoban.

9. For a tentative analysis of this kind of personal bubbles, see Casetti, *The Lumière Galaxy*, pp. 71–73.

10. According to Reddit users, the separation between the domestic space and the place from which to engage an online conversation or meeting is created at three levels. The first crucial element is the background: the place must have an appropriate appearance. A user asks the community: "Is it unprofessional to have a busy looking background on video calls?" Answers discuss the opportunity to have a very personalized or a neutral background; in both cases, it must not be confused with a casual slice of the domestic space. See kokomo318, "Is it unprofessional to have a 'busy' looking background on video calls?," https://www.reddit.com/r/workfromhome/comments/jieroc/is_it_unprofessional_to_have_a_busy_looking. The second crucial element is illumination. The spot for the online encounter requires an appropriate light, different from the everyday environment. A user opens a thread asking, "My home office has a lot of natural light on the side and back of my head. I got a ring light to try and balance the light from the front but my face looks so dark as the webcam auto balances the light. I'm wondering if you guys know of any better lighting solutions?" See revolvingneutron, "My home office has a lot of natural light . . . ," https://www.reddit.com/r/workfromhome/comments/ryqvlg/my_home_office_has_a_lot_of_natural_light_on_the. The third key element is the need for as specific look — a sort of photogenic look — through the use of appropriate makeup. A user asks for tips and shares tips in this post: "What makeup tips do you have for folks to look good on online/Zoom calls when working from home? Here's what worked for me." IndependentTerrible7, "WFH / looking good on Zoom

calls makeup tips?," https://www.reddit.com/r/muacjdiscussion/comments/qpxa2x /wfh_looking_good_on_zoom_calls_makeup_tips.

11. On Reddit, users share their discontent when an unplanned occurrence breaks or collides with the contexts imposed by digital bubbles. Here, the example of user gameld is quite telling. He reports a message that a friend of his wife received because her kids could slightly be heard during an online meeting: "My wife's friend got this email because her kids could briefly be heard laughing during a call. This somehow violates their 'quiet work area' policy." See gameld, " My wife's friend got this email . . . ," https://www.reddit.com/r/antiwork/comments/qxjo7c /my_wifes_friend_got_this_email_because_her_kids.

12. This mix of closeness and distance finds a dramatic echo in cases in which isolated individuals with suicidal thoughts look for support online, where someone distant can become crucially close. See Erin Taylor, "COVID-19 Anxiety Taking a Toll? There's a Subreddit for That," *The Verge*, March 25, 2020, https://www.theverge .com/2020/3/25/21193950/covid-19-coronavirus-anxiety-subreddit-community-support -group, or Allie Slemon, et al., "Reddit Users' Experiences of Suicidal Thoughts During the COVID-19 Pandemic: A Qualitative Analysis of r/Covid19_Support Posts," *Frontiers*, August 12, 2021, https://www.frontiersin.org/articles/10.3389/fpubh.2021.693153/full.

13. Karin Knorr Cetina, "The Synthetic Situation: Interactionism for a Global World," *Symbolic Interaction* 32.1 (2009), pp. 61–87.

14. Vittorio Gallese and Michele Guerra, *The Empathic Screen: Cinema and Neuroscience*, trans. Frances Anderson (Oxford: Oxford University Press, 2020), p. 24.

15. Giacomo Rizzolatti, Luciano Fadiga, Leonardo Fogassi, and Vittorio Gallese, "The Space around Us," *Science* 277 (1997), pp. 190–91; Claudio Brozzoli, Tamar R. Makin, Lucilla Cardinali, Nicholas P. Holmes, and Alessandro Farnè, "Peripersonal Space: A Multisensory Interface for Body-Object Interactions," in Micah M. Murray and Mark T. Wallace, eds., *The Neural Bases of Multisensory Processes* (Boca Raton: CRC Press, 2012), pp. 447–64; Eleonora Vagnoni and Matthew R. Longo, "Peripersonal Space: Its Functions, Plasticity, and Neural Basis," in Tony Cheng, Ophelia Deroy, and Charles Spence, eds., *Spatial Senses: Philosophy of Perception in an Age of Science* (New York: Routledge, 2019), pp. 199–225.

16. Rory J. Bufacchi and Gian Domenico Iannetti, "An Action Field Theory of Peripersonal Space," *Trends in Cognitive Sciences* 22.12 (December 2018).

17. Gallese and Guerra, *The Empathic Screen*, in particular the section "Positions,"

pp. 70–79, in which they recall—with references to Maurice Merleau-Ponty, among others—that our spatial orientation does not depend on fixed positions, but on contingent situations.

18. "The most intriguing finding, however, of this very interesting report is that some of these tonically discharging neurons continue to fire when, unknown to the monkey, the stimulus previously presented has been withdrawn, and the monkey 'believes' that it is still near its body. Space representation in the premotor cortex can be generated, therefore, not only as a consequence of an external stimulation but also internally on the basis of previous experience." Rizzolatti, Fadiga, Fogassi, and Gallese, "The Space around Us," p. 190.

19. Vittorio Gallese, "Embodied Simulation: From Neurons to Phenomenal Experience," *Phenomenology and the Cognitive Sciences*, 4 (2005), pp. 23–48.

20. Sofia Seinfeld, Tiare Feuchtner, Antonella Maselli, and Jörg Müller, "User Representations in Human-Computer Interaction," *Human-Computer Interaction* 36.5–6 (2021), pp. 400438.

21. Seinfeld et al. took into consideration other parameters, such as visual appearance, multimodal feedback, sense of agency, visual perspective, and body ownership. These parameters vary according to the different tools employed by the computer user and according to the User Representation.

22. On the processes of externalization, see Lambros Malafouris, *How Things Shape the Mind: A Theory of Material Engagement* (Cambridge, MA: MIT Press, 2012).

23. See Pietro Montani, "Techno-Aesthetics and Forms of the Imagination," in Simona Chiodo and Viola Schiaffonati, eds., *Italian Philosophy of Technology: Socio-Cultural, Legal, Scientific and Aesthetic Perspectives on Technology* (New York: Springer, 2021), pp. 247–61; Mark B. N. Hansen, *Feed-Forward: On the Future of the Twenty-First-Century Media* (Chicago: University of Chicago Press, 2014).

24. This extension of the idea of close-up helps to apply it to the images of the Phantasmagoria. When the magic lantern was moving away from the screen, the projected images became gigantic, imposing their presence on spectators.

25. Jean Epstein, "Magnification," trans. Stuart Liebman, in Richard Abel, ed., *French Film Theory and Criticism: 1907–1939, Volume 1, 1907–1929* (Princeton: Princeton University Press, 1988), pp. 235–40.

26. Ibid., p. 235.

27. Ibid., p. 239.

28. Ibid.

29. Ibid.

30. Ibid., pp. 239–40.

31. Hugo Münsterberg, *The Photoplay: A Psychological Study* (New York: Appleton, 1916).

32. Béla Balázs, *Visible Man, or the Culture of Film*, in *Béla Balázs: Early Film Theory: "Visible Man" and "The Spirit of Film*," ed. Erica Carter, trans. Rodney Livingstone (New York: Berghahn Books, 2010), pp. 1–90.

33. For a more recent approach to the questions elicited by the close-up in cinema, see Mary Ann Doane, "The Close-Up: Scale and Detail in the Cinema," *differences: A Journal of Feminist Cultural Studies* 14.3 (2003), pp. 89–111, and Doane, "Scale and the Negotiation of 'Real' and 'Unreal' Space in the Cinema," in Lúcia Nagib and Cecília Mello, eds., *Realism and the Audiovisual Media* (London: Palgrave Macmillan, 2009), pp. 63–81.

34. On the effects of split screen on our online conversations, see Malte Hagener, "Divided, Together, Apart: How Split Screen Became Our Everyday Reality," in Keidl, Melamed, Hediger, and Somaini, eds., *Pandemic Media*, pp. 33–40.

35. On the practices of excluding or including the environment in which participants in online conversations are located and in general on the ways of rendering the background, we can find useful remarks in Alberto Brodesco, "Questioni di sfondo: Come ci inquadriamo quando videochiamiamo," *Nazione Indiana*, June 2, 2020, www. nazioneindiana.com/2020/06/02/questioni-di-sfondo-come-ci-inquadriamo-quando -videochiamiamo and Brodesco, "Come ci inquadriamo quando videochiamiamo / 2: Sullo stendino," *Nazione Indiana*, October 21, 2020, www.nazioneindiana.com/2020/10/21 /come-ci-inquadriamo-quando-videochiamiamo-2-sullo-stendino.

36. Julian Hanich, *The Audience Effect: On the Collective Cinema Experience* (Edinburgh: Edinburgh University Press, 2018).

37. A Reddit user feels unprofessional when they must interrupt their zoom call because of their child and asks the community for advice. See Cherie Tseng, "Commentary: Is It Unprofessional When Your Child Interrupts Your Office Zoom Meeting?," *Channel News Asia*, December 22, 2021, https://www.channelnewsasia.com/commentary /children-interrupting-zoom-meetings-work-home-parents-2324541, via https://www .reddit.com/r/ChannelNewsAsia/comments/rlqo5p/commentary_is_it_unprofessional _when_your_child. On exiting from an online meeting, see Cetina, "The Synthetic Situation," pp. 61–87.

38. On the role of attention in a neoliberal society and in the media landscape, see Yves Citton, *The Ecology of Attention*, trans. Barnaby Norman (Cambridge: Polity, 2017), and Yves Citton and Estelle Doudet, eds., *Écologies de l'attention et archéologie des media* (Grenoble: UGA éditions, 2019). For a history of modern attention, see Jonathan Crary, *Suspensions of Perception: Attention, Spectacle, and Modern Culture* (Cambridge, MA: MIT Press, 1999).

39. "Enclosures are *molds*, distinct castings, but controls are a *modulation*, like a self-deforming cast that will continuously change from one moment to the other, or like a sieve whose mesh will transmute from point to point." Gilles Deleuze, "Postscript on the Societies of Control," *October* 59 (Winter 1992), p. 4.

40. On the combined processes of exteriorization and interiorization in a media environment, see the recent work by Pietro Montani, who provides a reconsideration of the "Material Engagement Theory" in the light of a theory of imagination. Pietro Montani, *Emozioni dell'intelligenza: Un percorso nel sensorio digitale* (Milan: Meltemi, 2020).

41. For a history of wearable media, see Errki Huhtamo, "Pockets of Plenty: An Archaeology of Mobile Media," in Martin Rieser, ed., *The Mobile Audience: Media Art and Mobile Technologies* (New York: Rodopi, 2011), pp. 23–38.

42. Paul Virilio, *Bunker Archeology*, trans. George Collins (New York: Princeton Architectural Press, 1994).

43. Jean Baudrillard, *The Ecstasy of Communication*, trans, by Bernard Schutze and Caroline Schutze (New York: Semiotext(e), 1988), p. 15.

44. "It is no longer the obscenity of the hidden, the repressed, the obscure, but of the visible, the all-too-visible, the more-visible-than-visible; it is the obscenity of that which no longer contains a secret, and it is entirely soluble in information and communication." Ibid., p. 22.

45. On spectators' isolation due to the dimming of the light, see the classical contribution of Eric Feldmann, "Considérations sur la situation du spectateur au cinéma," *Revue Internationale de Filmologie* 26 (1956), pp. 83–97.

46. Andrea Pinotti, "Towards An-Iconology: The Image as Environment," *Screen* 61.4 (Winter 2020), pp. 594–603.

47. On the anxieties tied to our being-there, see Martin Heidegger, *Being and Time*, trans. John Macquarrie and Edward Robinson (Oxford: Blackwell, 1962), pp. 228–35.

48. See Mark Zuckerberg's presentation, Meta, "The Metaverse and How We'll Build It Together — Connect 2021," *YouTube*, at https://www.youtube.com/watch?v=Uvufun6xer8&t=162s.

49. An unplanned intrusion into the digital bubble can cause a strong reaction from individuals who need to keep their digital context impersonal and stable. On Reddit, a woman shares her surprise at her husband's overreaction when she made herself visible during one of his meetings. "I was told this is one of the worst things I've done in this relationship, and that I sabotaged him and professionally embarrassed him, despite his thumbnail being so small and me being super far away. Am I the asshole for using the bathroom during his group's presentation?" See editedbysam, "AITA for walking behind boyfriend's computer during zoom presentation?," https://www.reddit.com/r/AmItheAsshole/comments/qof6hp/aita_for_walking_behind_boyfriends_computer. On the other hand, such intrusion can also create distress in the other participants of the online meeting—here, the case of an employee whose manager hosts his grandmother in business meetings: "At least, maybe twice a week, his grandmother comes up to him, gives him a big hug and starts waving at the camera. I get these things happen because working from home, but this has gotten to become a regular occurrence. I have started to get irritated, I find it EXTREMELY unprofessional and distracting to other employees. It also takes attention away from what we are currently talking about. In no scenario, if we were actually in office, would an employees grandmother be able to come and interrupt meetings to give their grandson a hug." See Infamous, "AITA if I were to confront an employee about his grandmother interrupting our zoom meetings," https://www.reddit.com/r/AmItheAsshole/comments/j7ffe9/aita_if_i_were_to_confront_an_employee_about_his.

50. It is worth noting that in all subreddits, there is a clear list of rules that each user must respect. These rules allow the community to maintain a protected environment and a certain conformity around its virtual dialogues. See, for example, the rules of the Subreddit r/covid19_support, a community "for people who need support in navigating the pandemic—advice on safe behaviour, support for difficult times, and resources for getting through. If you want to join the community, please message the moderators." See thatredditterapist, "Navigating COVID Support," https://www.reddit.com/r/COVID19_support/comments/i4jmwo/navigating_covid_support. The list covers three main areas. Tonality: be kind and reassuring; do not increase anxiety; offer support, not opinions; no rants, shaming, or complaining about others' behavior, (be civil). Type of content: only post topics that are appropriate to this subreddit; do not ask for donations; do not create posts regarding the wearing, purchasing or making of masks. Code of conduct: do not ask users to contact you off reddit, do not present oversensationalised media stories as "fact."

51. Peter Sloterdijk offers a brilliant characterization of the cell-like space in his description of the one-room apartment, Peter Sloterdijk is included in the narrative *Spheres, Volume 3, Foams,* pp. 529–42.

52. Epstein, "Magnification," p. 239. For the original text, see *Bonjour Cinéma* (Paris: Éditions de la Sirène, 1921), p. 106.

53. In a post from the Subreddit r/zoom a user asks the community "Anybody else find themselves only watching themselves?" In the post, the feeling of being on Zoom calls is compared with checking themself in a mirror, where the only possible area of action is to control facial expressions, adjust your own appearance. See made_up_name1, "Anybody else find themselves only watching themselves," https://www.reddit.com/r/Zoom/comments/lsosy8/anybody_else_find_themselves_only_watching. For a sociopsychological consideration of self-monitoring in conversations, see Mark Snyder, "Self-Monitoring of Expressive Behavior," *Journal of Personality and Social Psychology* 30.4 (1974), pp. 526–37.

54. The very fact that online conversations and meetings often elicit a state of numbness in which participants are unable to feel pleasure finds testimony is the following subreddit thread: projectedprotected, "Isolation & lack of emotions | an unavoidable consequence?," https://www.reddit.com/r/COVID19_support/comments/sknk3e /isolation_lack_of_emotions_an_unavoidable.

55. Yvonne Zimmermann detects with great precision the entanglement tied to the process of self-monitoring in communication platforms such as Zoom. In particular, she underscores how in the grid, the vignette of the user is an object simultaneously seen by the user and by the others: "Am I a virtual *me* or a virtual *you*? If the person I see on screen is *me*, it is suggested that it is me who looks at an image of myself on screen. I am the subject that looks at me — and at others. If the person I see on screen is *you*, the perspective changes. For this suggests that it is the others who look at an image of myself on screen. I am the object of *their* look — while I am at the same time the object of *my* look." Yvonne Zimmermann, "Videoconferencing and the Uncanny Encounter with Oneself: Self-Reflexivity as Self-Monitoring 2.0," in Keidl, Melamed, Hediger, and Somaini, eds., *Pandemic Media,* p. 100.

56. In the subreddit r/covidsupport we find countless posts about fears and anxieties generated by the isolation of digital bubbles can be found. A symptomatic example is the following: "I really just want to go to sleep for a year or two and wake up with this being over. I cannot cope to live in a world where there is no joy, no plans to

look forward to, no dating, no grabbing drinks with friends, no visiting older relatives, no gym classes, no going to the cinema, no going to restaurants. There is only fear. Fear of the economy. Fear of relatives dying. Fear of losing friends. Fear of never finding a partner due to not being able to date (also going through a messy break up right now). Fear of being alone. Fear of populist leaders taking over. Fear of the EU collapsing. Fear of not seeing my sister for a long long time due to her being abroad. How the fuck can one stay positive in times like these? These is nothing to be positive about? Luckily, I do have my highs and lows. I'm reading a lot of fiction, which is a great way to escape." See everythingzalright, "Has anyone's mental health been complete shit?," https://www.reddit.com/r/COVID19_support/comments/g6g3pj/has_anyones_mental_health_been_complete_shit.

57. Neta Alexander, "Rage against the Machine: Buffering, Noise, and Perpetual Anxiety in the Age of Connected Viewing," *Cinema Journal* 56.2 (2017), pp. 1–24.

58. Shane Denson, *Discorrelated Images* (Durham: Duke University Press, 2020). The idea of a gap between digital media and users' perception was firstly introduced by Hansen in *Feed-Forward*: according to him, this gap requires a "supplementary layer of mediation" to reconnect users with the "sensory basis for experience" (p. 43).

59. See Anthony Vidler, *Warped Space: Art, Architecture, and Anxiety in Modern Culture* (Cambridge, MA: MIT Press, 2000).

60. For Foucault, the cell is one of the constitutive elements of the Panopticon, and more generally, it is one of the outcomes of the spatial distribution that discipline promotes. See Michel Foucault, *Discipline and Punish: The Birth of the Prison*, trans. Alan Sheridan (New York: Vintage Books, 1995), pp. 200–209, where Foucault describes the Panopticon, and p. 221, where Foucault states that "the disciplinary pyramid constituted the small cell of power within which the separation, coordination and supervision of tasks was imposed and made efficient."

INTERMEZZO FOUR: FRAMES AND FOLDS

1. On Warhol's *Screen Tests*, see Callie Angell, *Andy Warhol Screen Tests: The Films of Andy Warhol. Catalogue raisonné, Volume 1* (New York: Harry N. Abrams, 2006).

2. "In the case of the natural entity, boundaries are simply the site of continuing exosmosis and endosmosis with everything external; for the work of art they are the absolute ending which exercises indifference towards and defense against the exterior and a unifying integration with respect to the interior in a single act. What the frame

achieves for the work of art is to symbolize and strengthen this double function of its boundaries." Georg Simmel, "The Picture Frame: An Aesthetic Study," *Theory, Culture, and Society* 11.1 (1994), p. 12.

3. André Bazin exemplifiesd this duality by speaking of the cinematic frame either as a *cadre* or as a *cache*. See *What Is Cinema?: Essays, Volume 1*, trans. Hugh Gray (Berkeley: University of California Press, 1967), in particular, the essays "Theater and Cinema, pp. 76–124, and "Painting and Cinema," pp. 164–72.

4. Guy Debord, *The Society of the Spectacle*, trans. Donald Nicholson Smith (New York: Zone Books, 1995), p. 20.

5. "Inflection is the ideal genetic element of the variable curve or fold. Inflection is the authentic atom, the elastic point." Gilles Deleuze, *The Fold: Leibnitz and the Baroque*, trans. Tom Conley (London: Athlone, 1993), p. 14.

CHAPTER FIVE: STRATEGIES OF MITIGATION

1. Marshall McLuhan, *Understanding Media: The Extension of Man* (New York: McGrow Hill, 1964).

2. Edgar Morin states: "[Lumière] had *understood that a primal curiosity was directed to the reflection of reality*. That people above all else marveled at seeing anew that which did not fill them with wonder: their houses, their faces, the settings of their familiar lives." Yet Morin adds: "*That is, what attracted the first crowds was not an exit from a factory, a train entering a station (it would have been sufficient to go to the station or the factory), but an image of a train, an image of workers leaving a factory. It was not for the real but for the image of the real that people flocked to the doors of the Salon Indien*." Edgar Morin, *The Cinema, or The Imaginary Man*, trans. Lorraine Mortimer (Minneapolis: University of Minnesota Press, 2005), p. 14 (italics in the original).

3. "Le cinéma est justement un acheminement vers cette suppression de l'art qui dépasse l'art, étant la vie.... Ce n'est plus un film. C'est la vérité naturelle." Louis Delluc, "La beauté du cinéma," (1917), in *Cinéma et cie*, vol. 2.1 of *Écrits cinématographiques*, ed. Pierre Lherminier (Paris: Cinémathèque Française, 1986), p. 31.

4. "C'est de la vie pure." Louis Delluc, "La mauvaise Étoile," in *Cinéma et cie*, p. 35.

5. Among the many, it is worth of noting the French director Marcel L'Herbier: unlike the immaterial arts, "the goal of cinema is, on the contrary, to transcribe as faithfully, as verily as possible, without transposition or stylization, and by the means of exactitude which has its own specific characteristics, the whole truth phenomenon."

Marcel L'Herbier, "Hermès ou le silence," *Le Film*, nos. 110–111, April 29, 1918, p. 9 (translation mine).

6. Walter Serner, "Cinema and Visual Pleasure," in Anton Kaes, Nicholas Baer, and Michael Cowan, eds, *The Promise of Cinema: German Film Theory, 1907–1933* (Oakland: University of California Press, 2016), pp. 41–45.

7. A philosophical and historical reconstruction of the desire to be the spectator of deadly events is Hans Blumenberg, *Shipwreck with Spectator: Paradigm of a Metaphor for Existence*, trans. Steven Rendall (Cambridge, MA: MIT Press, 1997).

8. Édouard Poulain, *Contre le cinéma, école du vice et du crime: Pour le cinéma, école d'éducation, moralisation et vulgarisation* (Besançon: Imprimerie de l'Est, 1917). On Poulain and the cultural context in which he writes, see Mélisande Leventopoulos, *Les catholiques et le cinéma* (Rennes: Presses Universitaires de Rennes, 2014), pp. 29–55.

9. A good example of Poulain's argument is that: "Police, criminal, licentious and demoralizing films, with the help of evocative posters, pave the way to future burglars, future rascals, future bandits." Hence the need of a moral reaction and action by the public authorities: "To react and protest against such moral poisoning is to serve our country." Ibid., pp. 29 and 31. In a relevant, though almost forgotten essay published in 1953, Edgar Morin discusses Poulain's book and implicitly accuses him of adopting "the magical idea that the representation entails the act." See Edgar Morin, "Le problème des effets dangereux du cinéma," *Revue internationale de filmologie*, nos. 14–15 (July–December 1953), p. 218, recently republished in Edgar Morin, *Le cinéma: Un art de la complexité*, ed. Monique Peyrière and Chiara Simonigh (Paris: Nouveau Monde, 2018), pp. 171–88.

10. For Italy, see, among others, the priest Mario Barbera, "Cinematografo e moralità pubblica," *Civiltà Cattolica* 4.1546, November 13, 1914, pp. 421–40, the psychiatrists Umberto Masini and Giuseppe Vidoni, "Il cinematografo nel campo delle malattie mentali e della criminalità: Appunti," *Archivio di Antropologia Criminale, Psichiatria e Medicina Legale* 26.5–6 (1915), and the prosecutor Pietro Pesce-Maineri, *I pericoli sociali del cinematografo* (Turin–Genoa: Lattes, 1922). For France, see the criminologist Maurice Rouvroy, "Le cinéma public et l'enfance: Étude psycho-criminologique," *Revue Internationale de l'enfant* 5.29 (May 1928). For Germany, in the framework of the so-called *Kinodebatte*, see Albert Hellwig, *Schundfilms: Ihr Wesen, ihre Gefahren und ihre Bekämpfung* (Halle an der Saale: Buchhandlung des Waisenhauses, 1911), The *Kinodebatte* is well documented in Kaes, Baer, and Cowan, eds. *The Promise of Cinema*.

11. "It is typical of these left-wing French intellectuals—exactly as it is of their

Russian counterparts, too—that their positive function derives entirely from a feeling of obligation, not to the revolution, but to traditional culture." Walter Benjamin, "Surrealism: The Last Snapshot of the European Intelligentsia," trans. Edmund Jephcott, in *Walter Benjamin: Selected Writings, Volume 2, Part 1, 1927–1930*, eds. Michael W. Jennings, Howard Eiland, and Gary Smith (Cambridge, MA: Belknap Press of Harvard University Press, 1999), p. 213.

12. This is precisely what the influential French literary critic Paul Souday asked in a celebrated conflict with his colleague Émile Wuillermoz. The polemical exchange between the two critics is collected and commented in Pascal-Manuel Heu, *Le temps du cinéma: Émile Wuillermoz, pére de la critique cinématographique, 1910–1930* (Paris: L'Harmattan, 2003).

13. Siegfried Kracauer, *Theory of Film: The Redemption of Physical Reality* (New York: Oxford University Press, 1960). On the genesis of the book, see Miriam Hansen, "'With Skin and Hair': Kracauer's *Theory of Film*, Marseille 1940," *Critical Inquiry* 19.3 (1993), pp. 437–69, and her excellent introduction to the reprint of *Theory of Film* (Princeton: Princeton University Press, 1997), pp. vii–xlvi.

14. Kracauer, *Theory of Film*, p. 305.

15. "The mass of salaried employees differ from the worker proletariat in that they are spiritually homeless." Siegfried Kracauer, *The Salaried Masses: Duty and Distraction in Weimar Germany*, trans. Quintin Hoare (London: Verso, 1998), p. 88.

16. Ibid.

17. "In Berlin, special shelters for the homeless are erected. Shelters in the literal sense are those gigantic taverns in which, as one garrulous fellow once put it in a Berlin evening paper, 'for not much money you can get a breath of the wide world.'" Ibid., p. 91. Kracauer would return on the metaphor of shelter for the homeless both in *Theory of Film* and in his American writings, where the two concepts take on greater latitude. While "homeless" connotes the modern man who lives "with a shadowy awareness of things in their fullness" (*Theory of Film*, p. 291), "shelter" now applies to a vast array of dispositifs, including art: "Thus Art is assigned the task of providing a shelter for all those in need of a roof above their heads. Improbable as it is that the increasing talk about poetry should reflect an increasing interest in it, it certainly gives the people the pleasant illusion that there is something somewhere which can be believed in if one has the gift of believing. The idolatry for art does, for a moment, away with the fear of the vacuum." Siegfried Kracauer, "Art Today: A Proposal," in *Siegfried Kracauer's American Writings: Essays on Film*

and Popular Culture, eds. Johannes von Moltke and Kristy Rawson (Berkeley: University of California Press, 2012), p. 117.

18. The claim is both in *The Salaried Masses* and in his famous essay "Cult of Distraction: On Berlin Picture Palaces." See, for example: "Like hotel lobbies, [picture palaces] are shrines to the cultivation of pleasure; their glamour aims at edification." Siegfried Kracauer, "Cult of Distraction: On Berlin Picture Palaces," in *The Mass Ornament: Weimar Essays*, ed. and trans. Thomas Y. Levin (Cambridge, MA: Harvard University Press, 1995), p. 323.

19. Kracauer, *The Salaried Masses*, pp. 91–92.

20. The sentence spectacularly ends Kracauer's essay "Cult of Distraction," p. 328. According to Kracauer, this closeness to the truth principally affects the proletarian masses.

21. *Affiches, annonces et avis divers, ou Journal Général de France*, no. 350, Sunday, December 16, 1792, p. 5189.

22. "What is decisive today is . . . the necessity, inherent in the system, of never releasing its grip on the consumer, of not for a moment allowing him or her to suspect that resistance is possible. This principle requires that while all needs should be presented to individuals as capable of fulfillment by the culture industry, they should be so set up in advance that individuals experience themselves through their needs only as eternal consumers, as the culture industry's object." Max Horkheimer and Theodor W. Adorno, *Dialectic of Enlightenment: Philosophical fragments*, ed. Gunzelin Schmid Noerr, trans. Edmund Jephcott (Stanford: Stanford University Press, 2002.), p. 113.

23. Michel Foucault, *Discipline and Punish: The Birth of the Prison*, trans. Alan Sheridan (New York: Random House, 1975), p. 148.

24. Ibid., p. 141.

25. According to Foucault, this is the process that transforms a space into an "analytical" entity. "Disciplinary space tends to be divided into as many sections as there are bodies or elements to be distributed." Ibid., p. 143.

26. Jean-Baptiste Chaussard, *Le nouveau diable boiteux: Tableau philosophique et moral de Paris, au commencement du XIXe siècle*, 2 vols. (Paris: Barba, 1803), vol. 2, p. 173.

27. Foucault, *Discipline and Punish*, pp. 143–44.

28. See ibid., in particular, pp. 145–46.

29. Ibid., p. 167.

30. National Council of Public Morals, Cinema Commission of Inquiry, *The Cinema:*

Its Present Position and Future Possibilities (London: Williams and Norgate, 1917). The report is based on more than fifty interviews with educators, policemen, judges, trade representatives, parents, and children. The interviews are included in the publication as part 2, whose pages are numbered in arabic, while the report's pages are numbered in roman. The report praises both the cinema for its "intensely realistic" and largely informative images (p. lxviii) and the film theater for providing the entertainment and relief that other public spaces are unable to offer, in addition of keeping adolescents out of streets (p. xlv). At the same time, it identifies some problems that had to be fixed and offers a number of recommendations to public authorities and public opinion.

31. Ibid., pp. xxviii–xxix.

32. The report complained of the risk of the "permanent aggravation of defective eyesight." Ibid., p. lxxv.

33. Ibid., p. lxxvi.

34. An effect of the cinema is "to lower the standard of reverence for women, and familiarising the minds of our young people with loose ideas of the relations of the sexes." Ibid., p. xxx.

35. "The evidence before us shows that there is a need for a stricter censorship than has been exercised in the past." Ibid.

36. Ibid., p. 235.

37. Indeed, the report's recommendations can be seen as part of widespread "practices of confinement"—confinement of the audience, of the images, of the cinema itself—that undergirded the full institutionalization of filmgoers as a "good" public, of filmgoing as a "good" act, and of cinema as a "good" object.

38. For the dangers tied to filmgoing, see Gary D. Rhodes, *The Perils of Moviegoing in America, 1896–1950* (New York: Continuum, 2012); for the undisciplined status of audiences, see Caetlin Benson-Allott, *The Stuff of Spectatorship: Material Cultures of Film and Television* (Berkeley: University of California Press, 2021); for unbearable forms of representation on screen, see Nicholas Baer, Maggie Hennefeld, Laura Horak, and Gunnar Iversen, eds., *Unwatchable* (New Brunswick: Rutgers University Press, 2019).

39. See the "Instructive Program" published by Robertson around 1800 as promotional leaflet, now reproduced in Laurent Mannoni, Donata Pesenti Campagnoni, and David Robinson, *Light and Movement: Incunabula of the Motion Picture, 1420–1896* (Pordenone: Le giornate del cinema muto / Cinémathèque Francaise-Musée du Cinéma / Museo Nazionale del Cinema, 1995), pp. 118–19.

40. We can find a summary of Filidor's address in 1792 either in "La Phantasmagorie: Description d'un spectacle curieux, nouveau et instructif," *La feuille villageoise* 3.22, February 28, 1793, pp. 489–510, or in Chaussard, *Le nouveau diable boiteux*, pp. 179–83.

41. Roberto Esposito, *Immunitas: The Protection and Negation of Life*, trans. Zakiya Hanafi (London: Wiley, 2011).

42. "In experiencing the rows of calves' heads or the litter of tortured human bodies in the films made of the Nazi concentration camps, we redeem horror from its invisibility behind the veils of panic and imagination." Kracauer, *Theory of Film*, p. 306

43. Walter Benjamin, "The Work of Art in the Age of Its Technological Reproducibility: Second Version," trans. Edmund Jephcott and Harry Zohn, in *Walter Benjamin: Selected Writings, Volume 3, 1935–1938*, eds. Howard Eiland and Michael W. Jennings (Cambridge, MA: Belknap Press of Harvard University Press, 2003), p. 118

44. Ibid.

45. Ibid., pp. 130–31.

46. Marshall McLuhan, *Understanding Media: The Extension of Man* (New York: McGraw-Hill, 1964).

47. Ibid., p. 64.

48. Ibid.

49. Ibid., p. 66.

50. See Michel Foucault, "Governmentality," in *Power*, ed. James D. Faubion, trans. Robert Hurley et al. (New York: New Press, 2000), pp. 201–22.

51. See Jonathan Crary, "Géricault, the Panorama, and Sites of Reality in the Early Nineteenth Century," *Grey Room*, no. 9 (Autumn 2002), pp. 5–25.

52. "Laughs follow silence and boos alternate with applauses, according to the grace that ghosts put in their roles, or according to the ideas that they raise." Chaussard, *Le nouveau biable boiteux*, p. 187.

53. "Collective laughter is one such preemptive and healing outbreak of mass psychosis." Benjamin, "The Work of Art in the Age of Its Technological Reproducibility," p. 118.

54. "On the one hand, film is the celebration of movement, the proof of its superiority over all the other media; on the other hand, however, it places its audience in a state of unparalleled state of physical and mental immobility." Boris Groys, "Iconoclasm as an Artistic Device: Iconoclastic Strategies in Film," in *Art Power* (Cambridge, MA: MIT Press, 2008), p. 71.

55. Jonathan Crary, *24/7: Late Capitalism and the End of Sleep* (London: Verso, 2013).

56. About the current domination of the logic of exchange over the logic of production in the art world, see David Joselit, *After Art* (Princeton: Princeton University Press, 2012).

57. For the passage from diffusion to integration, see Guy Debord, *Comments on the Society of Spectacle*, trans. Malcol Imrie (London: Verso, 2011) and Crary, *24/7*, pp. 72–74.

58. Sigmund Freud, *Beyond the Pleasure Principle*, trans. James Strachey (New York: Liveright, 1950), p. 18.

59. Ibid., p. 21.

60. Walter Benjamin, "On Some Motifs in Baudelaire," trans. Harry Zohn, in *Walter Benjamin: Selected Writings, Volume 4, 1938–1940*, ed. Marcus Bullock et al. (Cambridge, MA: Belknap Press of Harvard University Press, 2002), pp. 313–55.

61. Wolfgang Schivelbusch, *The Railway Journey: The Industrialization of Time and Space in the Nineteenth Century* (Berkeley: University of California Press, 1986).

62. See Gilles Deleuze, "Postscript on the Societies of Control," *October* 59 (Winter 1992), pp. 3–7.

63. On the flexibility of Freud's shield, see Catherine Malabou, "Plasticity and Elasticity in Freud's *Beyond the Pleasure Principle*," *Diacritics* 37.4 (Winter 2007), pp. 78–85. On the concept of plasticity, see Catherine Malabou, *Plasticity at the Dusk of Writing: Dialectic, Destruction, Deconstruction* (New York: Columbia University Press, 2010).

64. Freud, *Beyond the Pleasure Principle*, p. 18.

EPILOGUE: PROTECTION, OVERPROTECTION, AND THE FORCE OF SCREENED IMAGES

1. See the accurate account and interpretation of these experiments in Federica Cavaletti and Giancarlo Grossi, "Take a Deep Breath: Virtual Reality and Real Anxiety," in Luca Malavasi and Sara Tongiani, eds., *Technophobia and Technophilia in the Media, Art, and Visual Culture* (Canterano: Aracne, 2020), pp. 103–18.

2. Michele Cometa, *Perché le storie ci aiutano a vivere* (Milan: Cortina, 2017).

3. See Wendy Brown, *Walled States, Waning Sovereignty* (New York: Zone Books, 2010).

4. On the expansion of visuality at the end of eighteenth century, with a focus on the English context, see see James Chandler and Kevin Gilmartin, "Introduction: Engaging the *Eidometropolis*," in James Chandler and Kevin Gilmartin, eds., *Romantic Metropolis: The Urban Scene of British Culture, 1780–1840* (Cambridge: Cambridge University Press,

2005), in particular, pp. 8–11. See also Jonathan Crary, "Géricault, the Panorama, and Sites of Reality in the Early Nineteenth Century," *Grey Room*, no. 9 (Autumn 2002), pp. 5–25.

5. Luciano Floridi, ed., *The Onlife Manifesto: Being Human in a Hyperconnected Era* (Heidelberg: Springer Open, 2015).

6. Georges Duhamel, *America the Menace: Scenes from the Life of the Future*, trans. Charles Miner Thompson (Boston: Houghton Mifflin, 1931). Originally, *Scènes de la vie future* (Paris: Mercure de France, 1930).

7. Ibid., p. 34. The description of film continues: "It is a spectacle that demands no effort, that does not imply any sequence of ideas, that raises no question, that evokes no deep feeling, that lights no light in the depths of any heart, that excites no hope, if not the ridiculous one of someday becoming a 'star' at Los Angeles."

8. "For great men *were* being murdered. All those works which from our youth we have stammered with our hearts rather than with our lips, all those sublime songs which at the age of passionate enthusiasms were our daily bread, our study, and our glory, all thoughts which stood for the flesh and blood of our masters, were dismembered, hacked to pieces, and mutilated." Ibid., p. 30.

9. Speaking of Duhamel, Benjamin says: "How difficult to bear is the strained uprightness, the forced animation and sincerity of the Protestant method, dictated by embarrassment and linguistic ignorance, of placing things in some kind of symbolic illumination." Walter Benjamin, "Surrealism: The Last Snapshot of the European Intelligentsia," trans. Edmund Jephcott, in *Walter Benjamin: Selected Writings, Volume 2, Part 1, 1927–1930*, eds. Michael W. Jennings, Howard Eiland, and Gary Smith (Cambridge, MA: Belknap Press of Harvard University Press, 1999), p. 213.

10. Duhamel, *America the Menace*, pp. 24 and 25.

11. Ibid., p. 28.

12. Ibid., p. 27.

13. According to Duhamel, advertising is "a tremendous business of coercion and brutalization." Ibid., p. 130.

14. Giorgio Agamben, "L'invenzione di un'epidemia." *Quodlibet*, February 26, 2020, https://www.quodlibet.it/giorgio-agamben-l-invenzione-di-un-epidemia, originally published as "Lo stato d'eccezione provocato da un'emergenza immotivata,' *Il Manifesto*, February 26, 2020. About the state of exception, see Agamben's extensive research in *State of Exception*, trans. Kevin Attell (Chicago: University of Chicago Press, 2005).

15. See Droid2Win, "Isolation and lack of a life is sending me into a depres-

sion spiral," https://www.reddit.com/r/COVID19_support/comments/ljxvlw
/isolation_and_lack_of_a_life_is_sending_me_into_a.

16. See Plato, *Phaedrus*. The term and its former context are the object of a celebrated text by Jacques Derrida, "Plato's Pharmacy," in *Dissemination*, trans. Barbara Johnson (Chicago: University of Chicago Press, 1981), pp. 63–171.

17. Jacques Derrida, "Autoimmunity: Real and Symbolic Suicide," in Giovanna Borradori, ed., *Philosophy in a Time of Terror: Dialogues with Jürgen Habermas and Jacques Derrida* (Chicago: University of Chicago Press, 2003), pp. 85–136.

18. In a endnote, Derrida explains this "interiority" of the terror: "I underscored 'terrifying' in the above in order simply to suggest a hypothesis: since we are speaking here of terrorism and, thus, of terror, the most irreducible source of absolute terror, the one that, by definition, finds itself most defenseless before the worst threat would be the one that comes from 'within,' from this zone where the worst 'outside' lives with or within 'me' My vulnerability is thus, by definition and by structure, by situation, without limit." Derrida, "Autoimmunity," p. 188.

19. Donna J. Haraway, *How Like a Leaf: An interview with Thyrza Goodeve* (London: Routledge, 2000).

20. Roberto Esposito, *Immunitas: The Protection and Negation of Life* (London: Wiley, 2011); Esposito, *Terms of the Political: Community, Immunity, Biopolitics*, trans. Rhiannon Noel Welch (New York: Fordham University Press, 2013).

21. For an application of Derrida's argument to the world of media, see, among others, Francesco Vitale, *La farmacia di Godard* (Naples: Orthotes, 2021).

22. Vilém Flusser, *Into the Universe of Technical Images*, trans. Nancy Ann Roth (Minneapolis: University of Minnesota Press, 2011), in particular pp. 5–10.

23. Gary Tomlinson, *Culture and the Course of Human Evolution* (Chicago: University of Chicago Press, 2018)

24. Pietro Montani, *Technological Destinies of the Imagination* (Milan: Mimesis International, 2022).

25. Jacques Rancière, "Aesthetic Separation, Aesthetic Community," in *The Emancipated Spectator* (London: Verso, 2011), pp. 51–82.

26. Sherry Turkle, *Alone Together: Why We Expect More from Technology and Less from Each Other* (New York: Basic Books, 2011).

27. Denson writes: "As a technological artifact, the screen remains a practico-inert object, storing the labor of factory workers and engineers while embodying a dumb

physicality: it sits there, inert on my desk or in my lap, a material barrier between me and my interlocutors. But in operation, the screen instantiates a new temporality that transcends its physical inertia. Its protentional, predictive processes endow it with greater agency as its anticipatory dimensions intertwine with my own being-towards-the-future" Shane Denson, "'Thus isolation is a project': Notes toward a Phenomenology of Screen-Mediated Life," in Philipp Dominik Keidl, Laliv Melamed, Vinzenz Hediger, and Antonio Somaini, eds., *Pandemic Media: Preliminary Notes Toward an Inventory* (Lüneburg: Meson Press, 2020), p. 320.

28. Emmanuel Alloa, *Looking through Images: A Phenomenology of Visual Media*, trans. Nils F. Schott (New York: Columbia University Press, 2021).

29. Mary Ann Doane, "The Indexical and the Concept of Medium Specificity," *differences: A Journal of Feminist Cultural Studies* 18.1 (2007), pp. 128–52.

30. The concept of "precession," originally suggested by Maurice Merleau Ponty, has been expansively explored by Mauro Carbone in *The Flesh of Images: Merleau-Ponty between Painting and Cinema*, trans. Marta Nijhuis (Albany: State University of New York Press, 2015), pp. 56–61. See also the more recent reconsideration of the concept in Mauro Carbone, "Falling Man: The Time of Trauma, the Time of (Certain) Images," *Research in Phenomenology* 47.2 (June 2017), pp. 190–203, in which the images of falling men from the Twin Towers appears able to anticipate the work of mourning required by 9/11. See also the readaptation of the concept in Jean Baudrillard, *Simulations*, trans. Paul Foss, Paul Patton, and Philip Beitchman (New York: Semiotext(e), 1983). The idea of "premediation" is proposed in Richard Grusin, *Premediation: Affect and Mediality after 9/11* (New York: Palgrave Macmillan, 2010).

31. The epigraph reads: "Cinema replaces our gaze with a world in harmony with our desires"; in French, "Le cinéma substitue à notre regard un monde qui s'accorde à nos désirs." Godard attributes incorrectly the sentence to Andre Bazin, when it is a sentence by the French critic Michel Mourlet in his essay "Sur un art ignoré," published by *Cahers du cinema* in 1959, then collected in a volume with the same title published by La Table Ronde, 1965.

32. Flusser, *Into the Universe of Technical Images*.

33. Mark B. N. Hansen, *Feed-Forward: On the Future of Twenty-first-Century Media* (Chicago: University of Chicago Press, 2015); Shane Denson, *Discorrelated Images* (Durham: Duke University Press, 2020).

34. Fausto Maria Martini, "The Death of the Word," in Francesco Casetti, Silvio

Alovisio, and Luca Mazzei, eds., *Early Film Theories in Italy, 1896–1922* (Amsterdam: Amsterdam University Press, 2017), pp. 75–79.

35. Ibid., p. 76.

36. Ibid., p. 78.

37. Jean Epstein, "The Senses 1 (b)," trans. Tom Milne, in Richard Abel, ed., *French Film Theory and Criticism: 1907–1939, Volume 1, 1907–1929* (Princeton: Princeton University Press, 1993), p. 244. In the same essay, there is the celebrated description of the camera as a mechanical brain: "The Bell and Howell is a metal brain, standardized, manufactured, marketed in thousands of copies, which transforms the world outside it into art. The Bell and Howell is an artist, and only behind it are there other artists: director and cameraman. A sensibility can at last be bought, available commercially and subject to import duties like coffee or Oriental carpets." Ibid., pp. 244–45.

Bibliography

This bibliography includes only references that are directly tied to the main argument that this book develops. Archival material is detailed in the endnotes.

Acland, Charles, and Haidee Wasson, eds. *Useful Cinema.* Durham: Duke University Press, 2011.

Agamben, Giorgio. "L'invenzione di un'epidemia," *Quodlibet,* February 26, 2020, https://www.quodlibet.it/giorgio-agamben-l-invenzione-di-un-epidemia. Originally published as "Lo stato d'eccezione provocato da un'emerganza immotivata." *Il Manifesto,* February 26, 2020, https://ilmanifesto.it/lo-stato-deccezione-provocato-da-unemergenza-immotivata.

———. *State of Exception.* Translated by Kevin Attell. Chicago: University of Chicago Press, 2005.

Alexander, Neta. "Rage against the Machine: Buffering, Noise, and Perpetual Anxiety in the Age of Connected Viewing." *Cinema Journal* 56.2 (2017), pp. 1–24, https://doi.org/10.1353/cj.2017.0000.

Alloa, Emmanuel. *Looking through Images: A Phenomenology of Visual Media.* Translated by Nils F. Schott. New York: Columbia University Press, 2021.

Ameri, Amir H.. "The Architecture of the Illusive Distance." *Screen* 54.4 (Winter 2013), pp. 439–62, https://doi.org/10.1093/screen/hjto38.

Andriopoulos, Stefan. *Ghostly Apparitions: German Idealism, the Gothic Novel, and Optical Media.* New York: Zone Books, 2013.

Angell, Callie. *Andy Warhol Screen Tests: The Films of Andy Warhol. Catalogue raisonné, Volume 1.* New York: Harry N. Abrams, 2006.

Avezzù, Giorgio. "The Deep Time of the Screen, and Its Forgotten Etymology." *Journal of Aesthetics and Culture* 11.1 (2019), pp. 1–15, https://doi.org/10.1093/screen/hjt038.

Baacke, Rolf Peter. *Lichtspielhausarchitektur in Deutschland: Von der Schaubude bis zum Kinopalast.* Berlin: Fröhlich & Kaufmann, 1982.

Baer, Nicholas, Maggie Hennefeld, Laura Horak, and Gunnar Iversen, eds. *Unwatchable.* New Brumswick: Rutgers University Press, 2019.

Balázs, Béla. *Visible Man, or the Culture of Film.* In *Béla Balázs: Early Film Theory: "Visible Man" and "The Spirit of Film."* Edited by Erica Carter. Translated by Rodney Livingstone, pp. 1–90. New York: Berghahn Books, 2010

Balzer, Richard. *Peepshows: A Visual History.* New York: Harry N. Abrams, 1998.

Barthes, Roland. "Leaving the Movie Theater." In *The Rustle of Language.* Translated by Richard Howard, pp. 345–49. Berkeley: University of California Press, 1986.

Baudrillard, Jean. *The Ecstasy of Communication.* Translated by Bernard Schutze and Caroline Schutze. New York: Semiotext(e), 1988.

_____. *Simulations.* Translated by Paul Foss, Paul Patton, and Philip Beitchman. New York: Semiotext(e), 1983.

Baudry, Jean-Louis. "The Apparatus: Metapsychological Approaches to the Impression of Reality in Cinema." In Philip Rosen, ed., *Narrative, Apparatus, Ideology*, pp. 299–318. New York: Columbia University Press, 1986.

Bazin, André. *What Is Cinema?* Translated by Hugh Gray, 2 vols. Berkeley: University of California Press, 2005.

Belton, John. *Widescreen Cinema.* Cambridge, MA: Harvard University Press, 1992.

Benjamin, Walter. "Experience and Poverty." Translated by Rodney Livingstone. In *Walter Benjamin: Selected Writings, Volume 2, Parts 1 and 2, 1927–1934.* Edited by Michael W. Jennings, Howard Eiland, and Gary Smith, pp. 731–36. Cambridge, MA: Belknap Press of Harvard University Press, 1999.

_____. "On Some Motifs in Baudelaire." Translated by Harry Zohn. In *Walter Benjamin: Selected Writings, Volume 4, 1938–1940.* Edited by Marcus Bullock, pp. 313–55. Cambridge, MA: Belknap Press of Harvard University Press, 2002.

_____. "One-Way Street." Translated by Edmund Jephcott. In *Walter Benjamin: Selected Writings, Volume 1, 1913–1926.* Edited by Marcus Bullock and Michael W. Jennings, pp. 444–87. Cambridge, MA: Belknap Press of Harvard University Press, 1996.

_____. "Paul Valéry: On His Sixtieth Birthday." Translated by Rodney Livingstone. In *Walter Benjain Selected Writings, Volume 2, Part 1, 1927–1930*, pp. 531–35.

———. "The Story-Teller: Reflections on the Works of Nicolai Leskov." Translated by Harry Zohn. In *Walter Benjamin: Selected Writings, Volume 3, 1935–1938.* Edited by Howard Eiland and Michael W. Jennings, pp. 143–66. Cambridge, MA: Belknap Press of Harvard University Press, 2003.

———. "Surrealism: The Last Snapshot of the European Intelligentsia." Translated by Edmund Jephcott. In *Walter Benjamin: Selected Writings, Volume 2, Part 1, 1927–1930*, pp. 207–19.

———. "The Work of Art in the Age of Its Technological Reproducibility: Second Version." Translated by Edmund Jephcott and Harry Zohn. In *Walter Benjamin: Selected Writings, Volume 3, 1935–1938*, pp. 101–33.

Bennett, Tony. *The Birth of the Museum: History, Theory, Politics.* London: Routledge, 1995.

———. "The Exhibitionary Complex." *new formations*, no. 4 (Spring 1988), pp. 73–102.

Benson-Allott, Caetlin. *The Stuff of Spectatorship: Material Cultures of Film and Television.* Berkeley, University of California Press, 2021.

Blumenberg, Hans. *Shipwreck with Spectator: Paradigm of a Metaphor for Existence.* Translated by Steven Rendall. Cambridge, MA: MIT Press, 1997.

Boeger, Peter. *Architektur der Lichtspieltheater in Berlin: Bauten und Projekte, 1919–1930.* Berlin: Arenhövel, 1993.

Bolter, Jay David, and Richard Grusin. *Remediation: Understanding New Media.* Cambridge, MA: MIT Press, 1999.

Bousquet, Antoine. *The Eye of War: Military Perception from the Telescope to the Drone.* Minneapolis: University of Minnesota Press, 2018.

Brodesco, Alberto. "Come ci inquadriamo quando videochiamiamo / 2: Sullo stendino." *Nazione Indiana*, October 21, 2020, www.nazioneindiana.com/2020/10/21/come-ci-inquadriamo-quando-videochiamiamo-2-sullo-stendino.

———. "Questioni di sfondo: Come ci inquadriamo quando videochiamiamo." *Nazione Indiana*, June 2, 2020, www.nazioneindiana.com/2020/06/02/questioni-di-sfondo-come-ci-inquadriamo-quando-videochiamiamo.

Brown, Bill. "Re-Assemblage (Theory, Practice, Mode)." *Critical Inquiry* 46.2 (Winter 2020), pp. 259–303, https://doi.org/10.1086/706678.

Brown, Wendy. *Walled States, Waning Sovereignty.* New York: Zone Books, 2010.

Brozzoli, Claudio, Tamar R. Makin, Lucilla Cardinali, Nicholas P. Holmes, and Alessandro Farnè. "Peripersonal Space: A Multisensory Interface for Body-Object Interactions." In Micah M. Murray and Mark T. Wallace, eds., *The Neural Bases of Multisensory Processes*, pp. 447–64. Boca Raton: CRC Press, 2012.

Bryson, Norman. *Vision and Painting: The Logic of the Gaze.* London: Macmillan, 1983.

Bufacchi, Rory J., and Gian Domenico Iannetti. "An Action Field Theory of Peripersonal Space." *Trends in Cognitive Sciences* 22.12 (December 2018), pp. 1076–90, https://doi .org/10.1016/j.tics.2018.09.004.

Bull, Michael. "'To Each Their Own Bubble: Mobile Spaces of Sound in the City." In Nick Couldry and Anna McCarthy, eds., *Mediaspace: Place, Scale, and Culture in a Media Age*, pp. 275–93. New York: Routledge, 2004.

Cahill, Leo, and Timothy Holland. "Double Exposures: Derrida and Cinema, an Introductory Séance." *Discourse* 37.1–2 (Winter–Spring 2015), pp. 3–21.

Campe, Rüdiger. "'Schutz und Schirm': Screening in German during Early Modern Times." In Craig Buckley, Rüdiger Campe, and Francesco Casetti, eds., *Screen Genealogies: From Optical Device to Environmental Medium*, pp. 51–72. Amsterdam: Amsterdam University Press, 2019.

———, and Julia Weber, eds. *Rethinking Emotions: Interiority and Exteriority in Premodern, Modern, and Contemporary Thought.* Berlin: De Gruyter, 2014.

Carbone, Mauro, "Falling Man: The Time of Trauma, the Time of (Certain) Images." *Research in Phenomenology* 47.2 (June 2017), pp. 190–203, https://doi .org/10.1163/15691640-12341365.

———. *Filosofia-schermi: Dal cinema alla rivoluzione digitale.* Milan: Cortina, 2016.

———. *The Flesh of Images: Merleau-Ponty between Painting and Cinema.* Translated by Marta Nijhuis. Albany: State University of New York Press, 2015.

———. "Thematizing the Arche-Screen through Its Variations." In *Screens.* Edited by Dominique Chateau and José Moure, pp. 62–69. Amsterdam: Amsterdam University Press, 2016.

———, and Graziano Lingua. "Being Screens, Making Screens Functions and Technical Objects." *Screen Bodies* 6.2 (Winter 2021), pp. 1–22, https://doi.org/10.3167/ screen.2021.060202.

Carey, James W. "A Cultural Approach to Communication." In *Communication as Culture: Essays in Media and Society.* New York: Routledge, 1992.

Casetti, Francesco. "A Countergenealogy of the Movie Screen; or, Film's Expansion Seen from the Past." In Richard Grusin and Jocelyn Szczepaniak-Gillece, eds., *Ends of Cinema*, pp. 23–52. Minneapolis: Unversity of Minnesota Press, 2020.

———. *The Lumiére Galaxy: Seven Key Words for the Cinema to Come.* New York: Columbia University Press, 2015.

_____. "Primal Screens." In Craig Buckley, Rüdiger Campe, and Francesco Casetti, eds., *Screen Genealogies: From Optical Device to Environmental Medium*, pp. 27–50. Amsterdam: Amsterdam University Press, 2019.

_____, and Sara Sampietro. "With Eyes, with Hands: The Relocation of Cinema into iPhone." In Pelle Snikars and Patrick Vonderau, eds., *Moving Data: The iPhone and the Future of Media*, pp. 19–32. New York: Columbia University Press, 2012.

Castle, Terry. *The Female Thermometer: Eighteenth-Century Culture and the Invention of the Uncanny*. New York: Oxford University Press, 1995.

Cavaletti, Federica, and Giancarlo Grossi. "Take a Deep Breath: Virtual Reality and Real Anxiety." In Luca Malavasi and Sara Tongiani, eds., *Technophobia and Technophilia in the Media, Art, and Visual Culture*, pp. 103–18. Canterano: Aracne, 2020).

Cavell, Stanley. *The World Viewed, Enlarged Edition*. Cambridge, MA: Harvard University Press, 1979.

_____. "The Fact of Television." *Daedalus* 111.4 (Fall 1982), pp. 75–96, https://www.jstor.org/stable/20024818.

Chandler, James, and Kevin Gilmartin, eds. *Romantic Metropolis: The Urban Scene of British Culture, 1780–1840*. Cambridge: Cambridge University Press, 2005.

Charney, Leo, and Vanessa R. Schwartz, eds. *Cinema and the Invention of Modern Life*. Berkeley: University of California Press, 1995.

Citton, Yves. *The Ecology of Attention*. Translated by Barnaby Norman. Cambridge: Polity, 2017.

_____, and Estelle Doudet, eds. *Écologies de l'attention et archéologie des media*. Grenoble: UGA Éditions, 2019.

Cometa, Michele. *Perché le storie ci aiutano a vivere*. Milan: Cortina, 2017.

Cooper, Gail. *Air-Conditioning America: Engineers and the Controlled Environment, 1900–1960*. Baltimore: John Hopkins University Press, 1998.

Corner, John, ed. *Popular Television in Britain: Studies in Cultural History*. London: BFI, 1991.

Crary, Jonathan. "Géricault, the Panorama, and Sites of Reality in the Early Nineteenth Century." *Grey Room*, no. 9 (Autumn 2002), pp. 5–25, https://doi.org/10.1162/152638102320989498.

_____. *Suspensions of Perception: Attention, Spectacle, and Modern Culture*. Cambridge, MA: MIT Press, 1999.

_____. *24/7: Late Capitalism and the End of Sleep*. London: Verso, 2013.

Crowley, John E. *The Invention of Comfort: Sensibilities and Design in Early Modern Britain and Early America.* Baltimore: Johns Hopkins University Press, 2001.

Cubitt, Sean. *Eco Media.* Amsterdam: Rodopi, 2005.

Deane, Cormac. "The Control Room: A Media Archaeology." *Culture Machine* 16 (2015), pp. 1–34.

Debord, Guy. *Comments on the Society of Spectacle.* Translated by Malcol Imrie. London: Verso, 1990.

———. *The Society of Spectacle.* Translated by Donald Nicholson-Smith. New York: Zone Books, 1994.

De Certeau, Michel. *The Practice of Everyday Life.* Translated by Steven F. Rendall. Berkeley: University of California Press, 1984.

De Gaetano, Roberto, and Angela Maiello, eds. *Virale: Il presente al tempo dell'epidemia.* Cosenza: Pellegrini Editore, 2020.

Deleuze, Gilles. *The Fold: Leibnitz and the Baroque.* Translated by Tom Conley. London: Athlone, 1993.

———. "Postscript on the Societies of Control." *October* 59 (Winter 1992), pp. 3–7.

———. "What Is a Dispositif?" In *Two Regimes of Madness: Texts and Interviews 1975–1995.* Edited by David Lapoujade. Translated by Ames Hodges and Mike Taormina, pp. 338–48. New York: Semiotext(e), 2006.

Delluc, Louis. *Écrits cinématographiques.* 3 vols. in 4. Edited by Pierre Lherminier. Paris: Cinématheque Française, 1985–1990.

De Mesel, Benjamin. "Competence in Compensating for Incompetence: Odo Marquard on Philosophy." *Pluralist* 13.2 (Summer 2018), pp. 50–71, https://doi.org/10.5406/pluralist.13.2.0050.

Denson, Shane. *Discorrelated Images.* Durham: Duke University Press, 2020.

———. "'Thus isolation is a project.': Notes toward a Phenomenology of Screen-Mediated Life." In Philipp Dominik Keidl, Laliv Melamed, Vinzenz Hediger, and Antonio Somaini, eds, *Pandemic Media: Preliminary Notes Toward an Inventory,* pp. 315–24. Lüneburg: Meson Press, 2020.

De Rita, Lidia. *I contadini e la televisione: Studio sull' influenza degli spettacoli televisivi in un gruppo di contadini lucani.* Bologna: Il Mulino, 1964.

Derrida, Jacques. "Autoimmunity: Real and Symbolic Suicide." In Giovanna Borradori, ed., *Philosophy in a Time of Terror: Dialogues with Jürgen Habermas and Jacques Derrida,* pp. 85–136. Chicago: University of Chicago Press, 2003.

_____ . "Cinema and Its Ghosts." An interview with by Antoine de Baecque and Thierry Jousse. Translated by Peggy Kamuf. *Discourse* 37.1–2 (Winter–Spring 2015), pp. 22–39.

_____ . "Plato's Pharmacy." In *Dissemination*. Translated by Barbara Johnson, pp. 63–171. Chicago: University of Chicago Press, 1981.

Dilhac, Jean-Marie. "The Telegraph of Claude Chappe: an Optical Telecomunication Network for the XVIIIth Century," https://ethw.org/w/images/1/17/Dilhac.pdf.

Doane, Mary Ann. "The Close-Up: Scale and Detail in the Cinema." *differences: A Journal of Feminist Cultural Studies* 14.3 (2003), pp. 89–111, https://doi.org/10.1215/10407391-14-3-89.

_____ . "The Indexical and the Concept of Medium Specificity." *differences: A Journal of Feminist Cultural Studies* 18.1 (2007), pp. 128–52, https://doi.org/10.1215/10407391-2006-025.

_____ . "Scale and the Negotiation of 'Real' and 'Unreal' Space in the Cinema." In Lúcia Nagib and Cecília Mello, eds., *Realism and the Audiovisual Media*, pp. 63–81. London: Palgrave Macmillan, 2009.

Duhamel, Georges. *America the Menace: Scenes from the Life of the Future*. Translated by Charles Miner Thompson. Boston: Houghton Mifflin, 1931. Originally, *Scènes de la vie future*. Paris: Mercure de France, 1930.

Easterling, Keller. *Medium Design: Knowing How To Work on the World*. London: Verso, 2021.

Elcott, Noam. "The Phantasmagoric *Dispositif*: An Assembly of Bodies and Images in Real Time and Space." *Grey Room*, no. 62 (Winter 2016), pp. 42–71, https://doi.org/10.1162/GREY_a_00187.

Ellis, John. *Visible Fictions*. London: Routledge, 1982.

Ellis, Markman. "'Spectacles within Doors': Panoramas of London in the 1790s." *Romanticism* 14.2 (2008), pp. 133–48, https://doi.org/10.3366/E1354991X0800024X.

Epstein, Jean. "Magnification." Translated by Stuart Liebman. In Richard Abel, ed., *French Film Theory and Criticism: 1907–1939, Volume 1, 1907–1929*, pp. 235–40. Princeton: Princeton University Press, 1988.

_____ . "The Senses 1 (b)." Translated by Tom Milne. In Richard Abel, ed., *French Film Theory and Criticism: 1907–1939, Volume 1, 1907–1929*, pp. 241–45. Princeton: Princeton University Press, 1993.

Esposito, Roberto. *Immunitas: The Protection and Negation of Life*. Translated by Zakiya Hanafi. London: Wiley, 2011.

_____ . "The Immunization Paradigm." Translated by Timothy Campbell. *Diacritics* 36.2 (2006), pp. 23–48, https://doi.org/10.1353/dia.2008.0015.

———. *Terms of the Political: Community, Immunity, Biopolitics*. Translated by Rhiannon Noel Welch. New York: Fordham University Press, 2013.

Eugeni, Ruggero. *Capitale algoritmico: Cinque dispositivi postmediali (più uno)*. Brescia: Morcelliana, 2021.

Farocki, Harun. "Phantom Images." *Public*, no. 29 (January 2004), pp. 12–22, https://public .journals.yorku.ca/index.php/public/article/view/30354.

Feldmann, Eric. "Considérations sur la situation du spectateur au cinéma." *Revue Internationale de Filmologie* 26 (1956), pp. 83–97.

Floridi, Luciano, ed. *The Onlife Manifesto: Being Human in a Hyperconnected Era*. Heidelberg: Springer Open, 2015, https://link.springer.com/content/pdf/10.1007%2F978 -3-319-04093-6.pdf.

———. "What the Near Future of Artificial Intelligence Could Be." *Philosophy & Technology* (2019) 32, pp. 1–15, https://doi.org/10.1007/s13347-019-00345-y.

Flusser, Vilém. *Into the Universe of Technical Images*. Translated by Nancy Ann Roth. Minneapolis: University of Minnesota Press, 2011.

Foucault, Michel. *Discipline and Punish: The Birth of the Prison*. New York: Random House, 1975.

———. "Governmentality." In *Power*. Edited by James D. Faubion. Translated by Robert Hurley et al., pp. 201–22. New York: New Press, 2000.

Fourastié, Jean, and Françoise Fourastié. *Histoire du confort*. Paris: Presses Universitaires de France, 1962.

Freud, Sigmund. *Beyond the Pleasure Principle*. Translated by James Strachey. New York: Liveright, 1950.

Frisby, David. *Fragments of Modernity: Theories of Modernity in the Work of Simmel, Kracauer and Benjamin*. Cambridge: Polity Press, 1985.

Furuhata, Yuriko. *Climatic Media: Transpacific Experiments in Atmospheric Control*. Durham: Duke University Press, 2022.

Gallese, Vittorio. "Embodied Simulation: From Neurons to Phenomenal Experience." *Phenomenology and the Cognitive Sciences* 4 (2005), pp. 23–48, https://doi.org/10.1007 /s11097-005-4737-z.

———, and Michele Guerra. *The Empathic Screen: Cinema and Neuroscience*. Translated by by Frances Anderson. Oxford: Oxford University Press, 2020.

Galloway, Alexander. *The Interface Effect*. Cambridge: Polity, 2012.

Gaudreault, André, and Philippe Marion. "A Medium Is Always Born Twice." *Early Popular Visual Culture* 3.1 (May 2005), pp. 3–15, https://doi.org/10.1080/17460650500056964.

Gehlen, Arnold. *Man, His Nature and Place in the World.* Translated by Clare McMillan and Karl Pillemer. New York: Columbia University Press, 1988.

———. *Man in the Age of Technology.* Translated by Patricia Lipscomb. New York: Columbia University Press, 1980.

Geoghegan, Bernard Dionysius. "An Ecology of Operations: Vigilance, Radar, and the Birth of the Computer Screen." *Representations* 147.1 (Summer 2019), pp. 59–95, https://doi.org/10.1525/rep.2019.147.1.59.

Gerbi, Antonello. "Iniziazione alle delizie del cinema." *Il Convegno* 7, nos. 11–12 (November 25), 1926, pp. 836–48. Republished in Antonello Gerbi, *Preferisco Charlot: Scritti sul cinema, 1926–1933.* Edited by Gian Piero Brunetta and Sandro Gerbi, pp. 35–49. Savigliano: Aragno, 2011.

Giddens, Anthony. *The Consequences of Modernity.* Stanford: Stanford University Press, 1990.

Giedion, Siegfried. *Mechanization Takes Command: A Contribution to Anonymous History.* New York: Oxford University Press, 1948.

Goffman, Erving. *The Presentation of Self in Everyday Life.* Edinburgh: University of Edinburgh, Social Sciences Research Centre, 1956.

Gomery, Douglas. *Shared Pleasures: A History of Movie Presentation in the United States.* Madison: University of Wisconsin Press, 1992.

Gorky, Maxim. "Lumière's Cinematograph." Translated by Richard Taylor. In Richard Taylor and Ian Christie, eds., *Film Factory: Russian and Soviet Cinema in Documents 1896–1939,* pp. 25–26. Cambridge, MA: Harvard University Press, 1988.

Grau, Oliver. *Virtual Art: From Illusion to Immersion.* Cambridge, MA: MIT Press, 2002.

Grimm, Jacob, and Wilhelm Grimm. *Deutsches Vörterbuch.* Leipzig: S. Hirzel, 1899.

Groys, Boris. *Art Power.* Cambridge, MA: MIT Press, 2008.

Grusin, Richard. *Premediation: Affect and Mediality after 9/11.* New York: Palgrave Macmillan, 2010.

———. "Radical Mediation. *Critical Inquiry* 42.1 (Autumn 2015), pp. 124–48, http://www.jstor.org/stable/10.1086/682998.

Gunning, Tom. "The Cinema of Attractions: Early Film, Its Spectator, and the Avant-Garde." In Thomas Elsaesser, ed., *Early Cinema: Space, Frame, Narrative.* London: BFI, 1900, pp. 56–62.

———. "Illusions Past and Future: The Phantasmagoria and Its Specters" (2004), http://www.mediaarthistory.org/refresh/Programmatic%20key%20texts/pdfs/Gunning.pdf.

———. "Phantasmagoria and the Manufacturing of Illusions and Wonder: Towards a Cultural Optics of the Cinematic Apparatus." In Andre Gaudreault, Catherine Russell, and Pierre Veronneau, eds., *The Cinema: A New Technology for the 20th Century*, pp. 31–44. Lausanne: Éditions Payot, 2004.

Hagener, Malte. "Divided, Together, Apart: How Split Screen Became Our Everyday Reality." In Philipp Dominik Keidl, Laliv Melamed, Vinzenz Hediger, and Antonio Somaini, eds., *Pandemic Media: Preliminary Notes Toward an Inventory*, pp. 33–40. Lüneburg: Meson Press, 2020.

Hanich, Julian. *The Audience Effect: On the Collective Cinema Experience*. Edinburgh: Edinburgh University Press, 2018.

Hänsel, Silvaine, and Angelika Schmitt, eds. *Kinoarchitektur in Berlin 1895–1995*. Berlin: Dietrich Reimer, 1995.

Hansen, Mark B. N. *Feed-Forward: On the Future of Twenty-First-Century Media*. Chicago: University of Chicago Press, 2015.

Hansen, Miriam Bratu. *Cinema and Experience: Siegfried Kracauer, Walter Benjamin, and Theodor W. Adorno*. Berkeley: University of California Press, 2011.

———. "Room-for-Play: Benjamin's Gamble with Cinema." *October* 109 (Summer 2004), pp. 3–45, https://doi.org/10.1162/0162287041886511.

———. "'With Skin and Hair': Kracauer's *Theory of Film*, Marseille 1940." *Critical Inquiry* 19.3 (1993), pp. 437–69.

Haraway, Donna J. *How Like a Leaf: An Interview with Thyrza Goodeve*. New York: Routledge, 2000.

Heard, Mervyn. *Phantasmagoria: The Secret Life of the Magic Lantern: A Full-Blooded Account of an Extraordinary Theatrical Ghost-Raising Entertainment of the Early Nineteenth-Century and the True Exploits of Its Mysterious Inventor, Paul de Philipsthal, in Britain and Abroad*. Hastings: Projection Box, 2006.

Heidegger, Martin. "The Age of the World Picture." In *Off the Beaten Track*. Edited and translated by Julian Young and Kenneth Haynes, pp. 57–85. Cambridge: Cambridge University Press, 2002.

———. *Being and Time*. Translated by John Macquarrie and Edward Robinson. Oxford: Blackwell, 1962.

Heu, Pascal-Manuel. *Le temps du cinéma: Émile Wuillermoz, pére de la critique cinématographique, 1910–1930*. Paris: L'Harmattan, 2003.

Hidalgo, Santiago, and Louis Pelletier. "Le mystère du 'grand tableau gris': L'animation des images fixes dans les premières projections cinématographiques." *1895, Mille huit cent quatre-vingt-quinze, revue d'histoire du cinéma*, no. 82 (Spring 2017), pp. 87–106, https://doi.org/10.4000/1895.5374.

Holmes, Su. *Entertaining Television: BBC and Popular Television Culture in the 1950s.* Manchester: Manchester University Press, 2008.

Horkheimer, Max, and Theodor W. Adorno. *Dialectic of Enlightenment: Philosophical Fragments.* Edited by Gunzelin Schmid Noerr. Translated by Edmund Jephcott. Stanford: Stanford University Press, 2002.

Huhtamo, Erkki. "Ghost Notes: Reading Mervyn Heard's *Phantasmagoria: The Secret Life of the Magic Lantern.*" *Magic Lantern Gazette* 18.4 (Winter 2006), pp. 11–12.

———. "Pockets of Plenty: An Archaeology of Mobile Media." In Martin Rieser, ed., *The Mobile Audience: Media Art and Mobile Technologies*, pp. 23–38. New York: Rodopi, 2011.

Jeong, Seung-hoon. *Cinematic Interfaces: Film Theory after New Media.* New York: Routledge, 2013.

Joselit, David. *After Art.* Princeton: Princeton University Press, 2012.

Kaes, Anton, Nicholas Baer, and Michael Cowan, eds. *The Promise of Cinema: German Film Theory, 1907–1933.* Berkeley: University of California Press, 2016.

Keidl, Philipp Dominik, Laliv Melamed, Vinzenz Hediger, and Antonio Somaini, eds. *Pandemic Media: Preliminary Notes Toward an Inventory.* Lüneburg: Meson Press, 2020.

Kiesler, Frederick. "Building a Cinema Theatre." In *Selected Writings.* Edited by Siegfried Gohr and Gunda Luyken, pp. 16–19. Ostfieldern bei Stuttgart: Verlag Gerd Hatje, 1996.

———. *Contemporary Art Applied to the Store and Its Display.* New York: Brentano's, 1930.

Keller, Sarah. *Anxious Cinephilia: Pleasure and Perils at the Movies.* New York: Columbia University Press, 2020.

Kittler, Friedrich. *Optical Media: Berlin Lectures 1999.* Translated by Anthony Enns. Cambridge: Polity, 2010.

Knorr-Cetina, Karin. "The Synthetic Situation: Interactionism for a Global World." *Symbolic Interaction* 32.1 (2009), pp. 61–87, https://doi.org/10.1525/si.2009.32.1.61.

Kracauer, Siegfried. "Art Today: A Proposal." In *Siegfried Kracauer's American Writings: Essays on Gilm and Popular Culture.* Edited by Johannes von Moltke and Kristy Rawson, pp. 115–17. Berkeley: University of California Press, 2012.

———. "Cult of Distraction: On Berlin's Picture Palaces." In *The Mass Ornament: Weimar Essays.* Edited and translated by Thomas Y. Levin, pp. 323–28. Cambridge, MA: Harvard University Press, 1995.

———. *The Salaried Masses: Duty and Distraction in Weimar Germany.* Translated by Quintin Hoare. London: Verso, 1998.

———. *Theory of Film.* New York: Oxford University Press, 1960.

Kuntzel, Thierry. "Sight, Insight, and Power: Allegory of a Cave." *Camera Obscura* 2.6 (Fall 1980), pp. 91–110, https://doi.org/10.1215/02705346-2-3_6-90.

Lacan, Jacques. "The Mirror Stage as Formative of the Function of *I* as Revealed in Psychoanalytic Experience." In *Écrits: A Selection.* Translated by Bruce Fink, with Héloïse Fink and Russell Grigg, pp. 3–9. New York: W. W. Norton, 2002.

Lajer-Burcharth, Ewa, and Beate Söntgen, eds. *Interiors and Interiority.* Berlin: De Gruyter, 2016.

Latour, Bruno. "Visualization and Cognition: Thinking with Eyes and Hands." *Knowledge and Society* 6.6 (1986), pp. 1–40.

Leventopoulos, Mélisande. *Les catholiques et le cinéma.* Rennes: Presses Universitaires de Rennes, 2014.

Levie, Françoise. *Étienne-Gaspard Robertson: La vie d'un fantasmagore.* Brussels: Le Préamble, 1990.

Li, Jinying. "Toward a Genealogy of the Wall-Screen." *differences: A Journal of Feminist Cultural Studies* 33.1 (2022), pp. 28–59, https://doi.org/10.1215/10407391-9735441.

Littré, Émile, ed. *Dictionnaire de la langue française.* Paris: Librarie Hachette, 1873.

Loiperdinger, Martin. "Lumière's *Arrival of the Train*: Cinema's Founding Myth." *Moving Image* 4.1 (Spring 2004), pp. 89–118, http://doi.org/10.1353/mov.2004.0014.

Lovink, Geert. "The Anatomy of Zoom Fatigue." *Eurozine*, November 2, 2020, https://www.eurozine.com/the-anatomy-of-zoom-fatigue.

Malabou, Catherine. *Plasticity at the Dusk of Writing: Dialectic, Destruction, Deconstruction.* New York: Columbia University Press, 2010.

———. "Plasticity and Elasticity in Freud's *Beyond the Pleasure Principle*." *Diacritics* 37.4 (Winter 2007), pp. 78–85, https://doi.org/10.1080/13534640902793000.

Malafouris, Lambros. *How Things Shape the Mind: A Theory of Material Engagement.* Cambridge, MA: MIT Press, 2012.

Maldonado, Tomas. "The Idea of Comfort." Translated by John Collars. *Design Issues* 8.1 (Autumn 1991), pp. 35–43, https://doi.org/10.2307/1511452.

Mannoni, Laurent. *The Great Art of Light and Shadow: Archaeology of Cinema.* Exeter: University of Exeter Press, 2000.

———, and Donata Pesenti Campagnoni. *Lanterne magique et film peint*. Paris: Éditions de la Martinière, 2009.

———, Donata Pesenti Campagnoni, and David Robinson. *Light and Movement: Incunabula of the Motion Picture, 1420–1896*. Pordenone: Le giornate del cinema muto / Cinémathèque Francaise-Musée du Cinéma / Museo Nazionale del Cinema, 1995.

Marquard, Odo. *In Defense of the Accidental: Philosophical Studies*. New York: Oxford University Press 1991.

———. "Indicted and Unburdened Man in Eighteen Century Philosophy." In *Farewell to Matters of Principle: Philosophical Studies*, pp. 38–63. New York: Oxford University Press, 1989.

———. *Krise der Erwartung — Stunde der Erfahrung: Zur aesthetische Kompensation des modernen Erfahrungenlustes*. Konstanz: Universitätsverlag Konstanz, 1982.

Martini, Fausto Maria. "The Death of the Word." In Francesco Casetti, Silvio Alovisio, and Luca Mazzei, eds., *Early Film Theories in Italy, 1896–1922*, pp. 75–79. Amsterdam: Amsterdam University Press, 2017.

McCalman, Ian. "Mystagogues of Revolution: Cagliostro, Loutherbourg and Romantic London." In James Chandler and Kevin Gilmartin, eds., *Romantic Metropolis: The Urban Scene of British Culture, 1780–1840*, pp. 177–203. Cambridge: Cambridge University Press, 2005.

McCarthy, Anna. *Ambient Television: Visual Culture and Public Space*. Durham: Duke University Press, 2001.

McLuhan, Marshall. *Understanding Media: The Extension of Man*. New York: McGraw Hill, 1964.

Melnick, Ross. *American Showman: Samuel "Roxy" Rothafel and the Birth of the Entertainment Industry, 1908–1935*. New York: Columbia University Press, 2014.

Metz, Christian. "Mirror Construction in Fellini's 8½." In *Film Language: A Semiotics of Cinema*. Translated by Michael Taylor, pp. 228–34. New York: Oxford University Press, 1974.

Michotte, Albert. "Le caractère de 'réalité' des projections cinématographiques." *Revue internationale de filmologie* 3–4 (October 1948), pp. 249–61.

Mitchell, M. J. T. "Screening Nature (and the Nature of the Screen)." *New Review of Film and Television Studies* 13.3 (2015), pp. 231–46, https://doi.org/10.1080/17400309.2015.1058141.

Montani, Pietro. *Emozioni dell'intelligenza: Un percorso nel sensorio digitale*. Milan: Meltemi, 2020.

———. "Techno-Aesthetics and Forms of the Imagination." In Simona Chiodo and Viola Schiaffonati, eds., *Italian Philosophy of Technology: Socio-Cultural, Legal, Scientific and Aesthetic Perspectives on Technology*, pp. 247–61. New York: Springer, 2021.

———. *Technological Destinies of the Imagination*. Milan: Mimesis International, 2022.

Moores, Shaun. "The Doubling of Place: Electronic Media, Time-Space Arrangements and Social Relationships." In Nick Couldry and Anna McCarthy, eds., *MediaSpace: Place, Scale and Culture in a Media Age*, pp. 21–37. London: Routledge, 2004.

Morin, Edgar. *The Cinema, or The Imaginary Man*. Translated by Lorraine Mortimer. Minneapolis: University of Minnesota Press, 2005.

———. "Le problème des effets dangereux du cinéma." *Revue internationale de filmologie*, no. 14–15 (July–December 1953), pp. 217–31. Reprinted in *Le cinéma: Un art de la complexité*. Edited by Monique Peyrière and Chiara Simonigh, pp. 171–88. Paris: Nouveau Monde, 2018.

Mulvey, Laura. *Visual and Other Pleasures*. Bloomington: Indiana University Press, 1989.

Münsterberg, Hugo. *The Photoplay: A Psychological Study*. New York: Appleton, 1916.

Murray, James A. H., ed. *A New English Dictionary on Historical Principles*. Oxford: Clarendon Press of Oxford University Press, 1914.

Naylor, David. *American Picture Palaces: The Architecture of Fantasy*. New York: Prentice Hall, 1981.

Oettermann, Stephan. *The Panorama: History of a Mass Medium*. Translated by Deborah Lucas Schneider. New York: Zone Books, 1997.

Ortoleva, Peppino, and Teresa Di Marco. *Luci del teleschermo*. Milan: Electa, 2004.

The Oxford English Dictionary, Second Edition. Prepared by J. A. Simpson and E. S. C. Weiner. Oxford: Clarendon Press of Oxford University Press, 1989.

Packer, Jeremy. "Screens in the Sky: SAGE, Surveillance, and the Automation of Perceptual, Mnemonic, and Epistemological Labor." *Social Semiotics* 23.2 (2013), pp. 173–95, https://doi.org/10.1080/10350330.2013.777590..

Paglen, Trevor. "Invisible Images (Your Pictures Are Looking at You)." *New Inquiry*, December 8, 2016, https://thenewinquiry.com/invisible-images-your-pictures-are-looking-at-you.

———. "Operational Images," *E-Flux*, no. 59 (November 2014), https://www.e-flux.com/journal/59/61130/operational-images.

Parks, Lisa, and Nicole Starosielski, eds. *Signal Traffic: Critical Studies of Media Infrastructures*. Champaign: University of Illinois Press, 2015.

Peters, John Durham. "The Charge of a Light Barricade: Optics and Ballistics in the Ambiguous Being of the Screen." In Craig Buckley, Rüdiger Campe, and Francesco Casetti, eds., *Screen Genealogies: From Optical Device to Environmental Medium*, pp. 215–35. Amsterdam: Amsterdam University Press, 2019.

———. *The Marvelous Clouds: Toward a Philosophy of Elemental Media*. Chicago: University of Chicago Press, 2015.

Peterson, Jennifer Lynn. "An Anthropocene Viewing Condition." *Representations* 157.1 (2022), pp. 17–40, https://doi.org/10.1525/rep.2022.157.2.17.

Phillips, Stephen J. *Elastic Architecture: Frederick Kiesler and Design Research in the First Age of Robotic Culture*. Cambridge, MA: MIT Press, 2017.

Pinotti, Andrea. "Towards An-Iconology: The Image as Environment." *Screen* 61.4 (Winter 2020), pp. 594–603, https://doi.org/10.1093/screen/hjaa060.

Pirandello, Luigi. *Shoot!: The Notebooks of Serafino Gubbio Cinematograph Operator*. Translated by C. K. Scott Moncrief. New York: E. P. Dutton, 1926.

Quaresima, Leonardo. "Luoghi dello spettacolo e spazi della visione." *Cinema & Cinema*, no. 47 (December 1986), pp. 35–37.

Rancière, Jacques. "Aesthetic Separation, Aesthetic Community." In *The Emancipated Spectator*, pp. 51–82. London: Verso, 2011.

———. *The Politics of Aesthetics: The Distribution of the Sensible*. Translated by Gabriel Rockhill. London: Continuum, 2004.

Rankin, William. *After the Map: Cartography, Navigation, and the Transformation of Territory in the Twentieth Century*. Chicago: University of Chicago Press, 2017.

Rapp, George L. "History of Cinema Theater Architecture." In Arthur Woltersdorf, ed., *Living Architecture*, pp. 58–59. Chicago: A. Kroch, 1930.

Rasmi, Jacopo. "Comment le cinéma atterrit-il?: Repérages cinématographiques au pays de la crise écologique." In Hélène Schmutz, ed., *De la représentation de la crise à la crise de la représentation: Esthétique et politique de l'Anthropocène*, pp. 327–51. Chambery: Presses Université Savoie Mont Blanc, 2019.

Rhodes, Gary D. *The Perils of Moviegoing in America, 1896–1950*. New York: Continuum, 2012.

Rizzolatti, Giacomo, Luciano Fadiga, Leonardo Fogassi, and Vittorio Gallese. "The Space around Us." *Science* 277 (1997), pp. 190–91, https://doi.org/10.1126/science.277.5323.190.

Robertson, Étienne Gaspard. *Mémoires récréatifs, scientifiques et anecdotiques du physicien-aéronaute E. G. Robertson: Connu par ses expériences de fantasmagorie, et par ses ascensions aérostatiques dans les principales villes de l'Europe.* 2 vols. Paris: Chez l'auteur ... et à la Libr. de Wurtz, 1831–1833.

Rogers, Ariel. *On the Screen: Displaying the Moving Image in the Long 1930s.* New York: Columbia University Press, 2019.

Rossell, Deac. "The 19th Century German Origins of the Phantasmagoria Show," 2001. Unpublished conference paper for the Lantern Projections Colloquium, London, February 2001.

Roth, Joseph. *Antichrist.* Translated by Moray Firth. New York: Viking Press, 1935.

——. "Filme." In *Drei Sensationen und zwei Katastrophen: Feuilletons zur Welt des Kinos.* Edited by Helmut Peschina and Rainer-Joachim Siegel, pp. 147–48. Göttingen: Wallstein Verlag, 2014.

Rust, Stephen, Salma Monani, and Sean Cubitt, eds. *Ecocinema Theory and Practice.* New York: Routledge, 2012.

Sartre, Jean-Paul. *The Imaginary: A Phenomenological Psychology of the Imagination.* Translated by Jonathan Webber. London: Routledge, 2004.

Sauvage, Monique, and Isabelle Veyrat-Masson. *Histoire de la télévision française de 1935 à nos jours.* Paris: Nouveau Monde, 2012.

Schivelbusch, Wolfgang. *The Railway Journey: The Industrialization of Time and Space in the Nineteenth Century.* Berkeley: University of California Press, 1986.

Schnödl, Gottfried, and Florian Sprenger. *Uexkülls Umgebungen: Umweltlehre und rechtes Denken.* Lüneburg: Meson, 2022.

Seinfeld, Sofia, Tiare Feuchtner, Antonella Maselli, and Jörg Müller. "User Representations in Human-Computer Interaction." *Human-Computer Interaction* 36.5–6 (2021), pp. 400–38, https://oi.org/10.1080/07370024.2020.1724790.

Simmel, Georg. "The Metropolis and Mental Life." In David Frisby and Mike Featherston, eds. *Simmel on Culture: Selected Writings*, pp. 174–85. Thousand Oaks: Sage, 1997.

——. "The Picture Frame: An Aesthetic Study." *Theory, Culture, and Society* 11.1 (1994), pp. 11–17, https://doi.org/10.1177%2F026327694011001003.

Simondon, Gilbert. *Du mode d'existence des objets techniques.* Paris: Aubier, 1958.

——. *On the Mode of Existence of Technical Objects.* Translated by Cécile Malaspina and John Rogove. Minneapolis: Univocal, 2017.

Siry, Joseph M. *Air-Conditioning in Modern American Architecture, 1890–1970*. University Park: Pennsylvania State University Press, 2020.

Slemon, Allie, et al. "Reddit Users' Experiences of Suicidal Thoughts During the COVID-19 Pandemic: A Qualitative Analysis of r/Covid19_Support Posts." *Frontiers*, August 12, 2021, https://www.frontiersin.org/articles/10.3389/fpubh.2021.693153/full.

Sloterdijk, Peter. *Spheres, Volume 1, Bubbles: Microspherology*. Translated by Wieland Hoban. Los Angeles: Semiotext(e), 2011.

———. *Spheres, Volume 2, Globes: Macrospherology*. Translated by Wieland Hoban. Los Angeles: Semiotext(e), 2014.

———. *Spheres, Volume 3, Foams: Plural Spherology*. Translated by Wieland Hoban. Los Angeles: Semiotext(e), 2016.

Snyder, Mark. "Self-Monitoring of Expressive Behavior." *Journal of Personality and Social Psychology* 30.4 (1974), pp. 526–37.

Somaini, Antonio. "Walter Benjamin's Media Theory: The Medium and the Apparat." *Grey Room*, no. 62 (Winter 2016), pp. 6–41, https://doi.org/10.1162/GREY_a_00188.

Spigel, Lynn. *Make Room for TV: Television and the Family Ideal in Postwar America*. Chicago: University of Chicago Press, 1992.

———. "The Suburban Home Companion: Television and the Neighborhood Ideal in Postwar America." In Beatriz Colomina, ed., *Sexuality and Space*, pp. 185–217. Princeton: Princeton Architectural Press, 1992.

———. *Welcome to the Dreamhouse: Popular Media and Postwar Suburbs*. Durham: Duke University Press, 2001.

Stafford, Barbara Maria. *Body Criticism: Imaging the Unseen in Enlightenment Art and Medicine*. Cambridge, MA: MIT Press, 1991.

Szczepaniak-Gillece, Jocelyn. *The Optical Vacuum: Spectatorship and Modernized American Theater Architecture*. Oxford: Oxford University Press, 2018.

———. "Revisiting the Apparatus: The Theatre Chair and Cinematic Spectatorship." *Screen* 57.3 (Autumn 2016), pp. 253–76, https://doi.org/10.1093/screen/hjw030.

———, and Stephen Groening. "Afterword: Objects in the Theater." *Film History: An International Journal* 28.3 (2016), pp. 139–42, https://doi.org/10.2979/filmhistory.28.3.07.

Taylor, Erin. "COVID-19 Anxiety Taking a Toll? There's a Subreddit for That." *The Verge*, March 25, 2020, https://www.theverge.com/2020/3/25/21193950/covid-19-coronavirus-anxiety-subreddit-community-support-group.

Tseng, Cherie. "Commentary: Is It Unprofessional When Your Child Interrupts Your

Office Zoom Meeting?" *Channel News Asia*, December 22, 2021, https://www.channel newsasia.com/commentary/children-interrupting-zoom-meetings-work-home -parents-2324541.

Tomlinson, Gary. *Culture and the Course of Human Evolution*. Chicago: University of Chicago Press, 2018.

Troy, William. "Beauty and the Beast." *The Nation*, March 22, 1933, p. 326. Reprinted in Stanley Kauffmann and Bruce Henstell, eds, *American Film Criticism: From the Beginnings to "Citizen Kane,"* pp. 281–82. New York: Liveright, 1972.

Turkle, Sherry. *Alone Together: Why We Expect More from Technology and Less from Each Other*. New York: Basic Books, 2011.

Turquety, Benoît. *Inventer le cinéma. Épistémologie: Problèmes, machines*. Lausanne: L'Âge d'Homme, 2014.

Uexküll, Jakob von. *A Foray into the Worlds of Animals and Humans: With a Theory of Meaning*. Translated by Joseph D. O'Neill. Minneapolis: University of Minnesota Press, 2010.

Vagnoni, Eleonora, and Matthew R. Longo. "Peripersonal Space: Its Functions, Plasticity, and Neural Basis." In Tony Cheng, Ophelia Deroy, and Charles Spence, eds., *Spatial Senses: Philosophy of Perception in an Age of Science*, pp. 199–225. New York: Routledge, 2019.

Verhoeff, Nanna. *Mobile Screens: The Visual Regime of Navigation*. Amsterdam: Amsterdam University Press, 2012.

Vidler, Anthony. *Warped Space: Art, Architecture, and Anxiety in Modern Culture*. Cambridge, MA: MIT Press, 2000.

Violi, Alessandra. *Il teatro dei nervi: Fantasmi del moderno da Mesmer a Charcot*. Milan: Bruno Mondadori, 2004.

Virilio, Paul. *The Administration of Fear*. Translated by Ames Hodges. Los Angeles: Semiotext(e), 2012.

——. *Bunker Archeology*. Translated by George Collins. New York: Princeton Architectural Press, 1994.

——. *War and Cinema: The Logistics of Perception*. London: Verso, 1989.

Vitale, Francesco. *La farmacia di Godard*. Naples: Orthotes Editrice, 2021.

Ward, Janet. *Weimar Surfaces: Urban Visual Culture in 1920s Germany*. Berkeley: University of California Press, 2001.

Wasson, Haidee. "Electric Homes! Automatic Movies! Efficient Entertainment!: 16mm and Cinema's Domestication in the 1920s." *Cinema Journal* 48.4 (Summer 2009), pp. 1–21, https://doi.org/10.1353/cj.0.0133.

———. *Museum Movies: The Museum of Modern Art and the Birth of Art Cinema*. Berkeley: University of California Press, 2005.

———. "The Reel of the Month Club: 16mm Projectors, Home Theaters and Film Libraries in the 1920s." In Richard Maltby, Melvyn Stokes, and Robert C. Allen, eds., *Going to the Movies: Hollywood and the Social Experience of Cinema*, pp. 218–20. Exeter: University of Exeter Press, 2007.

Weil, Mark S. "The Devotion of the Forty Hours and Roman Baroque Illusions." *Journal of the Warburg and Courtauld Institutes* 37.1 (1974), pp. 218–48, https://doi.org/10.2307/750841.

Williams, Raymond. *Television: Technology and Cultural Form*. New York: Schocken Books, 1974.

Wills, David. "Screen Replays." *Discourse* 37.1–2 (Winter–Spring 2015), pp. 74–86.

Winthrop-Young, Geoffrey. "Bubbles and Webs: A Backdoor Stroll through the Readings of Uexküll." In Jakob von Uexküll, *A Foray into the Worlds of Animals and Humans*. Translated by Joseph D. O'Neill, pp. 209–43. Minneapolis: University of Minnesota Press, 2010.

Yacavone, Dan. *Film Worlds: A Philosophical Aesthetics of Cinema*. New York: Columbia University Press, 2015.

Zhou, Chenshu. *Cinema Off Screen: Moviegoing in Socialist China*. Berkeley: University of California Press, 2021.

Zimmermann, Yvonne. "Videoconferencing and the Uncanny Encounter with Oneself: Self-Reflexivity as Self-Monitoring 2.0." In Philipp Dominik Keidl, Laliv Melamed, Vinzenz Hediger, and Antonio Somaini, eds., *Pandemic Media: Preliminary Notes Toward an Inventory*, pp. 99–103. Lüneburg: Meson Press, 2020.

.

Index

49, 50–52, 194 n.13, 197 nn.30,41, 201 n.71. *See also* Phantasmagoria.

Robespierre, Maximilien, 51, 64.

Rogers, Ariel, *On the Screen*, 96–97, 212 n.57.

Ross, Gary, *Pleasantville*, 109–113.

Roth, Joseph: *Antichrist*, 80, 106–108, 215 nn.86–88; on Berlin's film palaces, 86; review of *The Great White Silence*, 77, 78–79.

Rothafel, Samuel "Roxy," 81, 94, 104, 210 n.50, 214 n.79.

Rousseau, Jean-Jacques, 64; *Confessions*, 61.

Roxy Theater (New York), 80–81, 206 nn.11–12.

SAFETY AND EXPOSURE, 16, 42, 60, 80. *See also* Movie theaters; Projection/protection complex.

Salle de la Fantasmagorie, 58, 151.

Salon de Physique, 57–58, *57, 59*, 151.

Schiller, Friedrich, *The Ghost-Seer*, 50.

Schirm, 20, 190 n.54.

Schivelbusch, Wolfgang, 162, 204 n.8.

Schlanger, Ben, 97–98, 103.

Schröpfer, Johann, 193 n.10.

Scientific American, report on movie theaters, 80–84, *82–83*, 211 n.54.

Scott, Robert, 77, 205 n.1.

Screen-based bubbles: balance between enclosure and openness, 121, 136, 219 n.11; as bubbles, 120–22; and closeups, 127–28; compared with cinema and Phantasmagoria, 117, 128–31, 132–33; and the disciplinary and immune paradigms, 159–60; "docile" users, 153–54; as enclosed sphere of experience, 119–20, 131, 132, 134; historical context of, 166; internalization and externalization, 126, 130–31; link to television, 110; as peripersonal space, 125–26, 128; and the projection/protection complex, 116–17, 119, 132, 136–37, 160; as protective medium, 149, 167; as retreat or shelter, 33–34, 133–34, 136. *See also* Bubbles; Peripersonal space.

Screened images, 130, 172–75; in cinema, 140, 146, 149, 156, 159, 160; Lumière, 180 n.15; and protection, 154, 155, 163, 170, 171; Warhol's *Screen Tests*, 139–43.

Screens: agency of, 235 n.27; as canvas, 10–11, 24, 180 nn.15,28, 212 n/57; cinema, 9–12, 24,

33, 98–99, 140, 148–49, 187–88 n.35, 210 n.52; and enclosures, 32–36, 37, 39, 40, 116–17, 163–64; as filters, 13, 21, 23, 35, 117, 180–81 n.28; as frames, 140–42; magic lantern and, 184–85 n.14, 185 n.15; meanings of word, 20–21, 23, 91, 117–18, 183 n.7; as means of innervation, 28–29, 30; mobile, 115; mode of working, 22–24; online communication platforms, 117–19, 128, 221 n.35; Phantasmagoria, 20, 23, 53–55, 58, 183 n.7, 197 n.34; scenes displayed on, 19–20; as shelter, 20, 21, 23, 35, 91; size and materials, 96–97, 212 n.57; and space, 21–22, 24–27, 28–30, 32, 37, 39–40; split, 128; as "technical object," 24–25; television, 28–29, 97; in urban spaces, 26. *See also* Screen-based bubbles; Screened images; Screenscapes.

Screenscapes, 26–31, 36–39.

Screen Tests (Warhol), 139–43.

Sedgwick, Edie, 139.

Seinfeld, Sofia, *124*, 125, 220 n.21.

Sensoriums, 117, 131, 163.

Serner, Walter, "Cinema and Visual Pleasure," 146.

Shaeffer, Jac, *Wandavision*, 217 n.9.

Shelter, 35, 152, 176, 190 n.54; art as, 229 n.17; bubbles as, 119, 120. 130, 133–34, 136; atomic, 42–44, 192 n.2; homeless, 148, 228 n.15, 228–29 n.17; in *The Most Dangerous Game*, 72; movie theaters as, 13, 60, 105, 108, 149, 209 n.32; screen and, 20, 21, 23, 35, 91.

Shoedsack, Ernest B., *The Most Dangerous Game*, 71–75, 203 n.1.

Simmel, George, 34, 140, 226 n.2 (intermezzo).

Simondon, Gilbert, 22, 25, 184 n.13; "pure schema of functioning," 35, 190 n.51; technical object and associated milieu, 24–25, 31, 185 nn.19–22, 188 n.39.

simulacra (Baudrillard), 107.

Skype, 117, 120, 122, 133.

Slapstick, 156.

Sloterdijk, Peter, 120, 224 n.51.

Slow cinema, 140.

Smartphones, 14, 33, 110, 115, 120, 125, 130, 131, 145.

Smoking, 206 n.14.

Souday, Paul, 228 n.12.

Zone Books series design by Bruce Mau

Image placement and production by Julie Fry

Typesetting by Meighan Gale

Printed and bound by Maple Press